MW00605316

THE HEARTLAND'S HERITAGE

AN ILLUSTRATED HISTORY OF FRESNO COUNTY

Catherine M. Rehart

First Edition

ISBN: 1-886483-32-9
Library of Congress Card Catalog Number: 99-073080
Author: Catherine M. Rehart
Photo Editors: Stephen L. Brown, Douglas Stewart
Publisher: C.E. Parks
Editor-in-Chief: Lori M. Parks
VP/Corporate Development: Bart Barica
CFO: Randall Peterson
Production Manager: Deborah Sherwood
Managing Editor: Betsy Baxter Blondin
Art Director: Gina Mancini
Senior Designer: Susie Passons
Production Staff: Astrit Bushi, Jeff Caton, Dave Hermstead, Jay Kennedy, Vincent Kornegay, John Leyva, Marianne Mackey, Gavin Rattmann, Charlie Silvia
Project Editor: Elizabeth Lex
Coordinating Editors: Renee Kim, Betsy Lelja, Sara Rufner, Mary Ann Stabile, Adriane Wessels, John Woodward
Profile Writers: Donnalee Dunne, Susan Jensen, Rex Oppenheimer, Kelley Reynolds, Sandie Spalding
Human Resources Manager: Ellen Ruby
Administration: Juan Diaz, Debbie Hunter, Azalea Maes, Majka Penner, Scott Reid, Patrick Rucker, Cory Sottek

Published by

Heritage Media Corp.
1954 Kellogg Avenue
Carlsbad, California 92008
www.heritagemedia.com

Printed by Heritage Media Corp. in the United States of America

DEDICATIONS

In memory of my great-great uncles Clark and A.T. Stevens, who believed in the future of a little railroad stop called Fresno Station and played their part in its growth, and to my children Bill, Anne and Kate. May you never forget the legacy that is yours — one that is rooted in the heart of this great valley.

~

In memory of my lifelong friend Jerome D. Laval, with gratitude for preserving your grandfather's photographs of our valley and with the belief that this book fulfills the dream we shared of collaborating on a history project.

TABLE OF CONTENTS

TRIBUTE TO "POP" LAVAL

When a young Claude C. "Pop" Laval picked up his first "5 Crackerbox" camera from a friend (who couldn't make it work), never could he have imagined that his photographs would someday compose one of the most extensive and sought-after collections in the San Joaquin Valley. "Pop" was just making a living and "having a lot of fun."

Born in 1882 into a family blessed with a rich and colorful heritage, "Pop" took to commercial photography with a passion that would span more than 55 years. Always an innovator, "Pop" is recognized as having brought the first movie camera to the valley as well as taking the first aerial pictures of the Fresno area from a balloon. He also introduced the region to the panoramic camera and the smokeless flash. His equipment was cumbersome and the glass negatives fragile, yet "Pop" managed to capture the images of an age as no one else could.

"Pop" passed away in 1966 and his legacy was nearly destroyed by a fire in his Van Ness Avenue family home in 1968. Thanks in part to the quick work of the Fresno County Historical Society, much of the collection was saved. Beginning in 1975 Jerome Laval honored his grandfather's memory with the lauded *As "Pop" Saw It* series of historical books featuring but a small sampling of the collection's more than 100,000 original photographs from all across the San Joaquin Valley. Interspersed throughout the books are excerpts from the popular "Pop says..." series published by the *Fresno Guide* for nearly a decade.

The "Pop" Laval Collection is now a part of the Laval Family Trust, currently administered by Elizabeth, Jerome Jr. and Jennifer Laval. An extensive effort is under way to preserve the irreplaceable glass negatives used by "Pop" and to ensure that this unique treasure will be available for the pleasure of future generations of Fresnans. A percentage of the purchase price of this volume will go directly to the Restoration Project. On behalf of the Laval Family Trust, I would like to sincerely thank you for your support.

"Pop" Laval loved the valley and considered its beauty and majesty a gift to fortunate residents. The photographs in this volume aptly illustrate his lifelong philosophy: "What is this picture intended to say to those who see it?" Perhaps he was best known for his weekly sign-off from his guide column — "Bye now, I'll be seeing you." Because of his vision, everyone can "see" a piece of the valley's colorful past.

Elizabeth Laval-Leyva,
Trustee, Laval Family Trust

ACKNOWLEDGMENTS

I want to express my deep appreciation to all the historians, past and present, who have written books and articles on the history of Fresno County. In particular I want to thank Helen and Forrest Clingan, Charles W. Clough, Wallace W. Elliot, Edwin Eaton, Frank F. Latta, J. Randall McFarland, Brenda B. Preston, Gene Rose, William B. Secrest Sr., William B. Secrest Jr., Wallace Smith, Paul E. Vandor and Ben R. Walker.

I want to thank William V. Pipes, principal geologist/Central Valley manager for Geomatrix Consultants, for editing my copy and for making suggestions concerning the geological formation of the valley and mountains.

Historian Schyler Rehart's area of expertise is the history of government and politics in the city of Fresno. I am grateful to him for reading and critiquing the chapter on Fresno's government and for providing material from his files for this work.

Tammy Lau, head of Sanoian Special Collections Department, Henry Madden Library, California State University, Fresno, and her assistant, Jean Coffey, have been very helpful to this project. Carol Cousineau and her staff in the Microforms Department of the Henry Madden Library have provided assistance also.

The California History Room of the Fresno County Free Library has an informative, helpful staff who has provided answers to questions and pointed the way to materials and books. To Joseph Augustino, Mike Schimmel, Bill Secrest Jr. and Bill Secrest Sr. I offer my deepest thanks.

Many thanks also go to Madera County Librarian Linda Sitterding who provided invaluable help as the project progressed.

The library of *The Fresno Bee* is a rich resource for a project of this kind. Thank you to all the staff members. You have provided tremendous help to this writer.

I want to thank the people who have graciously granted me interviews. They are listed in the bibliography at the end of this book.

A special word of gratitude to Fresno County historian Robert M. Wash who read my copy, and double-checked dates and facts. He made excellent suggestions and allowed me to use books from his extensive library.

FOREWORD

The history of the San Joaquin Valley and Fresno County is as richly textured as its land and its people. It has been the center of my life and that of my entire family for nearly 100 years. My family and that of my wife, Maurine, came from states as diverse as Texas and Nebraska, and the countries of Holland and Sweden. Like so many early settlers in the Central Valley, our descendants came in search of California's promise. I was born in Coalinga in 1949. At the time, my father was working for the Harris Ranch, an enterprise begun by a pioneering family who came west together with my grandfather at the turn of the 19th century. That same year my father purchased a ranch near Firebaugh. Three generations of the Jones family have farmed that land over the past 50 years. Without question, the roots of our families have run deep into the lifestrands of Fresno County and the San Joaquin Valley.

After having served in the California State Assembly for 12 years, I was fortunate enough to be elected in 1994 as California's Secretary of State and re-elected in 1998. During the entire time I have served in Sacramento, Maurine and I have always maintained our residence in Fresno, preferring to raise our two daughters in our home county, remaining close to family, friends and the community we love.

As secretary of state, I have been closely involved in the development of the Golden State Museum in Sacramento. This facility tells the story of California through four major galleries — the Place, the People, the Politics, and most importantly, the Promise, for it has been the promise that has brought the people to California, and indeed to Fresno County. The promise of a job, a healthy environment, a good place to raise children, and the opportunity for a better life are all promises that Fresno County has fulfilled for generations of people who have made it their home.

It is with this background that I read The Heartland's Heritage, a book that tells the interwoven story of the land, the people and the promise of our beloved corner of the planet Earth. Land and water, coupled with the hard-working, energetic and visionary settlers who tilled the soil, resulted in the creation of an agricultural industry that feeds much of our nation and indeed a significant part of the world. But, besides agriculture, Fresno County plays a unique role in this huge state that is 1,000 miles long and 350 miles wide — it is the glue that holds California together. For here, traditional values, the closeness one feels to the land and a slower-paced life provide a stability that balances other parts of the state where life moves more quickly in their rush for change.

With the arrival of the new millennium have come new challenges and changes, but I believe Fresno County will always be tied to its agricultural base. Critical to our future growth will be astute land planning and the defining factor — the availability of water for agricultural, urban and environmental uses.

Yes, The Heartland's Heritage is about Fresno County's history, but as the story unfolds, you will also find drama, excitement and a deeper understanding of this place we are proud to call home.

Bill Jones

PROLOGUE

This is the story of Fresno County. Within its boundaries are two great rivers — one named the San Joaquin, for the father of the Virgin Mary, and the other named the Kings, for the Holy Kings who brought gifts to the Christ Child on the first Epiphany. Fresno County stretches westward to the Panoche and Big Blue Hills of the Coast Range Mountains and eastward to the crest of the majestic Sierra Nevada. Fresno County is the heartland of the great state that draws its name from a fabled island that contained boundless gold and precious stones. The island was ruled by a queen named Califia and lay at the right hand of the Indies near the terrestrial paradise. The Spaniards called the state California.

CHAPTER 1

The story of California's great Central Valley begins approximately 185 million years ago. What would later become the state of California was under the waters of the Pacific Ocean. Emergence of this land began when the Pacific plate (the outer layer of the earth is divided into independently moving plates) was forced beneath the North American plate that held the North American continent. A process began that went on for eons — water eroded the higher land masses of the continent depositing sediment that formed the Pacific continental shelf and slope. Volcanoes were driven up from the bottom of the ocean. Together with other upthrusts in the earth's crust, a higher and larger ancestor of the Sierra Nevada Mountains, called the Nevadan Mountains, was formed providing an additional source of sediment. As this process ended, the rocks and sediment shed from this upheaval shifted westward to form the valley floor.

Unless otherwise noted all images this chapter courtesy Laval Historical Collection

The Formation of the Valley 1

The Railroad Creates a Town 2

The Blossoming of the Desert 3

The Settlements of the Heartland 4

The Sierra Communities 5

Fresno Comes of Age 6

About 70 million years ago another period of upheaval caused the present day Sierra Nevada Mountains to form. About 11 million years ago, the Coast Range Mountains formed finally creating a barrier between the ocean and the valley floor. Sediment shed from the mountains built up on the valley floor eventually bringing it above sea level. Large glaciers moved over the adjacent mountains carving mountain peaks and canyons and exposing mineral deposits, including one that would change the area's history — gold. As the glaciers melted, the channels for two great rivers were formed — the San Joaquin and the Kings. The ocean would not intrude again. However, Mother Nature was not finished. As the Sierra Nevada and Coast Range Mountains continued to jerk and thrust upward along numerous faults, many other rivers, creeks and streams flowed from the mountains, creating the great alluvial fans that form the current floor of the Central Valley.

The mountains of the Sierra Nevada became home to a wide variety of forest and timber trees. Most notable among them was the Sequoia gigantea that, at the higher elevations, can grow to a height of 275 feet. Sugar pine and tamarack were found at elevations above 4,000 feet. In the mountain, foothill and valley areas were digger and yellow pine, foothill and burr oak, poplars, sycamore, dogwood, maple and ash trees. Wildflowers abounded in the foothills and on the valley floor. Fields of poppies, lupine, goldenrod and alfalaria covered the valley in spring. Tules grew in the marshes and along river banks.

As long as 10 million years ago, mastodons, coyotes, deer, horses, wolves, rabbits, and large cats roamed the valley floor. Later, antelope, elk, squirrels, gophers, weasels, woodchucks, moles, mice, horned toads, lizards, vultures, owls, woodpeckers, doves, quail, ducks, ravens and pheasants joined them. In the mountains, the grizzly bear made his appearance.

Native Americans

No one knows when the first human beings settled in the area known today as Fresno County. It was many years after the last glacier melted and the valley was formed — probably sometime between 50,000 and 7,000 years ago.

The origin of the American Indians who came to live in the valley remains a mystery. No one can be certain where they came from or by what route, but they settled up and down the length and breadth of the entire central valley, establishing 63 tribes. Known collectively as Yokuts, a word that is always used in its plural form, they were all related by blood and language. Each tribe had its own name. The Kahwatchwah, Tache, Wimilche, Apiche, Pitkache and Wechikit lived in the valley area of Fresno County. The foothill Yokuts were the Dumna, Tolteche, Gashou, Choinumne, Michahi, Itecha and Chukimena. Another tribal group apart from the Yokuts was the Monache who inhabited the mountain areas of the county.

According to Frank F. Latta in his *Handbook of Yokuts Indians*, each tribe was presided over by a chief. Each village within the tribe had a subchief. A winatun, a sort of secretary of state, conducted business between the chief and subchiefs. The winatun had another duty as well. If a traveler entered the village, after he met with the chief the winatun escorted him out of the village, bid him good-bye and watched him go — making sure he left. Each tribe lived within defined boundaries. Within these boundaries, they hunted, fished and gathered food.

To the men fell the job of hunting and fishing — tasks that they accomplished using bows and arrows, spears and traps. The bow and arrow was used to hunt large game like antelope, deer, elk and mountain lion, although usually, the animal was not killed outright. The hunter would follow the trail of the wounded animal, waiting

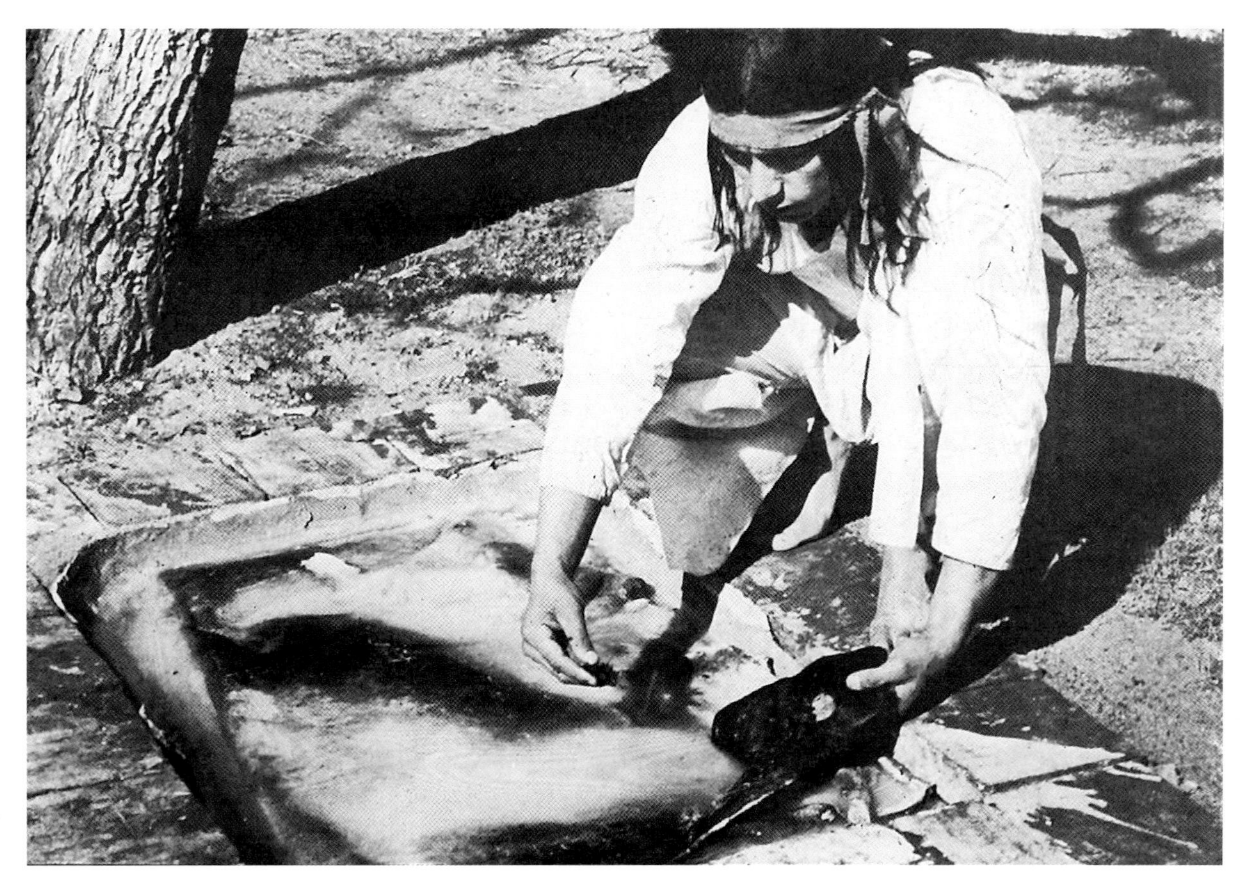

Grinding stones used by American Indians to grind acorns into meal

(Opposite page) The General Sherman Tree located in Sequoia National Park

(Chapter opening photo) A view of Yosemite Valley and the upper crest of the Sierra Nevada Mountain Range

until it became weak from loss of blood to complete the kill. Spears were used to hunt animals such as raccoons, badgers and bears. Fish were caught with nets.

Women gathered wild berries, tules, yucca roots, wild plums, birds' eggs, wild grapes, insects, and most important of all, acorns. The acorn was ground and then leached with hot water to remove the tannic acid. It was then used as flour and meal. It was the staple of the Yokuts diet.

The Yokuts manner of dress was simple. Men wore deerskin loincloths except in the summer when they went naked. Women wore skirts made of deerskin, willow bark or tule grass. Ear piercing — a common 20th century practice — was a popular custom. Decorating the body with tattoos was especially popular among the women. After cuts were made in the skin in decorative patterns, ashes were rubbed into the incisions.

The Yokuts practiced monogamy. Divorce and remarriage were allowed. It is also interesting to note that the Yokuts were one of the few North American tribal groups to develop a fairly good monetary system. Shells and beads were the medium of exchange.

The Yokuts also had a very good communication system between the tribes. When the Spanish, or any stranger entered the valley, this system was activated. If a group of Spaniards entered the valley from the south, the southernmost tribe would light a fire in a hole built for that purpose. When the fire was burning well, wet animal skins or wet tule mats would be held over the fire, interrupting the smoke creating puffs that could be used to send messages. Within four hours, the messages would be transmitted from one lookout station to another along both the Coast Range and Sierra Nevada mountains all the way from the south end of Kern Lake to the Cosumnes River near present-day Sacramento. Every tribe in the valley would know how many people were in the party, the direction of travel and whether or not they were hostile.

According to Frank F. Latta, some of the Yokuts tribes did not come into contact with the white man until well into the 1860s. By that time, Native American tribes in the East and Midwest had been in contact with the white man for well over 300 years.

An interesting footnote to this is that until 1917, when many Yokuts were drafted into the United States Army and taught to use guns, they had still been hunting using bows and arrows.

For the most part, the Yokuts were peaceful people living a fairly idyllic life. However, that was about to change. The next years would bring the white man and with him would come the beginning of a long, sad tale that would culminate in tragedy for the Native Americans of Fresno County.

The White Man Comes into the Valley

In 1769 Spain began colonizing Alta California by establishing missions along the coast. Alta California was the area north of the present-day Mexican border. The area below the border was called Baja California. Two expeditions, one headed by Don Pedro Fages and the other by Father Francisco Garces in 1776, came into the Central Valley. They left descriptions of a desert-like terrain and of the people who inhabited it. Until the early 19th century, few incursions had been made into the Central Valley and those had been of short duration — mostly to capture Indians to work at the missions on the coast or to chase Indians who had run away. There were several routes into the valley. Two of these were Indian trade routes that would become important roads for the Spaniards. One was El Camino Viejo, which extended from Los Angeles over the Tejon Pass, then north through the valley's west side and over the Altamont Pass to today's east Oakland. The other was the route over present-day Pacheco Pass.

By 1805 Spanish settlements on the coast were becoming crowded. Would the interior valley offer new possibilities for missions? In order to find out, and also to satisfy his own curiosity, Lt. Gabriel Moraga led an expedition into the valley. On January 6 he discovered a river that, since it was the feast day of the Holy Kings who brought gifts to the Christ Child, Moraga named Rio de los Santos Reyes (The River of the Holy Kings). Today it is called the Kings River. On March 20, 1805, his group reached another river that they named the San Joaquin River for St. Joachim, the father of the Virgin Mary.

A year later, in 1806, Moraga returned to the valley. This time he and his party traveled from Mission San Juan Bautista over what is now the Pacheco Pass. When they descended into the valley, they were greeted by swarms of yellow butterflies, mariposas, in Spanish. They came to a creek, which Moraga named El Arroyo de las Mariposas. When California later became a state, the name Mariposa was applied to the county that comprised most of the Central Valley.

In 1822 Mexico won its independence from Spain. Alta California was now part of Mexico. During the decade of the 1820s, fur trappers and traders began coming west to California. Outstanding among this group was Jedediah Strong Smith. Unlike other traders of that era, Smith was literate and a devout Christian. He even had some knowledge of Latin that, in the wilderness of the frontier, distinguished him as a superior person. Smith was the first white man to cross the Sierra Nevada Mountains and in 1827 became the first American to enter the area today known as Fresno County. Smith kept an extensive diary of his travels. He made note of the valley's excellent soil and predicted it would one day support farming — a prophecy that would come true in 40-50 years' time. He was followed by other trappers and

(Far right)
Gen. John C. Fremont played a major role in the acquisition and development of California. He served as one of California's first senators and as an officer in the Union Army during the Civil War.
Fresno County Free Library

Christopher "Kit" Carson later served as a colonel in the Union Army during the Civil War and held the position of superintendent of Indian affairs for Colorado territory until his death in 1868.

mountain men — two of the most famous of these were Joseph Rutherford Walker and in 1829 Christopher "Kit" Carson.

In 1843 a new expedition was planned into Alta California. The government of the United States was hoping to eventually wrest Alta California from Mexico. In order to obtain geographical information about the area, Brevet Capt. John Charles Fremont, a topographical engineer, was put in charge of the expedition. In his report on the expedition published first in 1845, Fremont gives colorful details of his journey. His guide for the trip was Thomas Fitzpatrick. On the trip west the group met up with Christopher "Kit" Carson, who was asked to join them. After enduring many hardships due to the winter snows, they crossed the Sierra in February 1844. They reached Sutter's Fort where they were received and entertained with great hospitality. They left the fort on March 24. They journeyed south, with the San Joaquin River to the west and the Sierra to the east. Fremont and his men reached the area that is now Fresno County on April 5, 1844. It was a spring in which the valley was filled with wildflowers. Late rains had left snow on the low peaks of the Sierra. Fremont was delighted by all he saw. The group camped along the San Joaquin River. The next day they continued their journey following the river until they could go no farther south. Turning east, they followed the river until they found a good ford (probably Gravelly Ford) and camped on the other side. They viewed droves of wild horses kicking up dust on the plains and saw columns of smoke in the afternoon sky — a signal that the Indians knew there were strangers in the valley. On April 7 the party continued across the valley, passing within sight of present-day Kearney Park. They continued south until they reached the Kings River and the approximate location of present-day Laton and then kept traveling south until they exited the valley.

The Gambetta Mine at Grub Gulch, whose main vein was eight inches wide, was discovered by a member of the J.B. Gullemin family. *Philip and Gay Wright*

In 1845 Fremont returned to California once again visiting the Central Valley. This time his expedition included Kit Carson and Joseph Walker as his guides. On this trip, Fremont explored the mountains of eastern Fresno County.

In 1848 the Mexican War that had begun in 1846, ended. Alta California became a territory of the United States.

Gold!

On January 24, 1848, James Marshall was building a sawmill at Coloma on the American River. He noticed specks of yellow in the water spilling along the tailrace. He took three ounces of the yellow material to his boss, John Sutter. It turned out to be gold. Even though they tried to keep it a secret, the news leaked out. By May the Gold Rush was on. Within a few months gold was discovered in the Chowchilla, Fresno and San Joaquin rivers. For the next few decades the area that would become Fresno County was a beehive of mining activity and became known as the southern mines. Settlements with colorful names began to dot the landscape. Coarse Gold Gulch, Texas Flat, Fine Gold, Gertrude, Fresno Flats, Narbo, Grub Gulch, Hildreth, and Rootville, a mining camp that within a short time changed its name to Millerton, began to swell in size as more miners poured into the area.

California's population grew dramatically as miners from all over the world headed there. The character of the territory became more cosmopolitan, but, with the huge immigration of people from the United States, it also became more American. These new arrivals joined their voices with those who were already clamoring for statehood. On September 9, 1850, after a constitutional convention was held in Monterey, California became a state of the United States of America. The state was divided into 27 counties. The largest of these was Mariposa County. It covered one-fifth of the state and encompassed the entire San Joaquin Valley.

Mariposa Indian War

Many of the valley Indians had been taken away from their people to work at the coastal missions. Many of them caught diseases from the white man and, when they escaped from the missions and came home, brought these diseases to their people. A significant number of Indians died as a result. After 1805 incursions by the Spanish military into the valley to capture Indians who escaped from the missions were made often. The Indians were dealt with cruelly. This only served to heighten fear and distrust of the white man. The influx of miners into the foothill areas of present-day Fresno County brought problems for both the Indians and the settlers. The Indians peaceful way of life was disturbed by people encroaching on their land. When all these things were added together, it wasn't surprising that trouble developed.

There were numerous skirmishes between Indians and the white men. There were deaths on both sides. More conflicts followed — leading to the Mariposa Indian War. When conflicts with the Indians reached their height, Gov. John McDougal gave orders for the Mariposa Battalion of 200 to be mustered in on January 24, 1851. Maj. James D. Savage was put in command. During their tour of duty, Savage and his men discovered Yosemite Valley. Most of the action took place near Mariposa, but soon it spread into the San Joaquin Valley. Wiley Cassity operated a trading post and ferry on the San Joaquin River several miles below Millerton. He had been warned about hostile Indians, but paid no attention. His body was found not too far from his store. Both his legs had been cut off, his tongue had been cut out and pinned to his chest with an arrow. Not long after this occurred four men were killed near Fine Gold.

Near the end of April 1851 the war ended. Plans were made for a peace conference at Camp Barbour that was located on the San Joaquin River near Rootville. According to Wallace W. Elliott, in his *History of Fresno County, California*, the camp had been established on April 14 by three federal Indian commissioners. The camp was named for one of them, George W. Barbour. The other two commissioners were Redick McKee and Oliver W. Wozencraft. It was their job to negotiate the treaty with the Indians. The treaty was drawn up by the commissioners and formally approved on April 29, 1851, by 16 tribal representatives. Under the terms of the treaty the Indians had to agree to stop fighting, to relinquish their lands and to move to the Fresno River Reservation, land that was set aside for them. A reservation agent was to look after their welfare. The treaty failed to mention that a military post would be established nearby staffed by soldiers who would see to it that peace prevailed. However, in less than a month — on May 26 — Fort Miller was established. Named for Maj. Albert S. Miller, a United States Army officer who had a distinguished career, the fort was located just one mile up the San Joaquin River from the little mining camp of Rootville, which would soon be called Millertown or Millerton. An interesting footnote is that the Camp Barbour Treaty and 17 other treaties with the California Indians were submitted to President Fillmore who submitted them to the Senate. The treaties were then referred to the Committee of Indian Affairs and were rejected. Instead, Congress authorized the establishment of seven reservations for the California Indians.

At this point, one of the most fascinating men in the early history of the valley made his appearance. Maj. James D. Savage, having just completed a tour of duty with John C. Fremont, left San Francisco and established a trading post and mining camp on the south fork of the Merced River about 15 miles below Yosemite Valley. The year was 1849. Early in 1850, members of the Yosemite tribe, attacked and tried to drive him off his property. According to Charles

Clough and William Secrest Jr. in their book, *Fresno County: The Pioneer Years*, Savage, in the summer of 1851, with Dr. Lewis Leach, Lorenzo D. Vinsonhaler and Samuel A. Bishop as his partners, built a trading post on the Fresno River. They had a contract to supply goods to the Fresno River Reservation and this site was a convenient distribution point. Although prices were high, business was brisk. Miners paid their prices rather than travel all the way to the stores in Mariposa. Savage became a wealthy man. In his early years Savage had been a trapper and mountaineer and had lived among the Indians learning their language and becoming acquainted with their culture. He was illiterate, yet he possessed a native shrewdness. Through some slight-of-hand tricks involving guns and bullets, he made the Indians think he was indomitable — they began to look on him as a god. He married the daughters of three Indian chiefs. Estimates of the number of wives Savage took run as high as 33. Some said he was the best friend the Indians ever had. On August 16, 1852, after the war ended, Savage went to Poole's Ferry on the Kings River to try to help ease tensions between members of the Choinumni tribe and a group of white men who tried to take their land and had murdered some of their people in the process. This group was led by Judge Walter Harvey of Tulare County. When Savage and Harvey met face-to-face, Savage told him that he abhorred his group's actions. Harvey drew his pistol and shot Savage, killing him. The seemingly invincible friend of the Indians was dead. Harvey was acquitted of the crime, but, for the rest of his life, was haunted by fear that he would be killed by vengeful Indians. Savage was buried near Poole's Ferry. His grave was later moved near the former site of his trading post on the Fresno River. When Hidden Dam was built and the waters of Lake Hensley covered the site of Savage's store, his grave was moved to a site overlooking the river and is marked by a tall monument with the simple inscription, "Maj. Jas. D. Savage."

The Fort Miller complex was located on the south bank of the San Joaquin River. The building in the center housed the adjutant's office and the officers quarters

The Blockhouse was built in 1851 and is the oldest building in Fresno County. The log walls had loophole openings for guns.

Fort Miller

Bertina Richter, in her book entitled, *Fort Miller, California, 1851-1865*, presents a comprehensive history of the fort. Fort Miller was located on the south bank of the San Joaquin River. It was situated on high ground as a preventive measure in case of floods. The main problem with the site was that in summer it was the hottest place in the area. The highest recorded summer temperature for 1853 was 121 degrees. It had some amenities — fertile soil, clear water and many trees. Adobe bricks, made on the site, were used in the construction of the buildings for the fort. Pine and oak trees supplied necessary components such as rafters,

Elisha Cotton Winchell and his family arrived in Millerton in 1859. He planted an orchard that provided the only fruit in the area. He practiced law and became the first county school superintendent. *Catherine Rehart Collection*

lintels and cross beams. Other materials came from Stockton in ox-drawn wagons. The Blockhouse, the first building to be constructed, was built in 1851. Other buildings including officer's quarters, junior commissioned officer's quarters, quarter master's building, kitchen and dining room, barracks, hospital, bakery, guard house, blacksmith shop and powder house were completed by 1855. One major event at Fort Miller that year occurred when the Episcopal Bishop of California, the Rt. Rev. Bishop William I. Kip, arrived to conduct a Baptism and Communion service.

One problem in the early days of Fort Miller involved treaty violations. Miners began trespassing onto the reservations and trading with the Indians. There were problems on both sides that the officers from the fort had to settle. The fort remained an active military post until 1858 when it was abandoned. During this period the family of Judge Elisha Cotton Winchell occupied the former hospital building. Winchell acted as a caretaker for the property. The family of James McKenzie also lived in a building on the grounds. Fort Miller was reactivated during the Civil War due to the presence of a strong, vocal group of Southern sympathizers in Millerton and other parts of the San Joaquin Valley. Lt. Col. James N. Olney and Company A of the 2nd California Volunteers arrived in the summer of 1863. Companies B, G and K soon followed. They were greeted without incident, but stayed at Fort Miller until December 1, 1864. From that time on the fort ceased to be a military outpost and became home to the Charles Hart and James McKenzie families. It remained in the care of their descendants until the waters of newly created Millerton Lake flooded the area in the early 1940s.

Millerton

The little gold mining camp of Millerton was a colorful place. It was one of the richest mining camps in the area and drew people from all walks of life. Spaniards, Indians, Chinese and Americans made up the diverse mix of peoples. Millerton started out as a "rag town," which meant that most of the dwellings were made out of canvas. Soon a few frame buildings were erected. The village consisted of one main street that ran parallel to the San Joaquin River. A few side streets intersected it. Wild hogs ran loose down these byways adding an interesting flavor to everyday life. Ownership of land was based on squatter's rights. Saloons were everywhere. They attracted a clientele not only interested in the liquid spirits they sold (whiskey, gin and brandy were not sold by the drink, but by the quart bottle), but in the gaming tables that were in continuous operation. Winnings were paid in gold dust. Soldiers from Fort Miller added to the local color. Millerton was never incorporated and never had a church although the circuit rider came occasionally to conduct a tent meeting. The arrival of the stagecoach brought excitement. The stage road from Los Angeles to Stockton followed a route through the foothills. Until a post office was established at Millerton on October 11, 1853, a mounted express rider handled the mail.

The town of Millerton is seen with Indian huts on the north bank of the river. The large building just left of the center of the picture is Fresno's County's first Courthouse building.

Millerton's earliest residents were David Bice James, a miner who left Col. Barbour's 1850 expedition through the Central Valley to head for the colorful gold mining camp; William Bowers, who was also a miner; and Jesse Morrow, a miner who would become a ferry operator and, later, a businessman in Fresno. Dr. Lewis Leach, who had been James Savage's business partner, was Millerton's resident physician. Other prominent residents of the settlement were J. Scott Ashman, who would serve as Fresno County's sheriff; Gillum Baley, who would be elected county judge; William Faymonville, who would serve as county recorder and auditor and, later, as the first mayor of Fresno; J.W. Ferguson, founder and publisher of the *Fresno Weekly Expositor* and the *Fresno Daily Expositor* newspapers; Charles A. Hart, who served as county judge; Clark Hoxie, who served as a county supervisor; Jefferson Shannon, who was a deputy sheriff and who would later become the land agent for the Central Pacific Railroad; E.C. Winchell, who served as county judge and district attorney; and Ah Kitt, who operated a blacksmith shop and would later enter into a partnership in Fresno with Jefferson Shannon.

Before the Courthouse was built, county offices were located in Henry's Hotel in Millerton. John C. Hoxie, an early Millerton resident, can be seen standing in front of the hotel.

In 1854 the first real hotels were built in Millerton. A year later Ira McCray, one of the hotel owners, purchased Jesse Morrow's ferry along with land on both the north and south sides of the San Joaquin River. On the north side he erected the $15,000 Oak Hotel that was said to be the finest between Los Angeles and Stockton. It had separate units, a large dining room and a bar with gaming tables, pictures of nude women and pool tables. It became a popular spot for the miners, many of whom lost their gold dust during an evenings play.

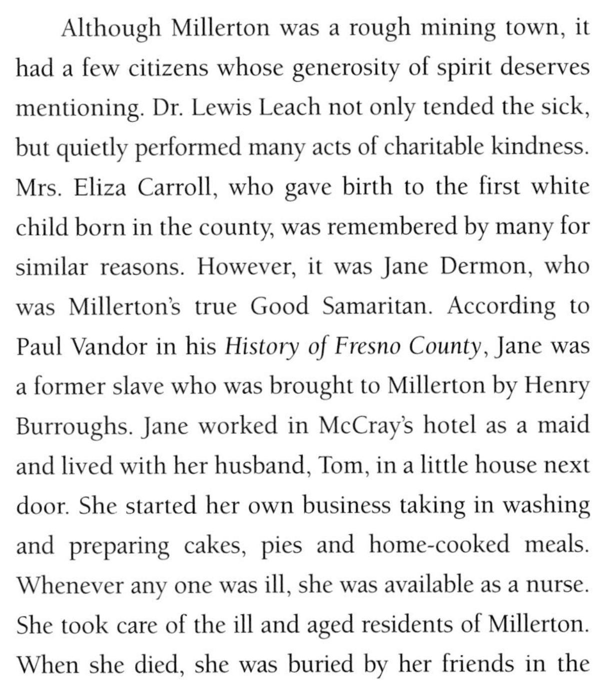

Although Millerton was a rough mining town, it had a few citizens whose generosity of spirit deserves mentioning. Dr. Lewis Leach not only tended the sick, but quietly performed many acts of charitable kindness. Mrs. Eliza Carroll, who gave birth to the first white child born in the county, was remembered by many for similar reasons. However, it was Jane Dermon, who was Millerton's true Good Samaritan. According to Paul Vandor in his *History of Fresno County*, Jane was a former slave who was brought to Millerton by Henry Burroughs. Jane worked in McCray's hotel as a maid and lived with her husband, Tom, in a little house next door. She started her own business taking in washing and preparing cakes, pies and home-cooked meals. Whenever any one was ill, she was available as a nurse. She took care of the ill and aged residents of Millerton. When she died, she was buried by her friends in the

Taken in 1914, this photo shows a deserted Millerton. The Courthouse is on the left. (Note the jail in the rear of the building.) On the right is the Court House Exchange — better known as Payne's Saloon.

nearby cemetery. Jane and Tom Dermon were probably the first African American residents of Millerton.

A County is Created

Soon after California was granted statehood and Mariposa County was created, the population of the area began to increase. It was not long before it was necessary to carve other counties out of Mariposa, the mother county. Mariposa's southernmost section went to Los Angeles in 1851. A year later Tulare County came into existence. In 1855 Merced County was formed.

If a citizen of Millerton needed to transact official business he had to travel a great distance over roads that were primitive and sometimes impassable to reach the county seat. As the area around Millerton grew in importance, the citizens felt neglected. They wanted to form their own county. On May 26, 1856, the California Legislature passed a creative enactment that allowed an appointed group of commissioners to form the county. Ira McCray, James Cruikshank, Hugh Carroll, Charles A. Hart, O.M. Brown, H.M. Lewis and J.W. Gilmore were given this task. They established 10 voting precincts. On June 9, 1856, the county election was held. The vote was favorable. At the first meeting of the newly elected Board of Supervisors on June 23, 1856, Fresno County was declared formally organized. Millerton, the largest community in the county, was the county seat. It was 10 years before a courthouse was built. Until that time, space for government offices was rented. Even though Millerton had now taken on the added importance of being the seat of county government, its lackadaisical, free-wheeling lifestyle did not change. The Board of Supervisors did not let its business meetings stand in the way of a good time — it might adjourn as many as 20 times a day to retire to the saloon for a drink. Court adjourned one day so the jury could attend a horse race. One piece of business, however, had to be taken care of immediately. A new jail had to be built. It was, but the men who built it cut every possible corner in its construction. When finished, it became a joke. It was so easy for anyone to break out of the building that prisoners did just that — returning only for the excellent meals that were provided by one of the hotels. Finally, the jail was torn down. When the courthouse was built in 1867 it contained a jail. Until then, lawbreakers were taken to Mariposa. Whoever held the post of county treasurer felt free to make loans to his friends from county funds — requiring only a personal note as collateral. The first treasurer skipped town taking a good part of the treasury with him. He was never caught.

On February 8, 1860, the Millerton School District was formed. The first classroom was in the dining room and kitchen of the old hospital building at Fort Miller. Rebecca Baley, the teacher, had 12 students. After three months classes ceased due in part to lack of funds and available teachers. It was not until spring 1864 that a school opened in the home of Laura Winchell.

At this point, mention should be made of the county's first newspaper, the *Fresno Times*. Conceived by Ira McCray, the editor was Samuel Garrison. It published just 10 issues and then ceased publication on April 28, 1865.

Millerton's location on the banks of the San Joaquin River made it vulnerable to flooding. Two major floods hit the town — one in the winter of 1861-62. It did a considerable amount of damage, but it was the Christmas Eve flood of 1867 that was the most devastating. No one was killed, but many businesses were wiped out. Most seriously damaged was Ira McCray's. His finances were precarious before the flood — he was deeply in debt. The flood completed his ruin. He left Millerton penniless. He would later die in Fresno cared for by Dr. Leach.

The First Fresno

Although gold mining attracted many settlers to eastern Fresno County, there was activity on the west side of the valley as well. In 1855 a small settlement named Fresno City was established near the present-day city of Tranquillity. It was located on the Fresno Slough, a branch of the Kings River that flows into the San Joaquin River. In the beginning, a warehouse, a store and a hotel, called the Casa Blanca, were the only buildings. C.A. Hawley and W.B. Cummings, who owned the Casa Blanca, had ambitious plans for the settlement. In 1860 they filed a town-site map showing the large community they wanted to develop. It consisted of a proposed 89-block area that measured 2.25 miles east and west and 1 mile north and south. Their agent, Abner J. Downey, was also the manager of the Casa Blanca and the postmaster.

It looked like the developer's vision might become a reality for several reasons. Fresno City was a stopping point on the Butterfield Overland Mail stage line that ran from St. Louis to San Francisco. It was a stopping point for steamboats that traversed the San Joaquin River, and Cummings and Hawley planned to build a ship canal southward. However, there were three problems: Fresno City's location on the slough made it prone to flooding, another stage stop at Hawthorne became more popular because it was in a drier area and steamboat travel began to die out. In 1863 the post office closed. The Casa Blanca continued to operate for a few more years. Then it, too, closed.

The stagecoach standing in front of Bear Valley's Oso House in 1854 has an illustrious traveler on board. Gen. John C. Fremont can be seen seated at the right on the top seat.

The Butterfield Overland Mail

On September 16, 1858, a new mail and passenger service between St. Louis, Missouri, and San Francisco, California, was inaugurated. It was called the Butterfield Overland Mail. Concord spring wagons, with four to eight horses depending on the terrain, transported their cargo of people and mail over many miles of inhabited and uninhabited land west of Missouri. Stage stations were opened along the way offering passengers and drivers an opportunity to rest and giving the hostlers a chance to change the horses. Most of the horses were wild mustangs. Even after they were broken in to harness, they were still fiery creatures. Only the best drivers — men who could be trusted, who were responsible, who could keep a cool head and who were fearless — were hired. The stage road through what is now Fresno County began at Kingston located on the Kings River. It then extended north to Elkhorn Station, Hawthorne Station, Fresno City and finally to Firebaugh's Ferry. From Firebaugh it went over the Pacheco Pass and on to San Francisco. On a good day a stagecoach could travel from Visalia to Firebaugh's Ferry in 17 hours.

Smith's Ferry

In the mid-1850s a pioneer arrived in the southeastern section of Fresno County. James Smith, who was born in Pennsylvania in 1821, was a school teacher in Ohio. He married and in 1848 left for the gold fields of California. He was the first to take up a claim at the site of the present-day town of Columbia. His mining operations proved fruitful. He decided to settle in California and brought his family to the San Joaquin Valley.

In 1855 he established a ferry on the Kings River just southwest of present-day Reedley. He and his family were the first residents in the area. The ferry was conveniently located on the Stockton to Los Angeles stage road. He built a two-story hotel on the hill above the ferry that was not only a home for his family, but also provided lodgings for travelers. The hotel did not have a saloon because he and his wife did not want their children to come under the evil influence that a saloon could bring.

The business operated for many years. Smith, in addition to his business responsibilities, served for two sessions in the California Legislature. After Smith died in 1862, his widow ran the business. She remarried several years later. Her new husband and later, other

The capture of Joaquin Murrieta by the California Rangers under the command of Capt. Harry Love

owners, kept the ferry going until 1874. By that time the railroad was in full operation through the valley and stagecoach travel was diminishing.

During the early years of Fresno County there were a number of colorful figures of less than sterling character. The story of two of these men follows.

Joaquin Murrieta

One of the most enduring legendary figures of Fresno County's history is Joaquin Murrieta, a man from the Pueblo de Murrieta in Sonora, Mexico. When gold was discovered in 1848, he left Mexico and headed for the mining camps of California. His first mining claim was in Calaveras County where a group of unruly men beat him, jumped his claim and assaulted his wife, Rosa. He and his wife moved to Angels Camp where another tragedy occurred. His brother, Jesus, was accused of stealing a mule that he had sold to a miner named Bill Lang. Jesus was lynched and Joaquin Murrieta was horsewhipped.

Because he had been honest in his dealings, but had been treated so outrageously, he turned against the law. Needing to avenge these acts, he found the miners who had abused his wife, roped them and dragged them behind his horse until they were dead. He knew a price was on his head so he sent his wife to a hideout in Niles Canyon in Alameda County.

Next he enlisted several relatives to help him command gangs he was forming. The gangs carried out various types of criminal operations — mainly horse stealing. Among the gang leaders was Manuel Duarte, better known as "Three-fingered Jack" because he lacked two fingers. The headquarters for the gangs was near present-day Coalinga at the Arroyo de Cantua. The hideout was in a perfect setting. There were several vista points that gave them a good view of the surrounding area. There was an adobe house, a barn and a corral. It was here that brands were changed on stolen horses before they were taken south to Mexico. On November 21, 1852, in Southern California, one of the members shot and killed Gen. Joshua Bean, a brother of Judge Roy Bean who was known as the "Law West of the Pecos." Murrieta's brother-in-law, Reyes Feliz, and two other men were hanged for the crime. The gang then moved into the gold country where they went on a rampage of robberies and murders that caused tremendous fear among the miners. Posses were formed, but the gang always eluded capture. Rewards, posted for the capture of Murrieta, went unclaimed. The situation became so desperate that the citizens of Mariposa petitioned the state to form a group of rangers to pursue the Murrieta gangs.

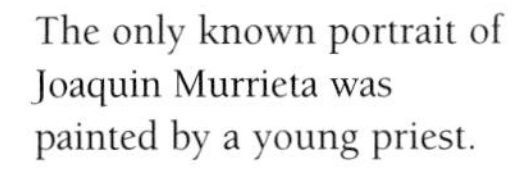

The only known portrait of Joaquin Murrieta was painted by a young priest.

The California Legislature took action by forming the California Rangers under the command of Capt. Harry Love. They were given a mandate — to bring the outlaws to justice. They forced the desperadoes to leave the gold country and move their operations to the west side of the San Joaquin Valley. Soon after this, the gangs split up. One gang went to Sonora, another went to Santa Barbara. Murrieta Joaquin Valenzuela, a cousin of Murrieta, and Manuel Duarte went to the hideout at Cantua.

On July 25, 1853, Capt. Love and his men came upon Murrieta's camp at Cantua Creek. One of the Rangers, Captain Byrnes spotted Murrieta. Murrieta saw him, jumped on his horse, pulled his gun and fired. The shot missed. The men chased Murrieta who, on horseback, jumped off a 12-foot cliff. He fell from his horse, but got back on and took off with the men in hot pursuit. Murrieta was severely wounded, but kept riding. He was shot again, fell from his horse, and although mortally wounded, tried to run toward the hills. Another shot rang out — this one pierced his heart. "Three-fingered Jack," seeing what

The Murrieta Rocks northwest of Coalinga was the site where the bandit Joaquin Murrieta was captured.

happened, tried to escape. It took 10 shots to kill him. The era of the Murrieta gang ended.

Tiburcio Vasquez

Tiburcio Vasquez was born near Monterey in 1835. He became one of the most notorious bandits of 19th century California — second only to Joaquin Murrieta. He was of Mexican and Native American ancestry. His life of crime began in a bar fight in Monterey. During the scuffle a constable was killed. Vasquez quickly left and launched a career of horse stealing in three counties. He was sentenced to three jail terms — one in each county — for his efforts. In 1871, after his release from the last prison, he and three accomplices lay in wait near Hollister for the Visalia stage. When it appeared, they held it up. One of the robbers was caught. The others fled. The Monterey sheriff tracked them down. In the gun fight that followed, one of the robbers was killed and the local marshal was wounded.

Vasquez formed a gang. Its focus of operation became the Central Valley. Its first raid was on Firebaugh's Ferry. Gang members walked away with $600. In 1873 Vasquez and his men came to Fresno to recruit more gang members. They rode into Russell Fleming's stables, turned their horses over to a frightened stable boy and refused to pay the boarding fee. Fleming soon returned and seeing them, grabbed his gun and demanded money from the outlaws. They jumped on their horses and rode off, calling to Fleming in Spanish, "bueno hombre" that means "good man."

Soon after this the gang raided Jones Ferry and made off with $1,000. Next, the men descended on Kingston, robbing the store of Jacob & Einstein, S. Sweet's store and the hotel. Their haul that day was over $2,500 in jewelry and money.

Tres Piños was the site of the gang's final robbery. While his cohorts were inside a store robbing it, Vasquez stood outside and killed several people.

This was the last straw. On January 24, 1874, Gov. Newton Booth posted a $3,000 reward for his capture. Sheriffs all over the state were on the lookout for Vasquez and his gang. He was trailed to a friend's house in Los Angeles, where he was apprehended while eating dinner. Vasquez was taken to San Jose where he was tried for murder. He was found guilty and sentenced to hang.

Tiburcio Vasquez was a lady's man in spite of being described by his contemporaries as being coarse, treacherous and brutish. The ladies seemed to find him irresistible. He was blessed with a magnetic personality that drew people to him. While in jail huge crowds of people came to see him. He entertained them all in his charming way, especially the ladies who made up half of his visitors.

The bravado that was one of his character traits was still in evidence the day before his hanging. He asked to see his coffin to make sure it was large enough to fit him. He was executed on March 18, 1875.

Land for Sale

In the mid- to late-1860s, the San Joaquin Valley Land Association, a San Francisco-based group of investors, acquired hundreds of thousands of acres of land in the San Joaquin Valley. They were speculators who were issued script by the federal government in the form of warrants. Each one of these warrants entitled the person who held it to 160 acres of land. Because most of these men were either recent German immigrants or of German descent, they were popularly called the German Syndicate. Among their number were William Chapman, Issac Friedlander and Frederick Roeding. This huge acquisition of land was not applauded by the few cattlemen who had settled in the valley.

One of the first settlers to acquire land from the syndicate was Anthony Y. Easterby of Napa, California. According to Charles W. Clough and William B. Secrest Jr., in *Fresno County: The Pioneer Years*, Easterby purchased 5,000 acres and set about planting wheat. Easterby had traveled extensively and had seen what could be accomplished when proper irrigation methods were applied to the land. He asked a friend of his, sheep man Moses Church, to join him in his new endeavor. The year was 1869. They dug an irrigation well on land near Millerton, but since there was little rain to augment the water supply and cattle from nearby grazing land trampled the wheat that did come up, the crop was ruined. In the following year, Easterby moved his operation to land nearer Fancher Creek east of what is now the city of Fresno. Church bought the Sweem Ditch and the Centerville Canal and formed the Fresno Canal and Irrigation Company. Church posted an appropriation for 3,000 feet of water and began building ditches bringing the water to Easterby's land. Wheat was planted and they waited to see what would happen. In 1872 the land produced 4 million pounds of wheat. Their venture was not only a success for Easterby and Church, but would shortly open up a new world of possibilities for Fresno County and the Central Valley.

Colorful stagecoach robber, cattle rustler and thief Tiburcio Vasquez had this photo taken to sell during his last trial.
William B. Secrest Sr.

CHAPTER 2

Fresno Station is Established

In 1871 the Central Pacific was building a railroad from Lathrop south through the Central Valley. A railroad stop was proposed at Sycamore (present-day Herndon) on the San Joaquin River. In November 1871 one of the owners of the railroad, Leland Stanford, was scouting the area on horseback with other officers of the line. They were not sure if Sycamore was a good choice and wanted to look at other options. The valley was desolate in winter, but then they saw a lush, green field of wheat — a verdant oasis in the brown desert. They called on the owner of the wheat field, Anthony Y. Easterby, and his associate, Moses J. Church, and were impressed with their irrigation accomplishments. Stanford saw very quickly what this could mean for his company. If more canals were built and people settled here farming this obviously fertile land, his railroad could make a great deal of money shipping crops out of the valley. Stanford made his decision very quickly. He would build his town near the wheat field — a town that he envisioned would become the major shipping point in the Central Valley.

Unless otherwise noted all images this chapter courtesy Laval Historical Collection

The Railroad Creates a Town 2

Soon after Stanford's visit a real estate subsidiary of the Central Pacific Railroad, the Contract and Finance Company, purchased land for the town site from the San Joaquin Valley Land Association, also known as the "German Syndicate." The area was known as the "Sinks of Dry Creek" because it was where three creeks, Dry Creek, Dog Creek and Red Bank Creek, drained into the plains. Stanford chose the location for the railroad stop, a site that today is marked by the Southern Pacific Depot.

The town site was now selected, but it did not have a name. Several versions of the naming of Fresno have been offered over the years. Some have said that it was named for Fresno County or the Fresno River. Dr. Raymond Wood, in his article entitled, "The Origin of the Name of Fresno," states that Leland Stanford, himself, selected the name Fresno because on the map it was directly opposite the old settlement called Fresno City. However, a letter from C.M. Wooster to George Cosgrave dated October 18, 1928, states what is perhaps the authentic story. C.M. Wooster was an employee of the Central Pacific Railroad and worked with the construction crews in 1872, when the railroad reached the new town site. He was in charge of drawing site maps of the new towns created by the railroad and of selecting names for them. He thought since the newest town site was slated to become a major city in the Central Valley, it should have an important name — perhaps the name of one of the railroad owners — Crocker, Huntington, Hopkins or Stanford. Others convinced him this was not a good idea because the area was so barren. Wooster, looking around, noticed that the only sign of life except for Easterby's wheat field was a lone tree next to a small spring. He was told it was an ash tree. He then said to himself "There's a Fresno!" (Fresno is the Spanish word for ash tree.) He named the new town site Fresno. The footnote to this story is that the tree was not an ash tree at all, but a nameless, ordinary green bush. The green bush and the spring that gave it life are memorialized on a plaque on the Mariposa Mall in downtown Fresno.

Railroad construction sped down the valley. A bridge and rail over the San Joaquin River were completed on March 23, 1872. A month later the new town site was reached. Fresno Station was born. In May the town was surveyed by Edward H. Mix. Streets were laid out parallel to the railroad with cross streets intersecting at a perpendicular angle. Since the railroad did not run on a due north and south axis, the downtown streets did not either. The streets that ran parallel to the railroad were given the names of letters — A, B, C and so forth. The intersecting streets were given the names of California counties. On June 26, 1872, a land sale was held. Lots measuring 25 by 150 feet were sold for $60 to $250 depending on where they were located.

A Raw Frontier Town

The first resident of Fresno Station, James Faber, arrived on the train. He came with more than a suitcase. He had made a number of purchases in Stockton hoping to open a general store in the new town. There was one small problem, however. There was a railroad regulation that stipulated freight could not be delivered south of Merced. Faber talked the railroad conductor into letting him drop his provisions off the train as he neared the Fresno Station stop. After he disembarked, Faber retrieved his goods, set up a tent near the railroad stop and opened his store, the first business in Fresno.

Faber's commercial venture was the first, but he was soon followed by others.

Otto Froelich opened a store across the tracks from Faber. A saloon and restaurant, owned by Anton Joseph Maassen; a livery stable run by John Wyatt; a variety store; a blacksmith shop; two other restaurants, one with a rooming house and the other with a hotel; and a lumberyard all opened soon after. Otto Froelich was the Wells Fargo agent and, in August 1872 Russell Fleming became Fresno Station's first postmaster.

The living conditions for these first residents were primitive. Simple frame houses were built. The railroad crews lived in tents. The first water had to be brought from the San Joaquin River in railroad tank cars. Anton Maassen dug the first well. Other residents were invited to fill their buckets at his well — for a fee, of course. The Fresno Water Works opened for business in July 1876. Owners Lyman Andrews and George McCullough drilled a 100-foot well. Using a steam pump, the water was raised to a 23,000-gallon tank that was about three-stories tall. It stood at the corner of Fresno and J streets. Underground water mains were laid throughout the town. Monthly rates were charged for the service including $1.50 for a family of five and 50 cents for the family cow. Many citizens dug their own wells in their backyards.

The first public water tanks in Fresno stood on the southwest corner of J (Fulton) and Fresno streets.

(Opposite page top)
In 1874 the office of the *Fresno Weekly Expositor* stood at the corner of J and Tulare streets. Today the Bank of Italy building sits on this site.

(Opposite page bottom)
This photo, taken in 1924, shows the first residence in Fresno. Built in 1872, it was located where the Helm Building stands at Fulton and Mariposa streets.
Catherine Rehart Collection

In 1873 regular passenger service on the railroad began. Large amounts of sheep, cattle and grain were shipped out of Fresno and 100 railroad cars filled with consumer goods came into Fresno. The town was beginning to grow.

In 1873 a school district was formed. Mary McKenzie was hired to teach the first class of students. They met on the second floor of Booker's store. A year later a school bond was approved. A school building was constructed at Tulare near M Street.

The first doctor in Fresno was Dr. H.C. Coley. He was followed by Dr. Lewis Leach, who moved from Millerton, and Dr. Chester Rowell, who arrived in Fresno from San Francisco in 1874. Fresno's first lawyer was A.C. Bradford. When Judge E.C. Winchell moved from Millerton to Fresno in June 1874, the two men became partners.

A New County Seat

Many of the settlers of Millerton, tired of the lack of progress and vision in the old mining camp, dismantled their homes and businesses. They loaded the lumber in wagons and headed for Fresno Station. The exodus began with a carpenter named Thomas Whitlock and steadily increased — leaving Millerton an empty shell

The Fresno County Courthouse is seen here as it looked in 1877. It was built for a cost of $56,000. Upwards of 800,000 bricks were used in its construction.

Looking east on Mariposa Street toward the Courthouse from J (Fulton) Street in 1882, the photo shows the unpaved streets and covered wooden sidewalks. In the distance can be seen St. John's Church, the White School and the Champion Mill.

of a town. As a result, Fresno's growth began to increase dramatically. The residents of Fresno County began to talk about moving the county seat from Millerton. A petition was submitted to the Board of Supervisors on February 12, 1874, requesting an election be held to decide the matter. The election date was set for March 23. Four communities were on the ballot — Millerton, Fresno, Centerville and Lisbon, a proposed town site northwest of present-day Clovis. Election day arrived. The votes were cast. Fresno won handily. In addition to the town's rapid growth, its substantial new population and its location in the valley as a rail center, another persuasive reason could be found for its strong support. Every voter who cast a vote for Fresno was given a ladle full of whiskey, courtesy of the railroad political machine.

The name Fresno was applied to the thoroughfare designated by the railroad to be the most important. At 80 feet across, it was the widest street in the new county seat. The railroad offered a four-block parcel at the corner of O and Fresno streets as a site for a courthouse park.

Dr. Lewis Leach arrived in California in 1850 and operated a trading post with James Savage south of Coarse Gold Gulch. He practiced medicine in Millerton and became the second doctor in Fresno. *Catherine Rehart Collection*

The railroad bosses had a vision for Fresno that included a wide, sweeping drive up Fresno Street to a grand courthouse. The offer was rejected. Many citizens felt it was too far from the business district developing near the railroad. They asked for a four-block parcel at Mariposa and L streets. This request was granted. It was on this site that a courthouse was constructed. On the day the cornerstone for the proposed courthouse was laid, District Attorney Cladius G. Sayle predicted it would "stand the heats of summer and the storms of winter for 1,000 years or more." This was a prediction that would long be remembered. The boxlike structure faced Mariposa Street and the railroad. Built by the California Bridge and Building Company of Oakland, the building was completed in August 1875. Until it was finished, some of the offices of county government were housed in a temporary building. Other offices were set up in anterooms of nearby saloons.

Now that Fresno was the county seat, it was called Fresno or Fresno City instead of Fresno Station. It was no longer a mere railroad stop — it was on its way to becoming a major town.

The business district was now beginning to expand beyond H or Front Street. Businesses began to open along Mariposa Street. The new town, however, was still more than a little rough around the edges. The streets were unpaved and often littered with rubbish; wooden sidewalks graced the business district; and cows, dogs and horses roamed at will. The most numerous businesses in town seemed to be the saloons. They could be found on every corner with several in the middle of each block as well. Having swinging doors with no locks, they were noisy, attracted an unsavory clientele, were unregulated and were open 24 hours a day, seven days a week. As the years progressed, the owners of these establishments would come to hold tremendous political power in the community. Later reformers would target the saloons as the primary source of all that was wrong with the city.

On October 4, 1874, Dr. Lewis Leach brought the patients from the county hospital at Millerton to Fresno. They made the journey in Russell Fleming's stagecoaches. Dr. Leach was the last county official to leave Millerton. On that same day the last county business was conducted in the Millerton Courthouse. Henry Clay

Daulton, a supervisor, presided over the meeting that concerned the Ne Plus Ultra Copper Mining Company. When this was completed, a resolution was passed transferring county business to Fresno. In keeping with the Millerton way of life, the assembled group adjourned to a nearby saloon to partake of some spirited liquid refreshment.

The new county seat was a crowded one. Hotels were filled — it was hard to find an empty bed. Reservations had to be made in advance. Although lumber was expensive, more hotels were being built. Some of the early hotels were Maassen's International, Larquier House, Washington Hotel and Henry House, which later became Morrow House. In the next decade the United States Hotel, the Star Hotel and the Grand Central Hotel would be fine additions to the town.

The town boasted a number of general merchandise stores. Some of the early owners of these establishments were Otto Froelich, L. Davis, Elias Jacob, George Bernhard, H.D. Silverman, Louis Einstein, Louis Gundelfinger, William Vellguth, Adolph Kutner and Samuel Goldstein.

Even though Fresno was a growing frontier town, by 1876 it still did not have a church building. Various religious denominations held services in rooms over saloons, in hotel anterooms or in private homes. It was a situation that bothered a number of people. Gillum Baley, the county treasurer, and his family had moved to Fresno from Millerton where he had served as county judge. He and his family had crossed the plains from Missouri and had suffered many hardships. A deeply religious man, he was instrumental in organizing the Methodist Episcopal Church South. The congregation had been meeting in a room over Shannon and Hughes Saloon. Often after church Baley would meet a notorious gambler named Mustang Ed as he came downstairs. Baley and other members had been trying to raise funds to build a church. One morning Mustang Ed asked Baley how the fund drive was going. Baley told him that it was not going well at all. The next day Mustang Ed won a poker game. The stakes had been high and the gambler fleeced his fellow players quite nicely. He swept his winnings off the table and presented them to Baley. This was the money that was used to build Fresno's first church — the Methodist Episcopal Church South at the corner of Fresno and L streets. Today, the church still is going strong, although at a different site, and is called St. Paul's Methodist Church.

Another important event in 1876 was the beginning of another Fresno newspaper. Dr. Chester Rowell was a native Midwesterner and a staunch Republican. During the Civil War he had fought in the Union Army. Fresno had many immigrants from Southern states — pro-Confederate sympathies were strong. He was concerned, but not surprised, that the other newspapers were very biased toward the Democratic Party line. Rowell wanted a voice for Republican politics. Using his own money and obtaining backing from a local group of Republicans known as "The One Hundred," he rented a store front, bought a press, hired a small staff and turned out a newspaper. The night before the first edition hit the streets, Rowell and his staff stayed at the office guarding the press so afraid were they that someone might vandalize it. On the morning of September 23, 1876, the first edition of the *Fresno Morning Republican*

Fresno's first church, the Methodist Episcopal Church South, was located at Fresno and L streets. Note the Mill Ditch running down Fresno Street in front of the church.

The Farmer's Bank building (right), located at Mariposa and I (Broadway) streets, was completed in 1889. It typifies the ornate architecture of the period.

The Mill Ditch ran down the middle of Fresno Street. The Black Hawk Stables and Methodist Episcopal Church South can be seen on the left. On the right are St. John's Church and the Champion Mill.

made its appearance. This newspaper was a success and in the years after 1900 would become Fresno's major newspaper and one of the most important newspapers in the state.

Near the end of 1874 Otto Froelich and Capt. Charles Barth built Fresno's first brick building to house their bank — Fresno's first. It was located on the north side of Mariposa Street between I Street (Broadway) and the alley to the west. Two years later in 1876 Capt. Barth experienced financial difficulties and resigned. The bank closed. In August of that year the Bank of Fresno opened its doors. Other banks opened during the 1880s including the Fresno County Bank with O.J. Woodward as president, which became the First National Bank of Fresno and was later absorbed by the Bank of America; Bank of Central California, organized by Louis Einstein; Farmer's Bank with Dr. Lewis Leach as president; Fresno National Bank; Fresno Loan and Savings Bank; Union National Bank; and the Fresno Savings Bank.

In 1877 Fresno's first flourmill was built on J (Fulton) Street by Calvin Jones, who owned the Jones Hotel next door. His wife had a corral in back where she kept cows. She milked them twice a day and had a number of customers. The cows were often let out of the corral to graze on nearby land. Jones' mill did good business until another mill opened nearby a year later. Jones closed his business and, with his family, moved away.

The new mill that opened in 1878 at the corner of Fresno and N streets was called Champion Mill and was owned by Moses J. Church. He ran a canal from Fancher Creek into Fresno on a 15-foot drop. The canal ran right down the middle of Fresno Street bringing clean water to power the mill. The refuse water was returned to the canal and conveyed through the canal to land Church owned in the country west of Fresno. The mill was enlarged in 1880 and eventually, in 1886, sold to the Fresno Milling Company. Later it was sold to Sperry Flour Company. The ditch, however, has a more colorful history. Church was a Seventh-day Adventist, a religious denomination that did not yet have a place of worship in Fresno. When he built his canal, he built a baptismal chamber between the mill's banks at a spot where the water ran clean between the canal and the mill. Here, baptisms were performed not only for the Seventh-day Adventists, but for the Baptists as well, until they were able to erect churches. The canal was open with slats laid across at intervals. Walkways were placed across it at intersections with cross streets so that people and animals could walk across — occasionally some fell in. As time went on, the mill ditch became a convenient place to dump refuse. In the summertime the heat caused the ditch to develop a rather unpleasant odor. It was also unsightly. For years the outcry raged — everyone from the general populace to the health board was crying for the ditch to be filled in. The city fathers ordered that the canal be discontinued. The matter got tied up in the courts. Finally, one Sunday in the late 1880s a group of people, led by Dr. W.T. Maupin, the health officer, gathered on the ditch's banks and, with shovels in hand and scrapers at the ready, filled in the offending ditch. The process took two days.

By 1879 the town was still a pioneer community. There were few trees, save in Courthouse Park where attempts were being made to landscape. The streets were still unpaved and filled with refuse. Cows and other domestic animals still wandered at will. People walking or riding four to six blocks in any direction would find themselves in the country looking at the barren plain.

West of the Southern Pacific Railroad track was Chinatown, where Fresno's large population of Chinese lived — apart from the Caucasian population — just as they had done at Millerton. According to Paul C. Vandor in his *History of Fresno County, California*, racial discrimination was as strong as ever. In 1874 there was a meeting of the residents of Fresno to write an agreement that no one would rent, lease or sell land east of the railroad to people of Chinese descent. Nearly every Fresno resident signed the agreement.

The decade of the 1880s was a dramatic period for the pioneer town. Two important changes occurred — incorporation and an unprecedented economic boom period that spurred major growth. As the story of the decade unfolds, these will be discussed.

In July 1882 telephone service arrived in Fresno. A 20-line switchboard was hooked up in the office of the *Republican*. Mrs. S.A. Miller was the operator. Some 15 people subscribed initially. A year later there were 20 subscribers. Those who had phone service were not only treated to Mrs. Miller's kind voice on the phone, but they also were able to hear the comments made by a parrot who held court rather vociferously nearby.

The early 1880s saw the building of a number of church structures. St. James Episcopal Cathedral, St. John's Catholic Church (at its first location at Fresno and M streets), Methodist Episcopal Church, First Baptist Church, First Congregational Church and African Methodist Episcopal Church were all built during 1881 and 1882.

Social clubs were important components of life in Fresno. In 1874 the Independent Order of Odd Fellows transferred its lodge from Millerton to Fresno, thus becoming the first club in the new county seat. The Good Templars and the Masons soon formed lodges. Clubs devoted to intellectual pursuits like the Fresno Social and Literary Club attracted members. Other clubs formed in the 1880s including the United Workman's Lodge, the Knights of Pythias, the Native Sons of the Golden West, the Atlanta Post No. 92 of the Grand Army of the Republic and the Martha Lodge No. 39.

Baseball was a favorite sport. The first recorded game was on Sunday, March 10, 1875, between the Fresno and Magnolia Clubs. As the years progressed Fresno would produce such top baseball players as Frank Chance, Dick Ellsworth, Jim Maloney and Tom Seaver. The names of Chance and Seaver are enscribed in the Baseball Hall of Fame.

The ever-present danger of fire was an issue with which Fresnans were all too familiar. Until the Fresno Hook and Ladder Company, a group of volunteers, was formed in 1877, the only help in fighting a fire was an ineffective Babcock extinguisher housed at the Jacob & Company store. Even with a volunteer fire brigade in place, efficiency and adequate equipment were still a problem.

Dr. Chester Rowell's nephew and namesake, Chester Harvey Rowell, arrived in Fresno from Illinois in 1895 to teach at Fresno High School. In his unpublished autobiography he relates the following: "Everybody carried a 'gun.' There were no fire alarms and the custom was for whoever saw a fire first to pull out his gun and fire five shots in the air. It was

A.H. Cummings (center) was the chief of Fresno's first volunteer fire department. Assistant Chiefs Ledyard Winchell (left) and Thomas Yost (right) are seated.

This group of Fresno citizens made up the first volunteer fire department.

taken quite for granted that the man who saw the fire would have a gun. The next man nearer the fire station would fire his, and the firemen, if sober, would finally hear and go out after the fire. Usually the first house was gone, but sometimes they saved the neighbors' houses. However, much of the town had been burned down several times." It was a revealing look at the Wild West nature of the community well into the 1880s.

Another difficult situation Fresnans faced was winter flooding. As stated at the beginning of this chapter, Fresno was situated on the confluence of three creeks. When heavy rains hit and those creeks overflowed, Fresno flooded. It was Mother Nature at work with a vengeance. The town did not have any kind of drainage system. The water came and it stayed. The worst instance of this was the flood of February 1884. The Sinks of Dry Creek filled like never before. People had to use rowboats to get from home to work. Basements flooded and those arriving on the train had to embark on flatboats to be transported into town.

The Pioneer Town Becomes a City

By 1885 talk of incorporation had been going on for a long time. Ever since Fresno had become the county seat, incorporation had been an issue for discussion. The town was growing; the Board of Supervisors was still governing it. Fresno was 13 years old and yet it still had no city government or city services. Those who settled Fresno were an interesting mix of people. There were the original Southerners who had come west after the defeat of the Confederacy in order to flee "carpetbagger" governments imposed on them by the Northern Unionists. Add to this a large number of immigrants from other parts of the country and from abroad. These newcomers were also strong-minded, independent and mistrustful of government. Even though many of them disagreed over politics, they believed, like the earlier pioneers, that Fresno's success depended on its unregulated saloons. They felt the saloons provided readily available "easy women," liquor and gambling, making it an entertainment center for miners, farmers and loggers who came to town and spent their money in the local businesses as well as the saloons. They felt that local government would enforce controls to the detriment of local business. Of course, there were some who did not agree with that view, but the majority did. Until 1885 any talk of incorporation was defeated each time it was put on the ballot.

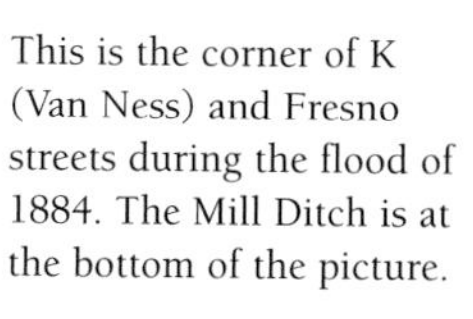

This is the corner of K (Van Ness) and Fresno streets during the flood of 1884. The Mill Ditch is at the bottom of the picture.

This scene during the 1884 flood shows the impact on the residential areas of Fresno. Water surrounds this home at K (Van Ness) and Tuolumne streets. The Courthouse can be seen in the background.

However, in 1885 the movement to create a city began to take root. Many of the citizens realized that the services a city could provide were sorely needed. A number of devastating fires and outbreaks of lawlessness provided incentive. On September 29, 1885, an election was held. The vote to incorporate was 277 to 185 — not a big voter turnout in a town of over 3,000 residents. It must be remembered that, at this point, women still did not have the right to vote. On October 12, 1885, the city of Fresno officially became, under California statute, a sixth-class city, the minimum form of municipality, but a city nonetheless. Five trustees were elected to the city's new governing body. The first meeting was held October 27, 1885, in the real estate office of Thomas Hughes. As events will show, even though a governing body was in place, it would be a number of years before really strong government would be a part of Fresno's life.

A harnessmaker, a doctor and three real estate men comprised the first Board of Trustees. William Faymonville, one of the real estate men, was elected

The officers of Fresno's first police department are shown here. J.D. Morgan (center) was the last city marshal and the first police chief.

president of the board, making him, in effect, the first mayor of Fresno. Famonville, A. Tombs and J.M. Braley each drew two-year terms. Dr. W.L. Graves and Thomas Hughes were to serve for four years. At that first meeting they began to create a city government. Taxes were set and ordinances were drafted. Some of the more interesting ordinances were: cows, sheep, horses, mules and goats could no longer be allowed to graze on public streets; carrying concealed weapons was no longer allowed unless the person carrying the weapon was a peace officer or a traveler; and anyone wishing to discharge a firearm within the city limits had to secure a permit from the city clerk two hours in advance.

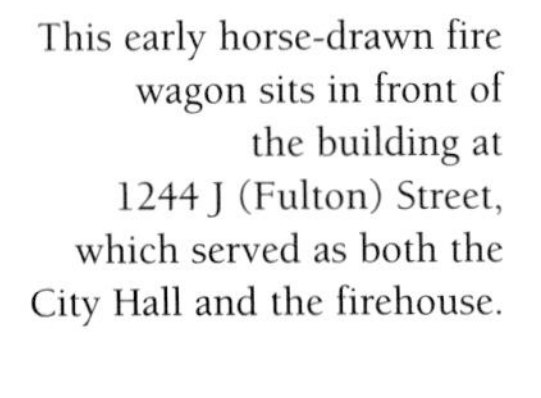
This early horse-drawn fire wagon sits in front of the building at 1244 J (Fulton) Street, which served as both the City Hall and the firehouse.

City offices were housed in leased quarters until a city hall could be built. In May 1888 such a structure was finally completed. The building was a combination city hall and firehouse. The city offices were on the second floor. The meeting room for the Board of Trustees doubled as a dormitory for the firemen — a situation that caused the trustees to pass an ordinance making it mandatory for firemen to remain clothed during meetings. The first floor was used for storing the fire engines and as a stable for the horses that pulled them.

Incorporation brought some real benefits. Main streets were graded and town lot numbers were put in place. Four years later some sections of I, J and Mariposa streets were paved. In July 1886 the Fresno Gaslight Company was granted an electricity franchise. In 1887 the first horsecar line franchise was given. The horsecars were trolleys pulled by horses. Track was laid and soon three different companies, each with a separate line, were offering this service to Fresnans. By 1889 Fresno's first sewer system was in place. In 1894 the owners of the Fresno Water Works decided to replace the old water tanks at O and Fresno streets. They hired Chicago architect George W. Maher to design a distinctive water tower. The result was a Romanesque structure that has become Fresno's foremost landmark. The Water Tower, with 250,000 gallon holding tank, would remain an integral part of the city's water system until 1963.

In 1886 a new newspaper devoted exclusively to legal notices and news appeared. Within a few months it was sold to Morris Webster. Now called the *Business Journal*, this newspaper continues to be owned and operated by the Webster family.

Fresno's Water Tower is listed in the National Register of Historic Places. It is the city's foremost symbol, reminding all who see it that it is water that allowed the valley's desert to become an agricultural paradise.

Land Boon

By the 1890s Fresno was beginning to look more like a city. Brick buildings graced the business district. Larger homes, including many in a fanciful Victorian style, were being built. This trend suddenly accelerated in 1887 when a tremendous period of economic boom took hold. Land values went up. Agriculture expanded. According to Paul Vandor in volume 1 of his *History of Fresno County, California*, "The year 1887 was one of dynamics; the town was one great real estate brokerage community; everyone was almost a land seller... Everyone was inoculated with speculative fever... The same piece of property was not infrequently turned over several times in a day, but always at an advance." There was an influx of new arrivals from other parts of the country wanting to invest in land. As the decade came to a close most of the land in the original town site had been developed.

Large business "blocks" were built by investors who believed in the city's future. Not only were these blocks large, they were opulent as well, ushering in an era of architectural elegance in the pioneer town. Not only business buildings, but residences took on more sophisticated styling. Large, distinctive homes began to be built particularly in the Nob Hill section of town.

This photo of J (Fulton) Street north from Kern Street shows some of the brick "blocks" built during the 1880s. Note the horsecar tracks down the middle of the street.

The Fresno Land Office housed in the Ogle House Hotel was one of many such businesses in 1880s Fresno.

The Hughes Hotel, which was built on the southwest corner of I (Broadway) and Tulare streets, had 145 rooms and its own electrical and ice plants.

An example of investing in Fresno's future was the four-story Hughes Hotel, built by real estate developer Thomas Hughes in 1888 at a cost of $300,000. It featured 200 rooms, each with an outside view, hot and cold running water, electricity and a large central court on the main floor overlooked by balconies surrounding the other three floors. The central court was graced with orange trees and flowers and presided over by a colorful peacock named Admiral Dewey who roamed at will. The Hughes remained, for many years, Fresno's finest hotel.

Another stately hostelry, built in 1887, was the Grand Central Hotel. Located at J (Fulton) and Mariposa streets, its owner was the colorful, delightful Fulton G. Berry. An uninhibited prankster, Commodore Berry had been known to play practical jokes on his good friend from his San Francisco days, Samuel Clemens (Mark Twain) and ride in parades on his white horse dressed up in the costume of a Spanish don wearing a huge sombrero. Berry was a staunch booster of Fresno — always ready to support whatever was best for the city. His good humor was always in evidence. When he died suddenly in 1910, he left specific instructions for his funeral that were carried out carefully. After the service, his coffin was borne through the streets of Fresno proceeded by a marching band playing "There'll Be a Hot Time In the Old Town Tonight" and other songs of a similar nature. At the corner of J (Fulton) and Mariposa streets the band paused and played "Auld Lang Syne." At this point a

The Barton Opera House provided not only a setting for Fresno's major cultural events, but also a place for community gatherings. Fresno High School's graduation ceremonies were held here for a number of years.

beer wagon appeared and dispensed drinks to all the mourners. It was the ultimate practical joke played by the greatest prankster of them all. In recognition of his love for Fresno and for all he had contributed to the community, J Street was renamed Fulton Street in his memory.

In 1890 the Barton Opera House and Armory Hall were built on the northeast corner of Fresno and J (Fulton) streets by vineyardist Robert Barton. The opera house became the major center of the performing arts. Fresno, located halfway between San Francisco and Los Angeles, was a perfect overnight stop for road companies and concert artists who were on tour. The Barton, with its plush red seats and elegant interior, was a sophisticated addition to Fresno. The finest artists of the day trod the boards of the Barton. John and Ethel Barrymore, George M. Cohan, Otis Skinner, Sarah Bernhardt, Lily Langtry, Mme. Schumann-Heink and Nellie Melba were some of the famous thespians and musicians who appeared on its stage. The Armory Hall next door was the headquarters for the Fresno National Guard and was also the setting for teas and dances.

The Kutner-Goldstein & Co. store on I (Broadway) Street offered the shopper dry goods, clothing, furniture, carpets, curtains and wallpaper.

Soon after the turn of the 19th century, H. Graff & Co. was offering delivery service using both horse-drawn and motorized vehicles.

During the 1890s general stores and grocery stores became more numerous. In the early days of the city, the butcher, the baker, the produce man and the rag man carried their goods in horse-drawn wagons and went door to door to offer their wares to local homemakers. Now stores with a new level of sophistication were opening all over Fresno. Some of the better known were: Kutner-Goldstein & Co., Radin and Kamp, Louis Einstein and Company, Sachs and Heringhi Grocery Store, H. Graff and Co. and Holland and Holland.

Also at this time the early privately funded library closed. In February 1893 a new library opened with Mrs. E.J. Latimer as the first city librarian.

One of outcomes of the boom years indeed of the whole decade of the 1880s, was the arrival of immigrants from many different countries. In 1881 the Seropian brothers arrived in Fresno. They paved

One of the stops on the "Pollasky" Railroad was the Tarpey Depot at Ashlan and Clovis avenues. Today the depot is located in Old Town Clovis.

Marcus Pollasky is seen here standing on the wagon supervising the first shipment of grapes from the Barton Vineyard on his rail line.

the way for a large migration to follow as the conditions leading up to and during the Armenian Genocide of 1915 by Ottoman Turkey played out. Like the Chinese before them, Armenians suffered prejudice for a number of years and, like the Chinese, formed churches and organizations that kept their heritage and culture alive. Their contributions to agriculture, cultural arts, business, and indeed, almost every field have enriched the Fresno community beyond measure. Other immigrants began to arrive including, among others, the Volga Germans, Japanese, Yugoslavians, Greeks, Portuguese, Danes, Swedes, Germans, Scots, English, Welsh, Irish, Russians, Finns, Italians and the Basques.

Madera County Created

Until 1893 the interests of the citizens who lived north of the San Joaquin River were represented by one member of the Fresno County Board of Supervisors. The area was growing in population. The city of Madera was founded in 1876 as the terminus for the flume built by the California Lumber Company from the mountains to the valley floor. Madera, the Spanish word for lumber, had grown to become the second largest city in Fresno County. There were many who felt it should become a county of its own. The drive for separation began in 1890. The state assemblyman from Madera, George Washington Mordecai, introduced a bill for county division into the legislature in 1892. State Sen. George Goucher of Fresno said that he would not sponsor such a bill until a meeting was held in Fresno where discussion of this matter could be held in a public meeting. A meeting was set for January 28, 1893, at Kutner Hall in Fresno.

There are several accounts of how Madera County was established. The most popular version is the one recounted by Charles W. Clough in his book, *Madera*. In the late afternoon of January 28, a special train pulled into the station at Fresno. The trainload of Maderans disembarked and walked to Kutner Hall to join the Fresnans already there. By 7:30 p.m. all the chairs were filled. Many people were standing in the back. The meeting began. Suddenly, a fire alarm sounded. Most of the men from Fresno, being able-bodied and members of the Volunteer Fire Department, sprang from their chairs and rushed out the door. Their chairs were appropriated by the men from Madera. Soon, the Fresno men returned because the alarm turned out to be a false one. The meeting droned on and on. Finally, a vote for separation was about to be taken. Someone asked that a standing vote be called for. The chairman said, "All those who favor the creation of a separate county for Madera please stand." Since all the chairs were filled with Maderans and the Fresnans were already standing, when the Maderans stood to register their favorable vote, everyone in the room was on their feet. The final count was 245 to 65 in favor of separation. This data was sent to Sacramento. On February 25, 1893, Madera County was officially created. As a result, the San Joaquin River became the northern boundary of Fresno County.

Two Railroads — Two Different Results

In 1891 a smooth talking promoter with a winning personality named Marcus Pollasky arrived in Fresno. He planned to build a new railroad on the east side of Fresno to Hamptonville (Friant) to the Sierra Nevada Mountains. To show everyone the extent of his wealth and good intentions, he built a large home with sumptuous gardens on an extensive parcel of land bounded today by Tulare, U, Divisadero and Mariposa streets.

The Southern Pacific Railroad was a monopoly in California controlling not only the state's politics, but the prices of shipping goods on its rail lines. It was not

The waiting room of the Santa Fe Depot located at Tulare and Santa Fe avenues

Shown here is suspected train robber John Sontag. He and his partner, Christopher Evans, became the objects of a manhunt and were met by a sheriff's posse at Stone Corral near Yettem, where a gunfight brought an end to Sontag's life.
William B. Secrest Sr. Collection

going to be easy for Pollasky to obtain a right-of-way for his railroad so he put together a group of the city's most influential citizens to help him. These men, who became directors and investors in his venture, included Thomas Hughes, Fulton G. Berry and John Gray. They launched a campaign to raise $100,000 to purchase the right-of-way that would run next to the Tarpey Winery, the new town of Clovis, and end at Hamptonville, which would be renamed Pollasky and, if Pollasky's vision became a reality, would become a major city.

The right-of-way was obtained, but there was one hitch. The rail line had to connect with the Southern Pacific line through Fresno. During construction many of the boxes and materials were marked "S.P." People asked him if that stood for Southern Pacific. "Oh, no," Pollasky said, "Those are the initials of my brother, Sam Pollasky." The line was finished in 1892.

Pollasky invited a large number of guests to a lavish barbecue to celebrate. They boarded flatcars with benches fastened securely to them and experienced a very dusty, hot trip. The barbecue took place, but rumors began to circulate that a buyout had taken place. It hadn't yet, but it was discovered that Pollasky had only invested a small amount of his own money in the scheme. He skipped town and his board sold its holdings to the Southern Pacific Railroad.

In 1894 there was a Pullman strike. This not only meant that food and supplies could not be brought to Fresno, but it posed a problem for mail delivery as well. Thanks to the ingenuity of Arthur Banta, who owned a bicycle shop, the mail was delivered on time. This is what he did. He got together teams of cyclists who rode in relays across the west side, over Pacheco Pass and on to San Francisco. Each rider waited at his destination for the south bound mail and carried it back to his original starting place. For three weeks in June and July of 1894, the Bicycle Mail teams performed their duty and saw to it that the mail went through. On July 18, 1894, the strike ended and the Bicycle Mail was consigned to history.

The next railroad venture was much more successful. The monopoly of the Southern Pacific Railroad had caused a public outcry for a long time. A group of farmers and businessmen and a few wealthy investors banded together to create a new railroad. Called the San Francisco and San Joaquin Valley Railroad, or the "Valley" or "People's" railroad, it reached Fresno on October 5, 1896. Two years later it became part of the Atchison, Topeka & Santa Fe Railway. This railroad was here to stay.

Colorful Criminals

No discussion of Fresno's history would be complete without including some of the scoundrels of the time, including John Sontag and Christopher Evans. John Sontag was, at one time, a brakeman for the Southern Pacific Railroad. Because he was injured on the job the railroad paid his medical bills, but refused to find him a less taxing job. He became very bitter. He went to Tulare County where he met Chris Evans, who was superintendent of a warehouse. The two men became friends. Sontag became engaged to Evans' daughter, Eva. They shared a dislike for the railroad and voiced their opinions to all who would listen. During the next two years four trains were held up on their Central Valley run. Suspicions pointed to Sontag and Evans. Then on August 3, 1892, a train was robbed near Collis (Kerman). In the course of the robbery the passengers were assaulted. This time enough of a description of the two men was given that there was enough evidence to arrest them. They had gone to Sontag's home in Visalia and it was there that Deputy Sheriff George Witty and the railroad's detective, Will Smith, arrived to take them into custody. When they entered the house, shots were fired. Witty and Smith were wounded. Sontag and Evans fled. A citizens' posse saw them. There was a confrontation, shots were exchanged and a member of the posse was killed. Sontag and Evans headed for the Sierra. By now rewards were being posted for their capture. U.S.

Marshall Vernon Wilson arrived with a posse and a group of expert Apache trackers. They began searching for the duo. They found them, but after another bloody confrontation the men escaped only to be pursued during the many months that followed. Finally, U.S. Marshall George Gard and another posse met up with them at the Stone Corral in Yettem on June 11, 1893. An all-out gun battle began. Sontag was critically wounded, was taken to Fresno and died there on July 3. Evans, although badly wounded, escaped, but surrendered soon after. He was incarcerated at the Fresno County Jail where he, with the help of an accomplice named Ed Morrell, made a daring escape. The pair eventually surrendered. Evans was put on trial and sentenced to life imprisonment at Folsom and San Quentin prisons.

Grat Dalton, one of the infamous Dalton brothers, is shown here. Dalton Mountain overlooking Wonder Valley is named for him.
William B. Secrest Sr. Collection

The infamous Dalton Gang made an appearance in Fresno County. James Louis and Adeline Younger Dalton had 15 children — 10 boys and five girls. According to Frank Latta in his book entitled, *Dalton Gang Days*, the family lived in Belton, Missouri. James Dalton was a ne'er-do-well whose string of race horses was his sole source of income. The older boys were disciplined, but the younger ones, Mason, Grat, Bob, and Emmett, were spoiled. They turned into a pretty wild bunch.

In the 1870s the boys began to travel with their father to race tracks in a number of California cities, including Tulare, Fresno and Stockton. Several of the boys got jobs doing general work on ranches throughout the Central Valley. Mason, called Bill, married and settled on a ranch near Paso Robles. Later, Lit became a muleskinner for Clovis Cole and his brother-in-law, Charles Owen.

Bob, Emmett and Grat returned to the Midwest. They and their brother, Frank, were all made deputy federal marshals in Oklahoma, then known as Indian territory. Frank was killed in the line of duty. Before long the remaining brothers were engaged in cattle rustling. They headed west for Bill's ranch, trying to keep one step ahead of the law. In January 1891 they traveled through what is now Tranquillity and on to Malaga where they hid out in a barn. Bob and Emmett rode their horses south. Grat took the train and met them in Traver. On February 5 the boys were seen in Delano drinking heavily. The next morning Bob and Emmett tethered their horses near the train tracks about one-half mile south of Alila, just a mile from the present-day city of Earlimart, and walked back to town. As the train pulled out of the station, they jumped on board the engine. They pulled out their guns and ordered the train to stop near the spot where their horses were tied up. Shots were fired. One man was killed, but the attempted robbery failed. The men jumped off the train and took off on their horses. While all this was happening, Grat was on a freight train headed for Fresno. However, since he was seen with his brothers the night before, it was assumed he took part in the attempted robbery that turned into a murder. In September 1891 Grat was arrested. On

Christopher Evans in his later years
William B. Secrest Sr. Collection

Sheriff Jay Scott (left) and Deputy Sheriff Lindsay P. Timmins (right) pose for this photo on the scaffold on which Dr. Frank Vincent was hanged.
William B. Secrest Sr. Collection

the night of September 20, he broke out of the Visalia jail with a hack saw that had been smuggled in to him. It was suspected that Chris Evans helped him, but it was never proven. With the help of his friend Joe Middleton, he headed for a mountain hideout where he holed up with a friend named Riley Dean. In late December, under pressure from the authorities, Middleton told the authorities of Grat's whereabouts. Fresno County Sheriff John Hensley and Visalia's Sheriff Eugene W. Kay and a posse headed for the mountain. Middleton was with them. It was night when they went up the mountain, but an almost full moon lighted their way. They saw Grat Dalton and shots were fired. Dalton picked up his rifle and shot it, just missing the head of one of the posse members. Grat dropped to the ground, made his way down a ravine, unhitched and jumped on a farmer's horse and rode off into the night.

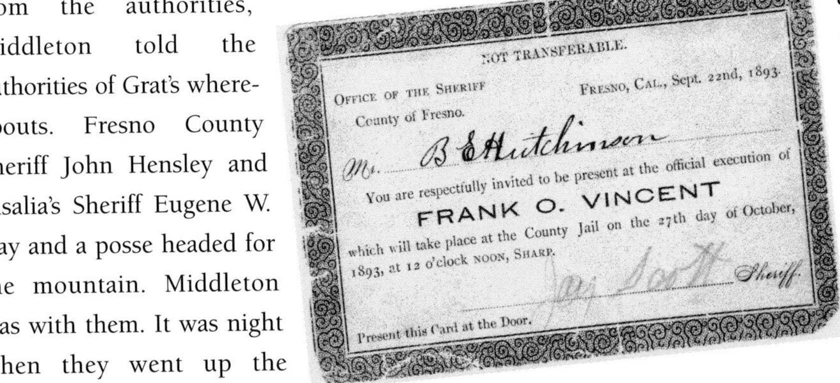

NOT TRANSFERABLE.

OFFICE OF THE SHERIFF
County of Fresno.

FRESNO, CAL., Sept. 22nd, 1893.

Mr. B E Hutchinson

You are respectfully invited to be present at the official execution of

FRANK O. VINCENT

which will take place at the County Jail on the 27th day of October, 1893, at 12 o'clock NOON, SHARP.

Jay Scott Sheriff.

Present this Card at the Door.

Shown here is the formal invitation that was sent to 600 Fresno residents inviting them to attend the hanging of Dr. Frank Vincent.
William B. Secrest Sr. Collection

So began a lawless journey that would end in the deaths of Bob and Grat and the wounding of Emmett on October 5, 1892, when they decided to rob two banks at one time in Coffeyville, Kansas.

There are two interesting footnotes to the story of the Daltons. The mountain where the hideout was located overlooks Wonder Valley. It has been named Dalton Mountain. The second footnote has to do with a side of the men that only a few had a chance to see. Bob, Emmett and Grat attended a number of socials in Kingsburg and Centerville. They appeared to be handsome, polite gentlemen, and were popular dancing partners for the local young ladies.

There were a number of other outlaws during this period, but the Daltons were probably the most famous. The one other notable criminal case involves the sad story of a marriage gone awry. It is the story of Dr. and Mrs. Frank O. Vincent.

The marriage of Annie and Frank Vincent had been in trouble for some time. In his despair, Vincent had begun drinking. His drinking spiraled out of control and he became a drunkard. Annie wanted a divorce. He confronted her and tried to get her to take poison. When she refused, he shot and killed her. A police officer heard the shot, ran into the house and prevented the doctor from drinking the poison himself. Vincent was arrested, charged with murder and confined to the Fresno County Jail. He was then tried, convicted of murder and sentenced to death. The sentence was appealed by Vincent's attorneys, but in fall 1893, the appeals process was over. Some 600 invitations were sent out, inviting people to witness the execution. A scaffold was brought from San Bernardino and erected in an enclosed area next to the jail. Just before noon on October 27, 1893, Dr. Frank O. Vincent was escorted to the scaffold. At noon, the only public execution by hanging in the history of Fresno County was carried out before 600 invited guests.

Culture

An interesting aspect in the life of the young city of Fresno was the creation of a number of women's study clubs. The women in this Wild West town wanted to improve their minds, perhaps, as an antidote to the community's rough edges. The saloons and related businesses were still, as late as the 1890s, very open.

In 1889 the Wednesday Club, the first of the study clubs, was formed. An active group, then and now, the members gave their own papers. In 1894 three more study clubs — Leisure Hour, Query Club and Parlor Lecture Club — were formed. In 1902 the Friday Club organized. Other clubs formed as well. Most are still in existence — a tribute to the passion for knowledge and the intellectual gifts of the women of Fresno.

Any discussion of women's clubs must include the name of one particular woman who played an important role in their development. Dr. and Mrs. William P. Miller moved to Sanger from Maine in 1888. In 1891 they moved to Fresno. Emma Miller was a classics scholar, well-versed in Latin and Greek. She was also an authority on Shakespeare and gave readings from his plays. She also reviewed modern literature. She became a patron of the first four study clubs for women in Fresno. She organized other clubs in Fresno and in other communities, including Sanger and Reedley. She later taught English and literature at Fresno State College. Her legacy is still in evidence in women's groups all over the Central Valley. A mention of her name brings smiles and nods of understanding.

Another cultural antidote was present in the 1896 founding of the Central California Conservatory of Music at Mariposa and O streets. Here, students studied piano, voice, harmony, violin and numerous other instruments. Many Fresno mothers felt that it was important for their daughters to study music. It was part of a young woman's education — as important

The members of the Parlor Lecture Club gathered in front of their clubhouse on Van Ness Avenue dressed in elaborate Chinese costumes

Dr. and Mrs. William P. Miller are shown here. Through her patronage, Emma Miller made lasting contributions to the intellectual life of the women of Fresno County. *Mary Helen McKay Collection*

as learning proper etiquette, developing needlework skills and learning to manage a home.

Government

As noted earlier in this chapter, the swelling economic growth of this period brought floods of immigrants to Fresno. The town grew in every direction. The minority population lived primarily in the area west of the Southern Pacific Railroad tracks in what came to be known as West Fresno or Chinatown. The largest concentration of saloons and brothels was now in this neighborhood. It was a colorful, but often violent section of town. Before incorporation there were no laws to regulate or license the saloons. The saloon owners had been the largest block of voters against incorporation. Now that a city government was in place, the saloon owners, who had acquired a great deal of political power, were adamant in their desire to keep the city fathers from enforcing any laws that were enacted. They also knew that if they wanted to control regulation, they had to control city government.

The major problem for citizens was to find a way to control the growing political power of West Fresno. It was hoped that creating a ward system in which the city would be divided into five geographical districts each with one representative on the Board of Trustees would solve the problem. This would give West Fresno one vote. Certainly, the other trustees from the other four wards would be able to outvote the West Fresno trustee. In reality, it had just the opposite outcome. Partisan politics played a big role.

In the early days of Fresno, according to Schyler Rehart book chapter entitled, "Fresno City: Its Leadership and Progress," in *Fresno County in the 20th Century*, city party conventions were held to nominate the people who would run for election. The Republicans nominated a slate of candidates, including a trustee for each ward, and so did the Democrats. Citizens went to the polls and voted for the party candidates of their choice. Often political "handlers," party loyalists, rounded up voters, gave them free drinks in return for favorable votes. The party who won the most seats on the Board of Trustees, controlled the board. Since all city jobs, with the exception of the elected position of city clerk, were appointed by the trustees, including the police and firefighters. The majority party on the board made all the appointments. It was pure political patronage — a political spoil's system. From 1885 until 1893 the Democrats controlled the board. Therefore, all the city employees were Democrats also. Instead of being accountable to the police marshall, police officers were accountable to the trustee of their ward. The same was true for other city employees. There was no discipline. As a result, many police officers were drunken and incompetent.

During the boom period and the bust that followed, the population of Chinatown grew dramatically. Fresno's Chinatown became the second largest in California. Only San Francisco's was larger. During the late 1880s and well into the 1890s, the trustee from the fifth ward, which was West Fresno, had become so powerful that he was the real boss of city hall.

The presidents of the board or mayors of Fresno during this time were Dr. W.L. Graves (1887), Dr. A.J. Pedlar (1889) and Stephen H. Cole, a realtor (1891). Cole and two other trustees, William Fahey and Bart Alford, made up a "triangle" on the board that became a scandal. Even though Cole was mayor, Fahey, the local head of the Democratic Party, was the real "boss" of Fresno.

In the election of 1893 Fresno's two leading newspapers, the *Expositor* and the *Fresno Republican*, began attacking each other over the issue of whether patronage would be in the hands of the Democrats or the Republicans. Ferguson, the editor of the *Expositor*, said the Democrats on the board were honest men who could better serve the Democratic majority of the electorate rather than the Republican candidates who talked about reform, progress and decency. He called them pretentious. However, when the votes were counted, the Republicans had won control of the Board of Trustees for the first time in the city's history. Firmin Church was the president of the board.

The election brought into power Joseph Spinney, the trustee from the fifth ward of West Fresno. He was the boss of West Fresno and controlled the vice interests. He was a brick maker of Portuguese extraction

Many Chinese people settled in West Fresno in the latter 19th century. This herbal nutritional store on China Alley was a popular shopping place.

who often contracted to build public buildings. He was illiterate and signed documents with an X. He ran as an independent Republican, but was a Republican in name only. A true opportunist, he voted which ever way the wind blew as long as it blew in his favor. He was probably the most corrupt politician the city of Fresno has ever seen. For the next eight years, he would dominate the board by keeping the other trustees divided so he would maintain the most power and control over political appointments and lucrative contracts. Whatever most benefited Spinney determined his position on issues. The office used as his headquarters was located at the Europa Hotel on G Street. At the first meeting of the Board of Trustees in 1895, Spinney was elected president (mayor). He gave a speech, made political appointments and resigned — all in the space of 10 minutes. He preferred to divide and control behind the scenes.

Another Republican was quickly elected to serve as president of the board, Columbus J. Craycroft. He was a brick contractor, but aside from that and his political affiliation, he bore no other resemblance to his predecessor. A native of Missouri, Craycroft's family later moved to Illinois. He served in the Union Army for five years during the Civil War. He married and came west to California, engaging in sheep raising. After his wife's death in 1886, he moved to Fresno and opened a brick-making plant. His bricks were used in the construction of many of the downtown buildings. Craycroft remained president of the board until the election of 1901.

In 1898 the *Fresno Republican* had a new editor. The nephew of Dr. Chester Rowell and his namesake, Chester Harvey Rowell, took over the reigns. Rowell was incensed at the lack of morality in his new home of Fresno, at the political system in general and the political boss of Fresno, Joe Spinney, in particular. Shortly after young Rowell arrived in Fresno, his wife gave birth to their son at Dr. Rowell's home. It was a hot 4th of July night and the saloons, as always, were open 24 hours a day. As his young wife went through a painful, difficult labor, the noise from the saloon across K Street wafted through their open windows. Around 2:00 a.m. a very drunken trumpeter held forth with various patriotic songs all played in a less than normal manner. The louder and longer the off-key trumpeter played, the angrier Rowell became. The next day he wrote an editorial about the previous night that appeared in the *Fresno Republican* on July 7, 1898. Then and there, he decided something had to be done to regulate the saloons. For him, it became a holy cause.

Chester H. Rowell was a Republican, but he did not believe in blind loyalty to a party. If a party did not live up to its principles, it should be

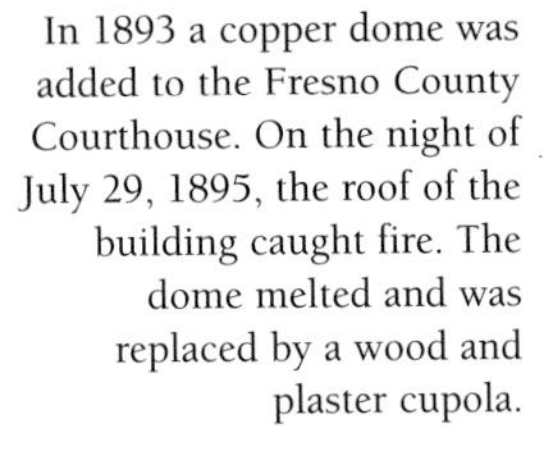

In 1893 a copper dome was added to the Fresno County Courthouse. On the night of July 29, 1895, the roof of the building caught fire. The dome melted and was replaced by a wood and plaster cupola.

This view is looking west down Mariposa Street from the Fresno County Courthouse in 1895; although the city has grown, rural farmland can be seen not far away.

held up to scrutiny. Rowell soon became the driving force in a movement for reform. A new city charter was envisioned that would create a stronger, more effective city government and would eliminate rule by political bosses. Using his editorials as a forum, he launched a vigorous campaign for a new charter, trying to educate Fresnans about the dangers of a thoroughly corrupt political system. It was not an easy task. Just as incorporation had been an unpopular cause, so too, was reform. The same business interests which felt, in 1885, that having unregulated saloons, brothels and gambling dens was good for business because of the money spent there by miners, farmers and loggers coming to town on the weekend, felt the same way now about a new charter. Good government was fine, they felt, as long as it didn't hurt business.

When the matter came to the public in the election of 1899, the new city charter passed. Under the new charter, the offices of assessor, tax collector and treasurer were abolished. These roles were now handled by the corresponding county officers. The mayor, city clerk and police judge were elected to four-year posts and made up the executive branch of the city government. Two elective boards, the Board of Trustees and the school board, each had eight members. The members were nominated, one from each of the eight wards, but they were all elected at large. Other city offices were filled by appointment of the mayor with the approval of the trustees. The school board chose the school superintendent. The police and firefighters were appointed by a commission. The members of that commission were the mayor and four people appointed by him. The fifth ward was divided into three wards, thus breaking the control of the boss of that district.

With the new system now approved, it was imperative to elect a man of character and integrity to the office of mayor. The Democrats, just a week before their city convention, were threatening to nominate a candidate who would be easily controlled by the party. The Republicans met first and nominated young Rowell, who accepted only because he felt it would force the Democrats to nominate a man of integrity. His ploy worked. The Democrats changed their minds and nominated Lewis Oliver Stephens, a religious man with a reputation for complete honesty. As the campaign progressed Rowell disappointed the Republican bosses by announcing he did not have time to campaign. He said that he and Stephens stood for the same ideals and to let the voters decide which man they wanted. If elected, he would serve. If not, he would support the administration of Stephens. On June 14, 1901, the citizens of Fresno elected L.O. Stephens as mayor of Fresno. A new era had begun.

CHAPTER 3

There were four industrial periods in the early history of Fresno County.

The first, the era of gold mining, began in 1848. When the placer mines gradually began to play out around 1860-1864, the period of stock-raising began. By 1874 cattle-raising began to decline although sheep-raising continued to be important for a number of years. In 1868 the era of agriculture was ushered in, first with grain farming, which was followed by the introduction of irrigation and the planting of a wide variety of crops. The year 1881 brought the era of viticulture — the beginning of the grape industry, in all its components, which today is still the foremost agricultural industry of Fresno County.

Cattle

The gold mining era brought thousands of new settlers to California. With this influx of people came the need to feed them. The era of agriculture had not yet begun and a practical means of shipping food from other parts of the country had not yet been found. The answer to the problem was to raise stock animals for food and profit. This was the beginning of Fresno County's cattle industry that, after gold, became the next major basis of the county's economy.

Unless otherwise noted all images this chapter courtesy Laval Historical Collection

The Blossoming of the Desert 3

The interior valley that was Fresno County was ideal for the cattle business. Range land seemed to be limitless. Cattle could roam at will from the Chowchilla River to the Kings River and from the foothills of the Sierra to the foothills of the Coast Range. There were plenty of native grasses for the animals to eat and the climate was ideal. If it got too hot, cattle could be taken into the higher elevations of the Sierra. The only time a rancher had to round up his herds was to drive them to market or, in the spring, to count and brand his stock. Each rancher had his own brand which was burned into the animal's left hip. It was a felony for anyone to obliterate or alter these brands.

One of the first cattlemen in what would become Fresno County was William Hazelton. Hazelton was born in Albany County, New York, on September 7, 1825. As a young man, he decided that the West offered adventure and promise. In 1849 he came to California and headed for the northern mines. He did fairly well but found the gambling tables a better source of cash. One night he and a friend, John Patterson, got into an all-night faro game. Luck was with them and they pocketed $20,000. The next day they made a pact to never gamble again. In 1853 they decided to head south to the upper Kings River area of what was then Mariposa County. They filed on a quarter section of government land.

Scottsburg, which would later be called Centerville, was the nearest town. Hazelton went south to Mexico to buy a herd of longhorn steers. When he returned, Patterson sold out his interest to Hazelton. As the years progressed, Hazelton added to his land holdings and became the largest land owner in the area. In 1857 he married Mary Akers. Their union produced 10 children. Although most of his neighbors had Southern sympathies, Hazelton stood firmly on the side of the Union during the Civil War years. This earned him the nickname "Yank."

In 1857 cattlemen Jefferson James, David Burris and John Sutherland came to Fresno County. James settled on the west side near Fresno City on the Fresno Slough. Burris and Sutherland ranged their cattle in the lower Kings River area. Cuthbert Burrel arrived about the same time. He settled on his Elkhorn Ranch, northwest of present-day Riverdale, with 1,300 head of cattle.

In 1874 Gustav Kreyenhagen sent his son, Emil, from Los Banos where the family owned a hotel and a store to Poso Chane, east of the present-day city of Coalinga. A year later Gustav and the rest of his family traveled along El Camino Viejo, the old Spanish road on the west side of the valley, to Poso Chane. Gustav purchased land between Garzas and Zapato Chino creeks and began raising stock on a large scale. About

1887 Gustav's four sons, Hugo, Adolph, Emil and Charles, took over the business. They had about 10,000 head of sheep and 600 head of cattle. Eventually, they disposed of their sheep and devoted their energies entirely to cattle raising. They were the largest individual cattle growers on the west side and they were the first to raise grain on the west side of the valley.

Another cattleman to settle in Fresno County was Henry Clay Daulton. A grandson of a Revolutionary War soldier, Daulton drove his sheep and cattle across the plains to California in 1853. After spending a few years in the San Gabriel Valley, he came to Fresno County where he purchased a tract of government land 12 miles northeast of present-day Madera. In 1857 he settled on the Santa Rita Ranch in northern Fresno County. Not only was he a successful cattleman, but he held public office. When Madera County was created in 1893, he served as the first chairman of the Board of Supervisors.

Any discussion of the early cattlemen of Fresno County must include Jesse Blasingame. Although he arrived later on the scene, in the late 1860s, he was an important part of the cattle industry and an influential citizen of the Big Dry Creek area in the Sierra foothills.

The last cattle barons to come into Fresno County were Henry Miller and Charles Lux. Miller, whose birth name was Heinrich Alfred Kreiser, was born in Germany to a peasant family. While tending pigs and calves one day, he fell asleep and dreamed that he saw huge herds of cattle with a Double H mark on their left hips. He left Germany and came to New York where he met a man named Henry Miller. Miller had a non-transferable ticket to California that he sold to Heinrich Kreiser for a reduced price. To use it, he had to use Miller's name — so he changed his name to Henry Miller. He arrived in San Francisco, got a job in a butcher's shop and saved his money. Dissatisfied with the quality of available beef, he decided that he wanted to produce beef of a higher quality. In 1851 he left for the San Joaquin Valley. He crossed the Coast Range Mountains on horseback. Descending into the valley, he saw huge numbers of cattle spread out across the plain. They all had the Double H mark on their left flank just as he had seen in his dream. The owner of the cattle ranch, Henry Hildreth, who was anxious to return to the gold fields, was willing to sell. Henry Miller bought his first land and cattle.

When Miller returned to San Francisco, he met with cattleman Charles Lux, his competitor for the San Francisco market. They formed a partnership. Miller would oversee the cattle raising and Lux would market the meat. They agreed to buy but never to sell land. Their holdings would grow over the years to such an extent that, after Miller's death in 1916, it was said that their holdings covered 22,717 square miles of California, Arizona, Oregon and Nevada. In addition to land and cattle, their firm owned slaughterhouses, stores, hotels and banks. It was said they could drive cattle through Central California from Arizona to Oregon and sleep every night on their own land. Their wealth was calculated at over $31 million.

During these years of the cattle barons, cattle roamed at will throughout the Central Valley. There were no fences or barriers. Only the cattle brand on each animal's left flank told who the owners were.

The era of the 1850s and 1860s was also important for sheep raising. The first sheep ranchers in Fresno County were Henry Clay Daulton and Jonathan Rea. They were followed by William Helm.

(Opposite page)
Two cowboys rounding up cattle in Fresno County

(Chapter opening photo)
These cattle grazing along the Kings River represent the second industrial period in Fresno County's history.

Flocks of sheep on the James Ranch near San Joaquin

Helm was born in Durham, Ontario, Canada, on March 9, 1837. He came to California in 1856 and tried his luck in the gold fields, but he soon found that unprofitable. After spending three years as a butcher in Placer County, he started raising sheep and became very successful. He married Frances Sawyer Newman in 1865. In that same year Helm brought his bride and his sheep and settled on 2,560 acres of land he purchased from William S. Chapman for $1 an acre. The land was 12 miles from the nearest neighbor and was just six miles from what is today the center of downtown Fresno. On this land Helm built the first house on the Fresno plains. The winter camp for his sheep was on the site of today's Courthouse Park. Helm became the largest wool grower in Central California. Over the years Helm would add to his land holdings. Several years after the town of Fresno was established, he built the Helm Block at the corner of J (Fulton) and Fresno streets. He was an organizer and vice president of the Bank of Central California.

Other prominent sheepmen were Thomas J. Hall, Thomas Hanes, Rickard Freeman, L.P. Clark and J.W. Potter. The first sheepmen in the Centerville area were Moses J. Church and John A. Patterson. In the mid-1860s, Frank Dusy purchased 1,900 acres of government land near Fowler. His holdings included 13,300 sheep that were allowed to graze on land that would become the town of Fresno.

During this period hog raising was also part of the economy. In 1854 Jefferson Shannon and S.B. Coffee were raising hogs at Millerton. They were followed a few years later by Scott Ashman, Charles A. Hart, Harvey Akers, Newton and Perry Murphy, F.C.B. Duff and Jesse Blasingame who had ranches in different areas of Fresno County.

The Ascendancy of Agriculture

The first hay and grain crops in Fresno County were harvested in the Big Dry Creek area of the Sierra foothills by William Lewis Lovely Witt and William Harshfield. The year was 1852. In the same year Samuel Bishop, who lived on the Fresno River Reservation, harvested a crop of wheat and Bud Akers planted grape cuttings near the Centerville area. In the early 1850s Billy Martin planted apples and peaches on his property at Temperance Flat on the San Joaquin River. William Hazelton planted the first orange trees on his property near Centerville. The first cotton was planted near the Kings River in 1865 by E.W. Burchfield and James Kincaid. These were all early attempts to grow crops with primitive methods of farming, without the irrigation methods soon to come, trusting nature to supply water and proper amounts of sunshine. Some of the planting succeeded, some did not.

Alabama Colony

In July 1868 Judge Samuel Holmes, Maj. C.A. Reading, and Levin A. Sledge, plantation owners from Mississippi and Alabama, came to California to buy land. The defeat of the Confederacy during the Civil War had robbed them of their economic and social positions. They wanted to start over in a new land. The property they were interested in was just southwest of the present-day city of Madera. They bought a large parcel for $2.50 an acre. They called their land the Alabama Colony and wrote to their friends urging them to come west and join them.

A number of settlers arrived in November 1868. Mr. Strudwick, father-in-law of Mr. Holmes; Dr. Joseph Borden and family; the Henry Pickens family; Mr. and Mrs. James N. Sledge; Major and Mrs. Dennett; and brothers James P. and Harry St. John Dixon were among the first arrivals. These settlers were the first group to attempt grain farming on the Fresno Plains. They were enthusiastic and hopeful that they could make a success of their venture.

Life was difficult. Millerton, the nearest town, was 20 miles away. Most goods came from Stockton on a wagon. A sense of humor helped and that this group had in great abundance. Many of them gave names to their homes that showed their sense of fun. The Pickens family named their spartan home "The Cradle of Innocence." The name "Hell's Half Acre" was applied to a bachelor's abode. Citing his change in circumstances, Harry St. John Dixon named his place "Refuge," which indicated that he saw it as a haven from past misfortunes.

Used to living a more gracious life with the help of servants and slaves, the new settlers were not used to hard work. However, they made a brave effort to begin their new life. Unfortunately, when the grain began to grow it was trampled and eaten by the bands of wild animals and cattle that roamed the plains at will. A series of drought years brought more hardship. By 1875 most of the settlers had left. One exception was Louise Dixon, the sister of Harry St. John Dixon. Louise married George Washington Mordecai, who had arrived in the area three months before the Alabama settlers. They purchased the Refuge from Dixon for $6. Here, they raised sheep and cattle and engaged in grain production. They made the land profitable. Their descendants still live on the Refuge.

Beginning of Irrigation

It is interesting to note that in 1872 Harry St. John Dixon, who had sold his Alabama Colony holdings, was the Fresno County Clerk and Recorder. After his experience in trying to grow crops on the Fresno Plains, he thought that Anthony Y. Easterby was crazy to even consider trying to cultivate grain on the flatlands of the valley. When Easterby brought his deed to record, Dixon hesitated to take the fees. What Dixon did not reckon with was Moses Church and his canal building project.

As was discussed in Chapter I, Easterby and Church began their irrigation project to divert water from the Kings River to Easterby's land. On July 7, 1870, Church purchased the Sweem Ditch, which extended from the west bank of the Kings River and began to lengthen it. When he reached the Centerville Canal, Easterby bought the canal. They formed the Fresno Canal and Irrigation Company. It was the job of Moses Church to dig more channels, which he did, and by the end of 1871, their irrigation system was operating — producing an incredible crop of wheat in 1872.

While Church was digging his canals, some serious problems developed. Yank Hazelton, pioneer cattleman in the Centerville area, did not like this intruder digging across land that had been his cattle range. Hazelton felt that he owned all the land from the

Many of Fresno County's crops are still irrigated by water channeled through canals to valley farms.

Sierra foothills to the west and was furious with Church. He began a war of nerves. He first instructed a band of his vaqueros (cowboys) to confront Church and order him to leave the area. They did and Church refused to go. The second confrontation was made by Hazelton and his men. This time threats were made against Church's life if he did not leave. The next morning, Church's barn and house were torn down while he was in Centerville. He became firm in his resolve to stay. Several attempts were then made on Church's life. They all failed. Easterby and Church walked into Jacob & Silverman's store in Centerville and were attacked by Hazelton's men. They fought back. Later, Church entered the post office in Centerville and a man by the name of Smith threw sand in Church's eyes. Another man, Paul Stover, kicked him in the jaw while another man, Bill Glenn, tried to kick him also. Church fought back furiously and by the time he got outside, his face was covered in blood. Church confronted the men and said, "If you want to kill me, why don't you do it?" The men, with guns drawn, walked toward him, then turned and walked into a saloon. Shortly after this, the attempts on Church's life ended.

Other irrigation projects by other pioneers followed. Wheat and grain production began to increase as settlers moved into the lands on the valley's east side and began farming. H. Voorman, George Eggers, and B.C, Libby were some of these early farmers. In 1873, L.A. Gould purchased the Fresno and King's River Canal bringing water to his ranch that today is bounded by Blackstone, McKinley, Belmont and First Street. Here he grew alfalfa, grain, fruit trees and vines. In the late 1870s and early 1880s, Francis Bullard purchased land stretching from the northern boundaries of Fresno to the San Joaquin River and bounded by Blackstone to the east and the Southern Pacific Railroad tracks to the west. He developed it into a 72,000-acre ranch where grain, mostly barley, was grown.

it would be a good forage crop for cattle as it did not cause animals to bloat. It had another side effect, however. It had a taproot that went down at least 40 feet and produced grass so high and thick that it was not only impossible to get rid of, but also it choked out everything around it. This unfortunate recommendation by Professor Sanders resulted in unleashing a scourge on the fields of the valley that even today causes gnashing of teeth when the good professor's name is mentioned.

The first wheat crops were grown primarily to feed cattle. The wheat was harvested by mule- or horse-drawn harvesters.

In 1875, six years before the Johnson Grass debacle, Professor Saunders was in Stockton giving a speech at a grange convention touting the valley's potential as an agricultural center. On that memorable evening one gentleman in the audience listened with growing interest. His name was Bernard Marks. He had had a successful career as a miner and a teacher, but what he wanted most was to be a farmer. He had tried to farm near Stockton but found it tough going. It was difficult and expensive for the small farmer to obtain water rights and build canals to bring the water to his land. As he listened to Sanders and his stories of Easterby and Church and their success, Marks began to have an idea. If it was hard for a man of moderate means to farm successfully, it might be a good idea for an investor to purchase a large acreage, buy the necessary water rights, see to it that the proper canals were built and sell off portions of the land to individuals who would be guaranteed water to irrigate their crops. This would make it possible for hundreds of people to go into farming. His vision would become known as colony farms.

Bernard Marks met with William Chapman who, according to Bob Long, was the principal owner of most of the land in Fresno County in the late 1860s and early 1870s. Chapman, at first, was hesitant about Marks' scheme but soon decided to go along with it.

The grain farmers did not appreciate the roving bands of cattle who wreaked havoc on their crops. Ranchers like Easterby could afford to fence their land; small farmers found this a hardship. A law that would require cattlemen to fence in their herds was presented in the California Legislature. State Senator Thomas Fowler, a cattleman, fought the law and paid a high price for it. Fowler was not re-elected in 1873. On February 4, 1874, the California Legislature enacted the "No Fence" law referring to the lack of fences surrounding cattle ranches but the need for them. Fences were built. An era began to fade away. No longer did cattlemen run the range — a new breed of farmer was settling the valley, one who planted many varieties of crops.

Colony Farms

In 1881 Professor W.A. Sanders introduced Johnson Grass to the farmers of Fresno County. He felt

Marks entered into a contract with Chapman for 21 square miles of prime land south of the new town of Fresno. They added another partner — William H. Martin, a San Francisco capitalist and general agent for the California Immigrant Union whose purpose was to publicize California attractions and resources to such far-flung areas as the eastern United States, England and Europe. During the summer of 1875, the union published a brochure advertising the colony. Then Marks began to lay out streets and farm sites. The Central California Colony was beginning to take shape. Seven streets, each two miles long, ran north and south through the colony. Each street was planted with a different tree and was given its name. The colony was bounded by North, East, South (today, American Avenue) and West avenues, with Central Avenue running through the center of the colony from east to west. Three canals were extended to bring water to the new site. Water rights were obtained from Moses Church's Fresno Canal and Irrigation Company.

All the new colony needed was colonists. The union's brochure had elicited a positive response. Quite a few lots were sold, but this was just a beginning — a number of lots remained. Chapman hired a new land agent and promoter named Martin Theodore Kearney, a bright young man who had recently come to San Francisco from Boston. Kearney had a talent for writing promotional material. His brochures were worded in a way that brought results. One of the most desirable features of the colony was the payment plan for land. Each lot sold for $100 down, $12.50 per month for five years with a final payment of $150 — and no interest. Lots began to sell. Houses soon appeared on the land and crops were planted. The first winter and spring were hard. Water delivery was an intermittent problem. By the next year, the land began to produce. Vines were growing, irrigated by water from the Kings River delivered by Church's canals. A school and church were built on colony land. Social events were organized and life for the colonists seemed good. Many of the early settlers were Danish, Swedish and Norwegian — a harbinger of the cultural diversity that would become such an important part of life in Fresno County.

The success of the Central California Colony paved the way for other colony developments. Within the next few years, many other colonies would dot the landscape around the pioneer town of Fresno Station.

Martin Theodore Kearney

The arrival of M. Theo Kearney brought a personage of intelligence, vision, wealth, arrogance, self-interest and mystery to the Fresno scene. Add to this mix his bachelor status and it is readily apparent why Kearney was the talk of Fresno until his death in 1906.

It is only in the last few years that Kearney's true origins have come to light. According to Schyler Rehart in an article titled "The Man Who Was M. Theo Kearney — New Facts Revealed," Kearney was born Martin Thomas Carney on February 5, 1842, in Liverpool, England, the son of Irish immigrants James and Ann Carney. James was a laborer. A few years later

M. Theo Kearney planted palm trees and oleanders on his 6.5-mile road from Fresno to his Fruitvale Estate. Today it is called Kearney Boulevard.

The Gatehouse Lodge at the entrance to Kearney Park burned down in the 1960s.

another boy was born to the couple. They lived on Banastre Street in Liverpool — an area of tenements and businesses near the Mersey River docks. It was an area teeming with people, diseases and, for many, despair. In 1854 the family immigrated to Malden, a suburb of mostly Irish immigrants just outside Boston. James suffered from alcoholism. His heavy drinking combined with his abusive treatment of his wife caused young Martin to take the temperance pledge at age 14. He was afraid that he might become a drinker also. His younger brother James did become an alcoholic and would die of the disease in 1881. Around 1858 both James and Ann died. By 1860 both boys had accepted a new spelling of their name — Kearney.

When Martin Kearney was 18, he left Malden and moved to Boston. He was hired by Nathan Neat as a clerk in his trunk manufacturing company. During the next few years he rose from the ranks to become the manager. As his prospects improved, so did his manners. He set about acquiring the education and social niceties of genteel society. When he entered polite society a couple of years later, it was without any trace of his Irish accent — he had acquired the polish of an English gentleman. It was the era of the Civil War. Kearney's sympathies were with the Confederate cause. His new friends were those whose beliefs were similar to his. During this period he also became a man of some wealth. He also traded his middle name of "Thomas" for "Theodore," which he shortened to "Theo." When he left Boston for California in 1868, he was ready to forget his past. For the rest of his life, his new persona was the only face the world would ever see.

After traveling overland through the Isthmus of Panama, Kearney took a steamer to San Francisco. On board ship he met Dr. Edward B. Perrin who owned large tracts of land in both Merced and Fresno counties. Perrin spoke enthusiastically of the agricultural potential of Fresno County. Kearney was convinced. When he arrived in San Francisco, he checked into the Lick House, a luxurious hotel. With his newly acquired sophistication and polish, he made his smooth entrance into the nouveau riche circles of San Francisco society. One of his first orders of business was to open a bank account and write out an $8,000 check to Perrin as partial payment on 8,640 acres of land east of the future town of Fresno that he would call the Fresno Vineyard Company. He traveled by stagecoach to view his holdings in March 1869. During the next two or three years, he would make numerous visits to Fresno not only to check on the progress of Church's irrigation scheme but to survey his land, plant a vineyard and view the developing agricultural scene. His work for Chapman as the manager and chief promoter of the Central California Colony began about this time. It is important to note that he was an investor in the colony as well. The ultimate success of the colony brought Kearney increased wealth. Kearney and Chapman had a falling out when Kearney struck out on his own in a new business enterprise. A lawsuit, which Kearney won, brought an end to their business dealings.

During the early 1880s Kearney's social life in San Francisco increased dramatically. He made frequent visits to Fresno, however, to oversee his vineyards and properties. On one of these trips, in March of 1883, he made a purchase of 6,000 acres west and southwest of Fresno — it was destined to become the Fruitvale

Estate. When it was completely developed, the Fruitvale Estate consisted of a 240-acre park; a boulevard that was 7 miles long — extending from Fresno to the park entrance; a large company town south of the park filled with numerous buildings including a store, stables, worker's bunk houses, tea house, blacksmith's shop, ice house, packing shed and small houses for families who worked on the estate; land under crop production and ranch lots that would be sold to individuals. Almost every kind of fruit crop was grown on the estate as well as chickens, hogs and sheep. It was essentially a self-productive operation. However, surplus crops were sold for profit. Raisins were one of the primary crops. During the development of the estate, Kearney embarked on his habit of visiting the spas of Europe — mostly in Germany.

In June 1889 he hired noted landscape architect Rudolph Ulrich to design a plan for the park. The plan included a small lake, tennis courts, fountains and winding roads. The landscaping of the Chateau Fresno Park and boulevard of the same name began in 1890-91. Today, primarily due to Ulrich's design, the park is listed in the National Register of Historic Places.

Ultimately, Kearney planned to build an elaborate chateau, patterned after Chateau do Chenonceaux near Tours, France, deep within the park. The immediate need was a home that would house the ranch office and living quarters. The Superintendent's Lodge was completed in 1902. It adjoined the Servants Quarters building to the south that had been completed earlier. Kearney moved into the Lodge and began, to collect objets d'art for his chateau while on his trips abroad.

During the panic of 1893 many of the people who had bought land on credit from Kearney defaulted. He was forced to foreclose on their property. However, he, like other growers, suffered heavy losses as well. Tariffs were removed on dried fruits causing prices on raisins to collapse. In 1898 he brought together a group of raisin growers and proposed the idea of a marketing organization called the California Raisin Growers' Association. Ideally, by banding together the growers could set prices, control quality and more effectively market their raisins. The group was formed and Kearney was elected president of the board. In the ensuing years, although profits went up, not everyone trusted Kearney. Some viewed him as a dictator who wanted to control the market for himself. It was a stormy few years. In 1905 the California Raisin Growers' Association voted to dissolve the organization. Shortly before his death, Kearney wrote his own epitaph in which he said that the effort to organize the growers killed him.

His health began to decline. Only his closest friends knew he had developed a heart condition. He was in San Francisco on April 18, 1906, and was jolted awake by the major earthquake that shook the city. He left quickly and returned to Fresno. He suffered a mild heart attack soon after. Early in May, he climbed into his car and asked his chauffeur to drive to the west side of the park. Here, he watched the workmen digging the foundation for the five-story chateau designed by Maurice Hebert. Then he ordered the chauffeur to drive on to Fresno where he boarded a train for what would be his final trip to Europe. On May 27, 1906, he suffered a fatal heart attack aboard the British liner, the *Caronia*. Work on the chateau ceased.

A portion of the Fruitvale Estate company town is shown here. Kearney's workers were paid in coins that he had minted and could only be used in the stores on the Fruitvale Estate.

A view of the gardens in Kearney Park

The Fresno Scraper being pulled by a horse on a Fresno farm

Today the Kearney legacy lives on. Kearney Park, Kearney Mansion and Kearney Boulevard are tangible reminders of the visionary man. One often-overlooked part of his legacy is that the concept of agri-business, the basis of Fresno County's economy, has its roots in the Kearney Mansion office on the Fruitvale Estate. His entire estate was left to the Board of Regents of the University of California. Today, Fresno County leases Kearney Park from the University.

James Porteous

As agriculture developed, it was necessary to provide new tools to make farming easier. At the forefront of this business was a Scots immigrant by the name of James Porteous. In 1874 he started a business in Fresno called the Fresno Agricultural Works. Porteous had learned the blacksmithing and wagon building trades from his father in Scotland. His new venture was an establishment that built wagons and carriages. His wagons were in great demand and were used to haul lumber from the camps in the Sierra as well as to haul goods in the new town of Fresno Station. Porteous was also an inventor. He began to work on a new implement that farmers and developers could use to level land. Others, including Abijah McCall and Frank Dusy, had experimented with such a device, but it was Porteous who conceived the final result. It was called the Fresno Scraper. When drawn by a horse, the scraper moved along the ground collecting dirt. When it was full, a lever was pulled to release the dirt. This revolutionalized the way large quantities of soil were moved. The Fresno Scraper was not only a boon to farmers but by 1891 it was being used all over the world. It was used in building the Panama Canal and helped to dig trenches for the U.S. Army on the European front in World War I. The name was commonly shortened to "Fresno" and took the name of Fresno all over the world. Porteous, in his career, invented numerous

By 1915 scrapers were pulled by motorized tractors like this one, which is leveling the Bullard lands north of Fresno.

other implements including the Porteous Header, which was used to harvest grain, and the End Shake North Porteous Raisin Mill. At the time of his death in 1922, over 200 patents were listed in his name in the U.S. Patent Office in Washington, D.C.

La Paloma Winery and Distillery, Fresno County's first winery, was located near Ashlan and Clovis avenues.

St. George Vineyard, one of the early wineries, had a wine storage tank that held 79,000 gallons.

Viticulture

The raisin industry in the central valley began because of a mistake that was made by a remarkable man, Francis T. Eisen, who became known as the father of both the raisin and the wine industries in Fresno County.

In 1873 Francis T. Eisen purchased land from the German Syndicate for $10 an acre. The parcel was bounded by the present-day Kings Canyon, Fowler, Belmont and Clovis avenues. There he established his ranch and planted table and wine grapes. It became the first commercial vineyard in the central valley. The summer of 1875 was very hot. Some of his grapes dried on the vine. Eisen picked them, removed the stems and sent them to market in San Francisco. He called them "Peruvian importa-tion's." They were an immediate hit and the raisin industry of the Central Valley was born.

A year earlier, in 1874, Francis Eisen asked his brother Professor Gustav Eisen, a wine expert, to come to Fresno. In 1875 they built the first winery and distillery in the area. The first year they produced 200 gallons of wine. As their business grew, they enlarged these facilities. By 1881 they were producing 80,000 gallons of wine a year. The varieties included Riesling, Zinfandel Claret, Zinfandel Port, Sweet Malaga, and Dry Sherry. In 1892 their wines won a gold medal at the Dublin Exposition. In 1896 Francis Eisen died. At the time of his death, the brothers were producing 300,000 gallons of wine per year. They had built a worldwide reputation for fine wines.

After Francis Eisen's success with raisins, many others began to plant vineyards with the intent of harvesting raisin crops. By August 1878, the vineyards of the Hedge-Row ranch were producing a substantial raisin crop. Located in the Central California Colony, Hedge-Row was owned by four San Francisco women schoolteachers — Minnie Austin, E.A. Cleveland, Lucy Hatch and Julia B. Short. They increased production each year. Profits rose accordingly. Hedge-Row was a success.

Other raisin growers followed suit, among them, Robert Barton, T.C. White, A.B. Butler, William N. Oothout, J.W. Gould and August Wiehe. Many growers began to produce wines including George H. Malter, Robert Barton, M. Theo Kearney, George and Herman Eggers, Herman Granz and later, Andrew Mattei. Mattei was awarded 22 prizes for his wines, including the Medal of Honor, at the 1915 Panama Pacific Exposition in San Francisco. By 1919 he was the largest individual vineyardist and vintner in the United States.

Minna Eshelman

Any discussion of agriculture in the early years of Fresno County must include the name of Minna Eshelman. Her story is remarkable. In 1877 her family moved west to Oakland because of father's failing health. Her father made a good income speculating in mining stocks. The market declined and thinking his

Minna Eshelman's home on her Minnewawa Ranch

stocks worthless, he threw them into the fireplace. His daughter entered the room and retrieved them. Later, the value of the stocks increased and he gave the money to his daughter, Minna.

Using the money, Minna Eshelman purchased 640-acres of farm land just east of Fresno. She planted Emperor and muscat grapes, olives, almonds, watermelons and peaches. She became fascinated with producing new varieties of crops. She pioneered in the shipment of table grapes to New York. An excellent businesswoman, she added to her holdings and built a large home surrounded by eucalyptus trees. Her estate was called "Minnewawa," a word that means wind in the trees. She took the name from Henry Wadsworth Longfellow's poem, "Song of Hiawatha." Eventually, she bred a strain of Holstein cattle that drew buyers from all over the country.

It was in her pioneering efforts in the dairy industry that she made her greatest contribution to Fresno County. In the 1880s dairy products were often unsafe to eat. Ms. Eshleman brought the latest scientific methods of cleanliness and sanitation to every stage of the operation of processing dairy products. The Minnewawa dairy produced only the highest quality butter, cream and milk. For her accomplishments, Governor Hiram Johnson appointed Minna Eshleman to the Board of Regents of the University of California — the first woman to be so honored. Tragically, she died before she could attend her first meeting.

Dairy Industry

Soon after the Washington Irrigated Colony was established (today the Easton and Oleander areas) in 1878, a group of farmers from the colony joined with settlers of the Central California Colony and formed a dairy. This became the first large-scale cooperative effort to supply milk, butter and cheese to people in Fresno County.

In 1895 a group of Danish immigrants led by Hans Graff formed a dairy cooperative called the Danish Creamery Company. They sold shares in the company for $100. They did not limit the number of shares one could buy. The result was that control of the company soon rested in the hands of a few people. At a meeting held on December 17, 1901, the controlling

The Danish Creamery plant at its original location on California Avenue and Fig Street in 1895

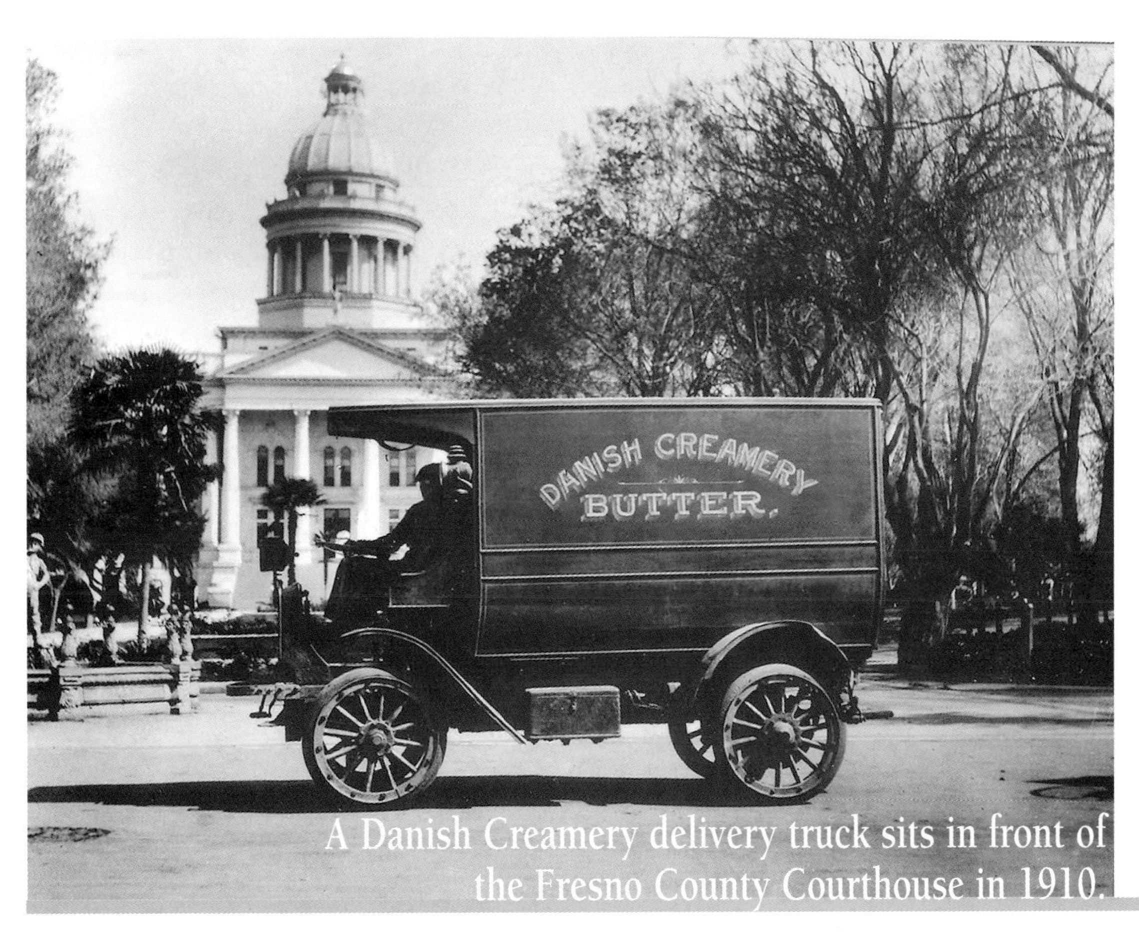

A Danish Creamery delivery truck sits in front of the Fresno County Courthouse in 1910.

George C. Roeding (left) played a leading role in the development of Fresno County's fig industry.

stockholders agreed to sell their shares. Then stock was reissued on a one-man, one-vote basis. Each stockholder was allowed to buy only one $50 share. The result of that meeting was that the organization was now a true cooperative bearing the name of the Danish Creamery Association. The company grew and by 1910 moved its plant from California and Fig avenues to its present site at E and Inyo streets.

In 1902 Danish Creamery joined Challenge Dairy Products. Now the plant not only produced butter, but also processed whole milk and made powdered milk. During the 1920s plants were acquired in Riverdale and Chowchilla. The Chowchilla plant was enlarged to produce evaporated milk in 1941.

Danish Creamery Association, the oldest and one of the largest dairy cooperatives in the United States, merged in August 1999 and became California Dairies Inc.

Other Agriculture Crops

At the same time vineyards were being planted, the seedlings of many varieties of fruits were finding their way into new orchards. Peaches, apricots, prunes, pears, plums and figs were growing well in the valley climate. One of these fruits — the fig — deserves special mention.

In 1883 Frederick Roeding, a nurseryman and vineyardist, made Gustav Eisen the manager of his Fancher Creek Nursery, located just east of the Eisen Vineyards. It was a good partnership. Roeding was a fine businessman and Eisen was an educated horticulturist. In 1885 White Adriatic Figs were being grown in Fresno County, but no one had been able to produce a mature Smyrna fig. Eisen began to research the Smyrna fig. Looking at some old documents one day, Eisen read that the Smyrna fig would not produce unless the pollen from a Capri fig was introduced into a Smyrna fig by a tiny Blastophaga wasp, an insect not found in Fresno County. He presented this finding to a group of Fresno horticulturists who laughed at him. Some time later, George Roeding, Frederick's son, received Capri figs from an agent of the U.S. Agriculture Department. The figs contained the Blastophaga wasps. Roeding used the wasps to pollinate the Smyrna fig. The result was named the Calimyrna fig. This discovery marked the real beginning of the fig industry in the central valley.

In 1882 Melcon Markarian and his family left Armenia and settled in Fresno. They farmed raisins and were so successful that they began packing raisins for the eastern market. Henry, one of the sons, managed the packing business.

Henry was not only interested in raisin production but was fascinated with the cultivation of figs. In 1894 he harvested and dried the figs. He shipped them, along with those from other farms, to St. Louis. These were the first California figs that were sent to an Eastern market.

Markarian purchased land north of downtown Fresno (today the location of Manchester Center) and planted all of it in figs. By 1910 it was producing well. It was called the "Fig Gardens" — the first time that term was used.

Jesse Clayton Forkner

At this point, a new figure entered the story. Jesse Clayton Forkner was a real estate developer from Southern California. Born in Kentucky, Forkner studied theology at the divinity school of Drake University and later was a member of the first law class of the University of Kansas. After graduating in the class of 1893, he practiced law for several years before leaving the field and turning to real estate as a career. He would later say that his combined training in the ministry and law combined with his "gift of gab" gave him the tools he needed to be a real estate promoter. He ventured first to southern California, then to the Tulare Lake area. He became involved in colony settlements and irrigation methods. In 1910 he was drawn to Fresno.

Fordson tractors are shown here leveling the "hog wallow" lands northwest of Fresno.

At that time, the area northwest of Fresno was called the "hog wallow badlands," because it was cursed with an underlying strata of adobe-like "hardpan" that was impenetrable. Everyone said it was totally unsuitable for cultivation. In the winter the land flooded and in the hot summer the land became hard as stone. Forkner looked on this as a challenge. He had seen seemingly impossible land before that when cultivated properly, supported crops. He took a one-year option to buy this land from the owner E.E. Bullard. Then he began to study the land and what it might produce. He was particularly interested in figs and met with Henry Markarian and hired him as a consultant. Markarian taught Forkner about blasting holes in the hardpan before planting. He and George Roeding taught him about the pollination methods that were required to fertilize the Smyrna fig. Before long, Forkner was claiming that his hog wallow land had the potential to grow the best figs outside of the Middle East. The tongues wagged among Fresnans who were suspicious of this new arrival in their community and of his seemingly impossible claims.

Forkner began leveling his land. He bought the first 48 Fordson tractors ever made to do the job. They were so effective that he ordered 80 more. Henry Ford, fascinated by the order that was placed with his company, journeyed to Fresno to see firsthand how they were being used. Ford drove up to Fresno from Los Angeles in his "Tin Lizzy" Model T coupe to meet with Forkner.

It took Forkner three years and 660,000 pounds of dynamite to tame the hog wallow badlands, but tame them he did. The planting began. He planted the 8-mile length of Van Ness Boulevard with deodors, cedars, eucalyptus and oleanders. He planted 600,000 fig trees in orchards stretching across the hog wallow lands. Soon, the badlands were bearing fruit and were transformed into a garden of Eden called the Fig Gardens.

Henry Ford (left) and J.C. Forkner (right) discuss the development of the Fig Gardens.

Grower Cooperatives

After 1900, farmers began to join newly formed cooperatives. The cooperatives were owned by the growers and initiated sales and marketing programs for their crops. They managed sales.

In the years after 1900, Fresno County became the grape-growing center of California. More acreage was planted in the Thompson seedless variety of grape than any other. After the failed efforts of M. Theo Kearney to form a raisin

A celebration of California's Admission Day was held at Zapp's Park on September 10, 1917. The Sun-Maid girls, representing several ethnic groups, played host at the California Associated Raisin Company's booth.

growers cooperative, other attempts were made. Finally in 1912 W.R. Nutting chaired a committee that formed the California Associated Raisin Company. They kicked off their advertising campaign by sending a 60-car freight train to Chicago with huge signs on each car reading "Raisins Grown by 6,000 California Growers." Three years later, they created the "Sun-Maid" brand.

In 1919 the California Fig Growers Association was organized. Many years later, in 1959, another fig grower cooperative, Valley Fig Growers, was formed.

Citrus growers had begun their efforts earlier. In 1891 the Orange Growers Union, which became the Southern California Fruit Growers Exchange two years later, was organized. In 1905 the word Southern was dropped from the title. Now it was called the California Fruit Growers Exchange. The cooperative marketed their citrus under the "Sunkist" label.

In 1927 the California Cotton Cooperative Association was organized and it eventually became Calcot Limited.

A worker packing raisins at the Sun-Maid raisin plant

Water

In the early years of the 20th century, there was a large influx of people into Fresno County who bought land and began farming. The majority of the farms were less than 50 acres in size. As more farms became productive, more water was needed to irrigate the new crops. Many farmers had to begin pumping water from the ground resulting in a lowering of the water table. Attempts were made to address this problem through legislation and eventually in 1921 the California Legislature authorized the drafting of a water plan. According to Richard D. Hall in "Agriculture and Water" in *Fresno County in the 20th Century,* the completed study was called the State Water Plan. Included in the plan was a proposed dam on the San Joaquin River and a plan for storing water from the Sacramento River for use on Fresno County's west side.

In 1933 the Central Valley Project Act passed the state legislature authorizing the building of dams and canals. Although the voters passed $170 million in bonds to implement the Central Valley Project, the state government couldn't sell the revenue bonds. It was the height of the Depression. When the state asked the federal government for help, the timing was right. President Franklin D. Roosevelt was putting people to work on government projects. In 1935 he turned the CVP over to the Bureau of Reclamation and earmarked monies for the project. Shasta Dam was

A young orange orchard on the east side of Fresno County

The proposed site of Friant Dam on the San Joaquin River

Simmons in *Westlands Water District: The First 25 Years*, in 1960 Congress passed the San Luis Act that authorized the federal government and the state of California to join together to build the San Luis Dam near Los Banos. Building the dam would create a 2,100,000-acre foot reservoir that would act as a holding tank for water — a portion of which would be distributed to users in the Westlands Water District through the San Luis Canal. It would supply the much-needed surface water for Fresno County's west side.

On August 18, 1962, President John F. Kennedy and California Governor Edmund G. Brown detonated the first dynamite in the groundbreaking ceremony for the San Luis Dam. The San Luis Dam was completed in 1968. The first water deliveries through the San Luis Canal began on November 10, 1967 and the major deliveries of water began in 1968.

enlarged and the Delta-Mendota Canal that carried Shasta's water to Fresno County was begun. In 1944 Friant Dam, located on the San Joaquin River, was completed creating Lake Millerton that covered the town site of Millerton, the first seat of Fresno County government. In 1951 the Delta-Mendota Canal was completed. Later, in 1954, Pine Flat Dam, which was not part of the CVP, was completed on the Kings River. The construction was authorized by the Flood Control Act of 1944 and was undertaken by the Corps of Engineers.

The 1960s brought a new focus for water needs — the county's west side. As more and more west side acreage was being used for farming, the need for water increased. The Westlands Water District had been formed in 1952 upon petition of landowners within the district who needed a supply of surface water to supplement the rapidly depleting underground water supply. Congress was urged by the district to authorize the San Luis Project that would bring the much-needed water to their district. According to Ed

Labor

Water is the most important resource for growing valley crops but once the crops ripen, they must be harvested. It is at this point that another important element comes into play — the labor force needed to harvest the crops. In the early years of Fresno County, the Chinese made up the largest component of the work force. By 1900 they had been replaced by the Japanese who quickly learned how to use strikes and boycotts to their advantage. By 1910 they had worked up to landowner status and by 1920 were only a small part of the laboring class. However, in 1915 the California Alien Land Law was passed. As John Walton Caughey in his book titled *California*,

The construction of Friant Dam is under way in 1941.

states, "Aliens who were not eligible to citizenship would not be permitted to acquire farmland or to lease parcels of agricultural land for more than three years. Ostensibly it applied to all Orientals and other aliens who could not or would not seek U.S. citizenship; practically its application was to the Japanese alone."

During this period the radical Industrial Workers of the World (IWW), the "Wobblies," became active in the valley. Their aims were: first, to unite the American working class with workers around the world into one large union that would hold a series of strikes and cause the capitalists to give up; and second, after the revolution that would follow, the leaders of the revolution would govern not only the workers, but everyone else as well.

Because the local in Fresno felt their meetings were being interfered with, the IWW decided to launch a free speech movement. One of their methods was to have IWW members get themselves arrested and fill the jail cells. Fifty Wobbly agitators were arrested after complaints were raised that they were intentionally creating a labor shortage. Following an announcement of the arrests to IWW members in Chicago, IWW members were urged to go to Fresno and get themselves arrested. The Wobblies stirred up local feelings to the point that on December 10, 1910, several hundred men marched on the local IWW headquarters and burned their possessions. Then they marched on the county jail demanding that the sheriff and police chief release the 50 Wobbly agitators into their hands. Two deputy sheriffs and Police Chief William Shaw blocked the door of the jail. Such mob action was roundly condemned.

The problem of the Wobblies did not go away, however. Three days before Christmas the IWW prisoners, whose numbers had now increased to 80, rioted. After being placed in total darkness on a diet of bread and water, they rioted again. This time the prisoners were sprayed with a high-pressure fire hose for 20 minutes. An agreement between the two sides was reached after this punishment. Two months later, the number of IWW prisoners had swelled to 116. The jail was so overcrowded that the Wobblies were moved to a stockade and put on street-cleaning detail. When word reached Mayor Chester Rowell that thousands of Wobblies were on their way to Fresno, he released the prisoners who left town soon after.

Many saw the IWW as a subversive organization even though many felt that the workers had a rightful cause. There were other Wobbly demonstrations throughout California. These brought the plight of the farm worker to the public's attention but by the mid-1920s, the IWW had faded to insignificance.

The World War I years saw the beginning of Mexican immigration into the valley to work in the fields. Mexican laborers were not brought in as a group. Those who came were allowed to remain. By the early 1920s, their numbers were increasing — many were coming in illegally. In 1924 the Immigration and Quota Act was passed. Under this act, Mexico did not have a quota. The term "non-quota" immigrant was used to define the Mexican worker who had now become the main source of labor in California.

The next group of immigrants to provide cheap farm labor were the Filipinos — the first group arriving in 1923. They were not excluded under the Immigration Act of 1924. By 1929 some 31,000 Filipinos had come to California.

The next group to arrive came in the 1930s while the Depression was in full swing. Many Americans who had lost their jobs headed for the fields of California. When they arrived, many residents found

Another view of Friant Dam during construction in 1941

they were having to compete with alien workers for employment. Hard on the heels of this came another wave of people. Some 350,000 refugees fled the Dust Bowl conditions in Alabama, Oklahoma and Texas and traveled to the San Joaquin Valley looking for

Farm workers in a field near Fresno

work. They arrived and were thrust into a nightmare situation — inadequate housing or no housing at all; malnutrition; and terrible sanitary conditions that resulted in disease. Some found shelter in government or private camps, and some lived under bridges or wherever they could find shelter. Their plight was described in John Steinbeck's novel, *The Grapes of Wrath*.

During World War II many of the white field workers moved into the factories.

Again, agricultural workers were needed. In 1944 Congress amended Public Law 45. This allowed prisoners of war to be used for farm labor. According to Bonnie Trask and Mary Graham in *Fresno County in the 20th Century*, in Fresno County alone, camps were set up near Coalinga, Firebaugh, Five Points I and II, Mendota, San Joaquin and Tranquillity. Most of the POWs in these camps had served with Hitler's Afrika Korps.

In 1942 the bracero program began using imported Mexican nationals contracted through the Department of Agriculture. Under this program, Mexican workers were brought to California for a specified length of time, then they had to return. Migrant labor camps were set up by the U.S. government, the state and the county. The federal government was the main stimulator for this, but sometimes the agencies overlapped. The bracero program ended in 1964, opening the way for more illegal immigration.

In 1965 Caesar Chavez rose to prominence. His organization, the National Farm Workers Association, held their first strike in Delano. Three months later he called for a national boycott of California table grapes. The strike lasted for several years and drew supporters of national prominence to Delano including U.S. Sen. Robert Kennedy and AFL-CIO President Walter Reuther. By 1970 Chavez's group had become the United Farm Workers of America (UFW), AFL-CIO. In 1975 the Agricultural Labor Relations Act was passed — a legislative victory for the workers. In more recent years, the UFW has declined in importance. What remains is the need to have enough workers to bring in the crops at every harvest season.

Crop Production

As Fresno County approaches the beginning of the 21st Century, it continues to be the No. 1 agricultural county in the United States. In order to give some idea of the impact of agriculture on the county's economy, this chapter will close with a listing of crop production figures for 1998. These figures were obtained from the 1998 Fresno County Agricultural Crop and Livestock Report provided by the Fresno County Department of Agriculture.

Fresno County's 10 leading crops (listed in order from No. 1 to No. 10) and their dollar values are: grapes, $569,208,000; poultry, $438,569,000; cotton, $308,231,000; tomatoes, $243,846,000; milk, $229,158,000; peaches, $137,915,000; almonds, $125,173,000; cattle and calves, $124,903,000; oranges, $124,899,000; and head lettuce, $112,924,000. The total dollar value of these Top 10 crops is $2,414,826,000. The total gross production value of all agricultural products for Fresno County in 1998 was $3,292,951,900.

A farm worker rolling grape trays in a Fresno County vineyard

CHAPTER 4

The communities that make up Fresno County developed for different reasons. Some are the offspring of the railroad and others owe their existence to lumber, coal or oil. Still others are located on old stage routes or on the sites of former ferry crossings, but they have one thing in common — they each possess their own unique history, their own individual story. When these stories are woven together, they create the colorful fabric that is Fresno County.

Friant

One of the oldest settlements in Fresno County can be found just minutes away from Fresno. Situated on the San Joaquin River, just a couple of miles downstream from the mining camp of Millerton, the location was perfect for a ferry business. In fact, such an operation was needed to provide a way for miners and those traveling the stage road along the foothills to cross the river. In 1852 Charles Porter Converse and W.W. Worland established a ferry. Converse, who by 1868 owned the entire business, sold it to James Richardson Jones. In addition to operating the ferry, Jones ran a

Unless otherwise noted all images this chapter courtesy Laval Historical Collection

The Settlements of the Heartland 4

store and hotel on the river's north bank. The settlement was popularly called Jonesville.

After Jones' death in 1877, the clerk in Jones' store, William R. Hampton, leased the businesses. Later, Hampton and his wife, Catherine, bought land on the south side of the river and built a new hotel and store. He also built a home for his family and changed the name of the settlement to Hamptonville.

In 1884 the Jenny Lind Bridge, the first reinforced concrete bridge in Fresno County, was built across the San Joaquin River. The ferry was no longer needed and ceased operation. The road through Hamptonville had grown quiet. Since the railroad had been built through the valley and the county seat moved from Millerton to Fresno, there was little commercial activity in Hamptonville.

Then in 1891 Marcus Pollasky built a railroad on the east side of Fresno. When the line reached Hamptonville, William Hampton sold his interests and moved his family to Fresno. The town was again renamed — now it was called Pollasky. Even though Pollasky skipped town and the railroad became part of the Southern Pacific line, the town kept its name until the early 1900s when the name was changed to Friant in honor of Thomas Friant who was a partner in the White-Friant Lumber Company.

When Friant Dam was being built in the early 1940s, workers flocked into town. With little available housing, some had to pitch tents. The town, once again, took on a frontier flavor as the town's 10 bars did a rollicking business.

Today Friant is still a small town clustered, for the most part, on the south bank of the San Joaquin River. It boasts 509 residents, a post office, a strip mall, several bars, a couple of restaurants and an antique store.

Centerville

Another Fresno County town that began its existence as a ferry crossing is Centerville. Like Friant, it has also had five names. In 1853 the Campbell brothers, William and Ed, began operating a ferry on the Kings River. The ferry was on a portion of the well-traveled Stockton-Visalia stage road. Business was good and the Campbells were soon joined by "Widow" Flanagan who opened the Falcon Hotel, J.B. Sweem who started a grist mill and William Y. (Monte) Scott who opened a saloon and restaurant. The town was on the south side of the river. The mill and residences were on the north side.

Three years later, in 1856, a post office was established and the community was named Scottsburgh in honor of William Scott. Shortly after this, the "h" was dropped and the name was then spelled Scottsburg. A school district was formed in 1860, and the winter of 1861-62 brought a great flood that completely destroyed the town. The river channel became so choked with trees and debris that the river abandoned its course and cut a new channel. The settlers rebuilt their town on the west side of the new river channel. In 1866 the town's name was changed to Kings River.

Another flood in 1867 caused the residents to move their town, once again, to higher ground. They relocated at the site of present-day Centerville and at this point, the town began to grow. A number of

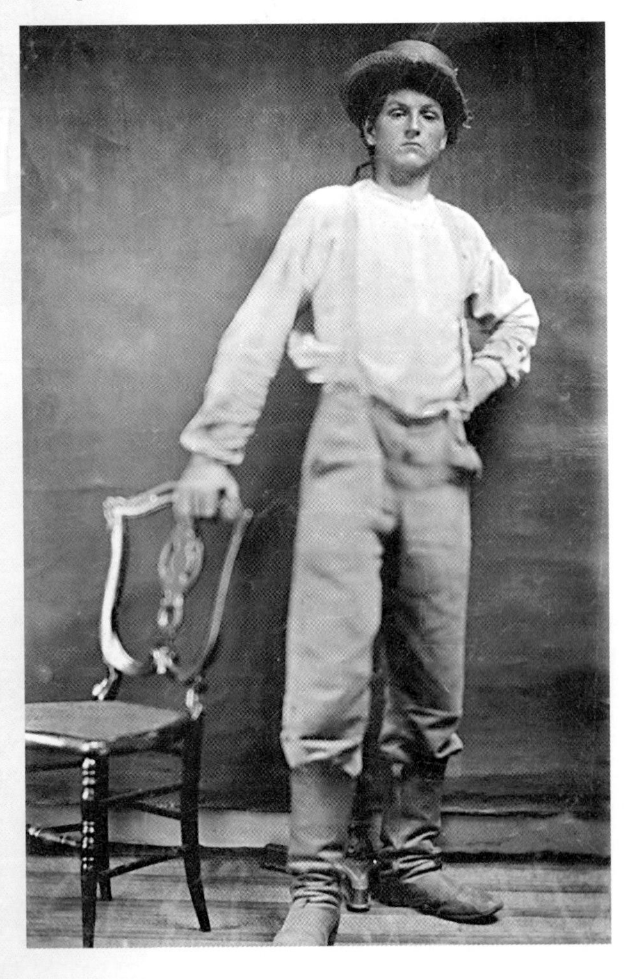

businesses opened including hotels, saloons, a drugstore, a carpentry shop, and a newspaper. Several doctors had moved to town and Clark Stevens was now running the four-horse stage line (originally operated by Jesse Morrow) with daily runs between Centerville and his livery stable in Fresno. Cattlemen and farmers in the area needed a commercial center nearby and Centerville provided those services.

From this point until April 30, 1905, the name changed three more times. The settlers called the relocated town Centerville, then it became King River (the "s" was omitted), and finally it was called Centerville again. When an election was held in 1874 to determine the new county seat, Centerville was one of the towns on the ballot. (Fresno won.)

In 1879 Centerville boasted a population of 300. Social clubs were formed and a number of buildings were constructed including the Independent Order of Odd Fellows building that still stands. The town began to go into a decline in the late 1880s when a rail depot was built in the new town of Sanger instead of at Centerville.

Today, Centerville remains small. Vineyards and orchards have replaced grain fields and cattle. Several old buildings dot Kings Canyon Road and an air of history hangs over the town.

Firebaugh

Firebaugh began its existence as a ferry crossing and a stop on the Butterfield Overland Stage route. Andrew Davidson Firebaugh was born in Virginia in 1823. In his early 20s, he left for Texas and signed on with the 1st Regiment of the Texas Mounted Riflemen Volunteers serving from 1845-48 in the war with Mexico. A year later he came west to California and joined Maj. James Savage's Mariposa Battalion. His unit discovered Yosemite Valley in 1851.

By 1854 he had moved to the west side of the valley and was farming near the Coast Range Mountains and the San Joaquin River — the second largest river in California. It was hard to cross. Firebaugh decided to start a ferry business and a trading post. Called Firebaugh's Ferry, the trading post was located on the site of the present-day city of Firebaugh.

In 1856-57, with the permission of the Monterey Board of Supervisors, Firebaugh built a toll road on the old Indian trail over the mountains that became known as Pacheco Pass. In 1858 Firebaugh's Ferry became a stop on the Butterfield Overland Mail route. On March 13, 1860, a post office was established. Firebaugh became so busy building his road that he sold his business. The ferry and trading post passed through several owners.

In the late 1870s a sheep-shearing corral was built in the town for the use of nearby sheepmen including the Miller and Lux ranches. The town began to grow. In 1885 a steel drawbridge was built across the river ending the ferry operation for good. Four years later the Southern Pacific Railroad built a branch line south from Los Banos to Fresno. It went through Firebaugh probably due, in large part, to a generous donation of land by Miller and Lux to the railroad.

Sheep brought business to Firebaugh, but it brought unsavory people as well. The itinerant sheep shearers were an unruly bunch — fist fights and shootings often filled the evening hours. By 1900 Firebaugh was, in essence, a Miller and Lux company town. Miller and Lux owned most of the surrounding land and most of the town. They also employed most of the residents.

Firebaugh was incorporated in 1914. It is situated in a very fertile section of the San Joaquin Valley. A wide variety of crops are grown in the Firebaugh area including cotton, alfalfa, melons, tomatoes, asparagus, cauliflower, broccoli and onions. Garlic is a leading crop. More garlic is grown in the Firebaugh area than in Gilroy. The 1999 population figure for Firebaugh is 6,200.

Kingston

Although nothing remains of this community except a park and a historic marker, it is still worthy of a brief mention. Kingston was located on the south bank of the Kings River near the present-day town of Laton. It was the site of the only ferry on this section of the Kings River. It was also a stop on the route of the Butterfield Overland Mail. L.A. Whitmore began operating the ferry in 1854. A post office opened in

(Opposite page)
Clark A. Stevens in 1868, five years before he and his brother, A.T. Stevens, left Michigan and settled in Fresno Station
Catherine Rehart Collection

(Chapter opening photo)
This 1918 photograph shows a street in Caruthers. The large wood-framed building was a hotel.

1859 and a school a year later. Whitmore was killed in 1859 and his ferry auctioned off to the highest bidder, James Denny. It was soon sold to Oliver Bliss. In 1870 Bliss had the town surveyed and platted. People began to settle there and businesses were established.

On Christmas Day in 1873, Tiburcio Vasquez and his gang — nine men in all — rode into town. Within five minutes they had tied up 30 men including Oliver Bliss and Louis Einstein. Then they proceeded to open safes in the various businesses. Eight hundred dollars in coin was taken from the safe in Jacob & Einstein's store. Not satisfied with only the money, they took jewelry from their captives as well. J.W. Sutherland and James E. Flood were told what was going on. They grabbed their rifles and headed for the store of S. Sweet who was at that moment being robbed. They shot at the robbers who decided it was time to leave town. Vasquez and his gang jumped into their saddles and rode out of town to the accompaniment of Sutherland and Flood's rifle shots. Some of the bullets hit their target wounding the bandits who made off with a total of $2,400 in coin and a lot of jewelry. The robbery gained statewide attention and made people very nervous wondering where the gang would strike next.

Soon after this, Kingston began to decline. The railroad was founding new towns nearby. The era of the stagecoach was almost over. The post office closed in 1890. Many of the residents moved to nearby Laton.

Laton

The town of Laton is situated on the north side of the Kings River on land that was once part of the Laguna de Tache Grant, a Mexican land grant given to Manuel Castro in 1846. Charles A. Laton of San Francisco, a colonizer for Manchester Trust Company, and L.A. Nares acquired a large portion of the grant for development purposes. A townsite, named for Laton, was surveyed and the plat was filed in 1899.

The main line of the Santa Fe Railroad was laid through the area in the late 1890s — today, the tracks bisect the town. A post office opened on March 5, 1900. The community has its own school district. Its situation adjacent to the Kings River offers many recreational opportunities. It has a fine park. The town was never incorporated and in 1996 it had a population of 1,250.

Burrel

In 1860 an Englishman named Cuthbert Burrel brought 13,000 head of cattle from Sonoma and established himself on the old 20,000-acre Elkhorn Ranch south and west of present-day Fresno. The Elkhorn Ranch had been a stage stop on the Butterfield Overland Mail. A town site was carved out of Burrel's holdings in the early 1900s and named for him.

The Southern Pacific Railroad came through Burrel and established a station in 1911. The settlement began to grow. A post office opened on June 4, 1912. A year later phone service reached the small community.

Burrel is a town surrounded by rich farmland. Dairy cows, cotton, alfalfa and potatoes fill the fertile fields of the area. The community did not live up to the potential for which its founders hoped. Although still on the map of Fresno County, Burrel has a population today of only 50 people.

Riverdale

There was a settlement called La Libertad on the El Camino Viejo, the old road that skirted the west side of the valley. It died out. Another one developed nearby and took its name of Liberty from the old Spanish settlement. On July 1, 1875, a post office was established there with Thomas Thompson as postmaster.

The area was filled with swamps, tules, sloughs, wild antelope, elk, horses, hogs and horned toads. The swamp around Liberty was called a river. Because of that the post office was renamed Riverdale in the early 1880s. The post office moved first to James Powell's ranch and then to the Elisha Harlan ranch in 1883 with Lucy Harlan as the postmaster. The mail was brought by a rider on horseback. Lucy sorted the mail on her dining table and everyone dropped by to get their mail, have something to eat and catch up on all the local news. In the 1890s, canals and levees were built to control flooding from the Kings River. The reclaimed land became lush pastureland — perfect for raising dairy cattle. In 1898 the San Joaquin Ice Company established a milk-skimming plant on the east side of present-day Valentine Avenue just north of the Burrel ditch. This was the first business in Riverdale. William Henson, the operator of the plant, built a general store next door. This was the beginning of the town.

As dairy farming increased, the farmers decided to unite their efforts by forming the Riverdale Cooperative Creamery in 1909. Managed by J.H. Jorgenson, it merged with Danish Creamery in 1930 and remained an important milk and cream processing plant until 1960 when the plant was closed. In 1909 the Cream City Celebration, an annual festival that included a parade, a carnival, games and other events began.

The milk produced in the Riverdale area today is sent to Fresno for processing. It is a significant part of the total dairy industry of California. Riverdale, although never incorporated, is still known as the Cream City.

Wildflower

At a point where Fowler Avenue crosses Clarkson Avenue and heads south toward the town of Laton, there is a tiny community called Wildflower. The first settler, B.M. Stone, arrived with his family in November 1975 from Louisiana. His brother-in-law, C. Joplin, and the Joseph Prather family joined him. In 1876 several other families moved to the area. They planned to plant crops and needed water so they built a ditch that was called the Emigrant Irrigation Ditch. Stone planted grain and in 1878 harvested his first crop. By 1882 his 320-acre ranch was producing wheat, alfalfa and fruit. Other families began moving into the area.

The community received its name from a gift provided by Mother Nature. In the spring, wildflowers cloaked the fields in a panoply of colors — they grew so high that they tickled the underbellies of the horses. So the area was called Wildflower. On June 21, 1878, a post office was established, which gave the community its official name. Exactly 20 years later on June 21, 1898, the post office was closed. However, the farming around the area continued to flourish. Today, the Wildflower Superette, a grocery store, continues in operation and provides the only indication of the area's name.

The establishment of blacksmith J.P. Jensen in Easton

Lone Star

In 1882 volunteers built a one-room schoolhouse on the northwest corner of Clovis and North avenues. Three of the students, Woodson Pool, Mellie Hughes and Jesse Weber, were asked to select a name for the school. They said that the small lone schoolhouse set in the middle of a huge grain field reminded them of a "Lone Star." In 1883 the Lone Star School District was formed and a larger two-room school was built on the same site.

In 1898 the Santa Fe Railroad branch line that ran east from Fresno was finished. Also in that year a large two-story Lone Star school was built on Fowler Avenue. A Lone Star Village developed nearby with a railroad station, post office, store and blacksmith shop. In 1899 volunteers built the Lone Star Hall, which became a gathering place for weddings, dances and other community events. The school was torn down in 1914 and a new school was built across Fowler Avenue. The area generally bound by Peach, American and Dockery avenues and the Southern Pacific rail line is still known as the Lone Star area.

Oleander

South and west of downtown Fresno there is a community where people began to settle in 1880. A post office was established on January 10, 1881. The developer of the area, Judge J.W. North, decided to name it Washington Colony. He wrote to Washington, D.C., for approval.

One day Judge North loaded his wagon with oleander cuttings he was going to plant that afternoon and went to pick up his mail. He was hoping a reply from Washington would be waiting for him.

The Easton Meat Market

The letter did not arrive until the next day and the request was denied. Evidently, there were too many communities named Washington. He looked at the wagon full of oleander cuttings and submitted the name "Oleander" to the postal authorities in Washington. It was approved and the new community was officially called Oleander. A school district was formed in 1883. By 1884, 30 houses dotted the area.

In 1887 the Valley Railroad laid tracks through Oleander. Several raisin and fruit packing companies were built nearby. As the community grew, a general merchandise store, blacksmith shop, service station, two churches and public hall were built. A Fresno County Library branch opened at Cedar and Adams avenues. The library and post office are gone, but Oleander is still an active community that counts among its residents the descendants of some of the early pioneers.

Easton

In 1878 the Washington Irrigated Colony was organized by Wendell Easton, J.P. Whitney, and Allen T. Covell on 7,040 acres of land south and southwest of the Central California Colony. They advertised and were not successful selling their lots at first, but it was not long before people began to buy. Soon 385 farms were sold — the colony was a success. Water rights were purchased from the Fresno Irrigation and Canal Company. Homes were built and vineyards and orchards were laid out. The stock animals were well fed by the colony's rich fields of alfalfa. Soon there was a surplus of milk. In 1880 a cheese factory was built. "Washington Colony Cheese" became a popular item with the public and was a source of pride for the colonists.

The plan for a town was laid out by Allen T. Covell. Four blocks were set aside for a school, a town hall and a public park. The town was named Covell for the man who planned it and was the first resident. Although many of the settlers called the town Easton — everyone still does today — the name of the town is legally designated on maps and legal documents by the name Covell. The town, had a population of 1,710 in 1996. It boasts Washington Union High school, churches and many businesses. The cemetery that serves the district bears the name Washington Colony and is a reminder of the area's history.

In 1872 the Central Pacific Railroad began to make its way south through Fresno County. The railroad brought tremendous change. No longer would the stagecoach be the major means of transportation for county residents. No longer would horse- or mule-drawn wagons be used to transport goods. The arrival of the railroad meant the creation of new towns not only along the main north-south line, but also on the west and east side of the county as spur lines developed.

Fowler

The story of Fowler begins with the railroad, a state senator and the senator's cattle. Thomas Fowler, an Irishman, and Thomas Davis came west to California in 1853 with the intention of heading to the gold fields. Instead they got into the cattle business. In 1868-69 they purchased a large acreage along the Kings River near Minkler and Sanger. Their cattle carried the "76" brand and ranged across the valley.

As his empire and his influence grew, Fowler decided to enter politics. In September 1869 he was elected to the state senate. He remained in office until he fought the "No Fence" law and did not win re-election.

When the Central Pacific Railroad began to lay its track south of Fresno Station, Sen. Fowler saw it as a perfect chance to find an efficient way to get his cattle to market. He arranged for a switch to be placed 10 miles south of Fresno — the most convenient spot for him. Fowler's first shipment of cattle left Fowler

Switch right after it opened on August 1, 1872. Fowler's neighbors Frank Dusy and Jefferson James also used the switch. Sheep-shearing pens, corrals and loading chutes were built by the switch.

From 1878-1881, Fowler Switch had one resident — John S. Gentry. Gentry was an eccentric bachelor who lived in a run-down cabin with a dirt floor. Gentry raised poultry, primarily turkeys, which seemed appropriate because his cabin had the look of a chicken coop. The cabin had a cellar where Gentry kept items to sell transients who came to the switch to find work during cattle shipping and sheep-shearing season — in effect, this made him the first merchant in Fowler.

By 1882 a few people were beginning to farm land around Fowler notably Amos Harris and his wife, Antoinette. A few stores and homes were built near Gentry's abode. In 1885 the Fowler School District was formed. When the people of Fowler began to discuss incorporating their town in 1908, there was one major issue — it centered around alcohol. Would alcoholic beverages be sold in

Merced Street in downtown Fowler in 1912

Fowler or not? Those who supported the saloon interests supported the Anti-Progressive Party; those who advocated closing the saloons supported the Progressive Party. The motto of the Progressive Party was, "Incorporate with No Saloons." The campaign was heated. On election day, May 26, 1908, 97 percent of the voters in Fowler voted and incorporation passed. Two weeks later the new board of trustees outlawed the sale of liquor in Fowler. It was not until the election of June 20, 1933, that voters narrowly approved the sale of 3.2 percent beer.

Fowler boasts a fine high school and a number of churches and businesses but still remains a small town set in the midst of lush vineyards and farmland. Its population in 1990 was 3,208.

Selma

As the Central Pacific Railroad continued laying track south of Fowler in 1872, it did not establish a station at Selma, but continued south. The railroad, however, did build a two-story frame section house and a few smaller buildings to house the Chinese section crew and their overseer, Pat Reardon, at a spot that would later be the city of Selma.

Meanwhile, a few hardy souls were beginning to come to the area to plant wheat and fruit. Many of the early settlers came from Mendicino County. They realized they needed water to grow crops and began negotiations with Moses Church and his Fresno Canal and Irrigation Company. Water was sent to them through an existing channel, but they found the channel was too small. They incorporated the Centerville and Kingsburg Irrigation Ditch Company in 1876 and began building their own canal. Each man worked on the project that was finished in 1877. It was an amazing feat. With irrigation, the land began to produce and the result was lush wheat fields and orchards.

On May 6, 1878, the Valley View School District was established. Two early settlers in the vicinity, Monroe Snyder and George B. Otis, gave land to the district so that a schoolhouse could be built.

This 1914 view of the city of Selma looks east along Second Street. Selma is known as the "Home of the Peach."

According to Selma historian Randy McFarland in an article titled, "City in the Country," "On June 26, 1880, Selma was established with an auction sale of lots by its founders, Jacob E. Whitson, George B. Otis, Monroe Snyder and E. H. Tucker." The next task was to lay out the town. County Surveyor Caleb Davis began the process. Using the Witness Tree, a massive oak tree located on Fourth Standard Parallel (Elkhorn Avenue) near Kingsburg that had been used to measure the Laguna de Tache Grant, Davis chained the necessary distance west and then north on the alignment of Highland Avenue. From there, streets were laid out. In the same year the first business was established by the Frey brothers — the Selma Flour Mill — which was located on the Selma Branch of the Centerville and Kingsburg Canal.

An early butcher shop in Sanger with a delivery wagon to the right

The town began to grow. The economic "boom" period in the late 1880s brought many people to Selma. In 1887 Jacob Whitson invested $50,000 in building a three-story hotel. Other fine buildings went up also. In March 1893 Selma was incorporated — the second city in Fresno County to achieve this distinction.

Although there has been some controversy over the naming of the city, historians feel that the city was named for Selma Michelsen Kingsbury Latimer. Selma was the wife of Sanford Kingsbury, an assistant of A.N. Towne, the general superintendent of the Central Pacific Railroad. It was Towne who suggested the new city be named for her.

Today, Selma is a charming city with a downtown filled with restored historic buildings. Set amid orchards and vineyards, Selma's nickname is the "Home of the Peach." It also hosts a raisin festival each year. With a population of 25,400 people, it no longer considers itself a small town, but rather an important city in the Central Valley.

Kingsburg

In May 1872 the Central Pacific Railroad tracks reached the Kings River. In 1873 the railroad decided to establish a switching point on the line near the Kings River. It was called the Kings River Switch. From the "Switch" goods could be unloaded from the train and grain could be shipped off to markets. The first settlers were Andrew Farley and Josiah Draper who each took a quarter section of land — Farley on the west side of the tracks and Draper on the east. Thomas Cowan arrived next settling northwest of Draper's land. The settlement, which was also called Drapersville or Farleyville, began to grow.

Looking east on Draper Street from California Street in downtown Kingsburg in 1915

In 1874 a post office opened bearing the name of Wheatville, giving the settlement a name. Andrew Farley, who by now had opened a general store, became the

In this 1914 view of Sanger the lumber flume is visible in the lower half of the photograph.

At this early-day livery stable in Reedley, a person could not only hire a horse, but a carriage as well.

first postmaster. Draper built a hotel. A blacksmith shop and several saloons also opened for business. The new town had an interesting reputation. Wheatville became known as "the toughest place" between Los Angeles and San Francisco because most of the buildings had acquired bullet holes. In 1874 the name of the town changed to Kingsbury for a clerk with the Central Pacific Railroad. Shortly after, the name changed again to Kingsburg.

In 1878 Frank D. Rosendahl arrived in Kingsburg. A native of Sweden, he was a landscape architect who had played a role in the design of New York's Central Park and of Golden Gate Park in San Francisco. He was made a justice of the peace in Kingsburg. Ten years later his brother, the Reverend E.G. Rosendahl, made his home in Kingsburg also. Other Swedish immigrants soon followed. By 1921, 94 percent of the population within a three-mile radius of Kingsburg was Swedish. No longer the toughest city between San Francisco and Los Angeles, Kingsburg had become a city with churches, parks and a thriving business community. Kingsburg was incorporated on May 11, 1908.

Today, downtown Kingsburg has brightly colored dala horses on the light standards lining downtown Draper Street carrying out its Swedish Village theme. Boasting a population of 8,900, Kingsburg hosts its annual Swedish Festival each May.

Sanger

In 1887 the Southern Pacific Railroad began building a rail line from Fresno across eastern Fresno County and then south to Porterville. A depot was built at a site a few miles east of Fresno. It was called Sanger Junction, named for Joseph Sanger Jr., secretary of the national Railroad Yardmaster's Association. Building lots were offered for sale. Soon people began to arrive at the new town. On June 26, 1888, the post office opened. Businesses and homes were being built. Sanger Junction was shortened to Sanger.

In the fall of 1889 the Kings River Lumber Company's flume, the longest in the world, was finished. It began in the foothill community of Millwood and had its terminus in Sanger — a distance of over 50 miles. The company built a finishing plant in Sanger. About this time, Valley Lumber Company, headquartered in Fresno, established an office in Sanger. The town's newspaper, the *Sanger Herald,* published its first edition on May 11, 1890. The town grew quickly and in July 1911 Sanger was incorporated.

In 1949 Sanger received recognition from the U.S. Postal Service. It was designated the "Nation's Christmas Tree City" because of its proximity to the General Grant Tree in Kings Canyon National Park. Sanger's population in 1999 was 18,847.

Reedley

As the Southern Pacific line continued south toward Porterville in 1888, another town came into being. Thomas Law Reed, a local wheat grower, gave the railroad a one-half interest in a 360-acre townsite. The townsite was in the middle of a huge wheat growing area — near the northern end of 76 Land and Water

Reedley's main street, G Street, in 1914

Company lands. The 76 Land and Water Company had completed canals through the area. The railroad called the town Reedley in honor of Reed.

Clovis Union High School in 1904

L.D. Norton surveyed the town in May 1888. Reed began selling lots. The first post office opened in June in the home of Mr. and Mrs. F.S. Knauer, who built the first house in the new town. William McCreary opened a livery stable and E. Hirschfield established a general merchandise store. Soon other businesses, homes and churches were being built. The town grew quickly. Reedley became an important commercial center. According to Charles Clough and William B. Secrest Jr., in their book *Fresno County: The Pioneer Years,* "In 1891 alone, 12,000 tons of grain and 1,031,957 feet of lumber left the town via teams and trains." The town continued to grow and the city was incorporated on March 14, 1913.

Soon after the town was founded, a large group of German Mennonites settled in Reedley. Today, only one other city in the United States, Hillsborough, Kansas, has a higher population of Mennonites. The Mennonite Central Committee's store in downtown Reedley is the scene of weekly quilting sessions.

"The Fruit Basket of the World" is Reedley's slogan. This eastern Fresno County town has a population of 20,187 people.

Clovis

Mr. and Mrs. Stephen H. Cole and their son, Clovis, came to Fresno from Vevay, Indiana, in 1873. They came to join an uncle, Jacob, who had already come to Fresno County. Stephen homesteaded a piece of land near the present-day Balfe Ranch.

When Clovis was 16, his father gave him four horses. Clovis started a teamster business hauling lumber from the mountains. In a few years he home-steaded a piece of land near present-day Clovis. He added to his holdings by purchasing 480 more acres of land for $4 an acre which later became the townsite of Clovis. By 1840 he owned 40,000 acres of land that he planted in wheat. Clovis Cole was said to be the wheat king of the nation.

The Coles went into the real estate business. When Marcus Pollasky's San Joaquin Railroad was built on the east side of the valley, one of its three stations was built at 4th and Clovis avenues on land donated by Cole. The station was named Clovis.

In 1891, Ingvart Teilman surveyed the land for a townsite and the Fresno Flume & Irrigation Company built a flume from Shaver Lake to the new town. The terminus of the flume was on 60 acres the company purchased from Cole. Also on this site was built a large lumber and finishing mill, a storage yard and a distributing plant. It was called the Clovis Mill.

The new town also was named Clovis. Developers began to subdivide large parcels of land and sell small lots to private investors. Clovis began to grow, mostly on more desirable land north and west of the depot because it was upwind from the rather odoriferous plant burners of the mill.

In February 1893 the Clovis post office was established By the mid-1890s a variety of businesses were doing well. By 1894 the mill was going strong employing between 300 and 500 people. The mill

The southeast corner of Pollasky and 4th streets in Clovis in 1914

The northeast corner of Pollasky and 5th streets in Clovis in 1915

plant also contained a box factory, planing mill, warehouse, drying kiln, housing for employees and 5 acres of pasture for the company horses. The town continued to grow and on February 27, 1912, Clovis was incorporated.

Today, Clovis continues its pattern of growth as the city spreads to the north and east. Clovis' population in 1999 was 68,900.

In 1883 I.N. Parlier planted a fig tree that grew to a height of 65 feet and spread its limbs over 100 feet. Although now gone, it was reputed to be the largest fig tree in the world.

Parlier

In the last years of the 19th century, the Southern Pacific Railroad built a line that extended southeast of Fresno. One of the new towns on the line was founded in 1898 and named Parlier in honor of Issac N. Parlier who had served as president of the Centerville and Kingsburg Irrigation Ditch Company. In 1876 Parlier had brought his family from Springfield, Illinois, to the site of the present-day city of Parlier. He opened a trading post, general store and post office.

The agriculture of the area was, in the beginning, small family wheat farms. Later, after irrigation opened the door to other possibilities, grapes, raisins and tree fruits became the focus of farming. Today, the area is still filled with vineyards and orchards. On November 14, 1921, Parlier was incorporated. Because so much fruit and grapes are grown, packed and shipped from Parlier, the city is known as "The Buckle of the Raisin Belt." Parlier's population in 1999 was 11,300. Parlier was recently ranked as California's second-fastest growing community.

Orange Cove

Elmer M. Sheridan owned a large acreage in the southeast corner of Fresno County adjacent to the foothills. He subdivided his land and contacted the officials of the Atchison, Topeka & Santa Fe Railway who decided to build a rail line through the area. They asked him to name the rail station. Although there were no citrus groves in the area, Sheridan suggested the name Orange Cove. Today, the area is a citrus growing center and proudly lives up to its name. The city of Orange Cove was incorporated in 1948 and in 1990 boasted a population of 5,604.

Kerman

About 1891 the Southern Pacific Railroad Company built a rail line that extended from Tracy to Fresno. At a point some 12 miles due west of downtown Fresno, a water tank and pump were erected next to the line. The tank had to be kept full so there would always be water for the engines. A caretaker was hired to see to this job, but he got so lonely that in a short time he quit.

In 1894 a post office was opened named Collis for Collis P. Huntington, the president of the railroad. In 1899 the post office moved to Rolinda. A large tract of arid land was purchased by the Bank of California as a speculative venture. The project's promoter died, the bank became insolvent and the property was sold to two capitalists from Los Angeles, William G. Kerckhoff and Jacob Mansar. Their purchase included the town site where the post office had been. The Enterprise

A view of the main street of Kerman in 1914

Canal had been built nearby and offered a potential for the colony development that Kerckhoff and Mansar promoted. Many people came to the new town and the post office was reopened in 1904. In 1906 the town was renamed Kerman — a name that used the first three letters of Kerckhoff and Mansar.

The town began to grow and by 1910 Kerman had a volunteer fire department and a branch library. The $15,000 Kerman Creamery Company plant opened. By the 1920s Kerman was known as "The Home of the Thompson Seedless Grape." Farms in the area also produced alfalfa, peaches, figs, nuts, berries, vegetables and honey. On July 2, 1946, the town of Kerman was incorporated.

Kerman's population today is 7,400 people. Some of the major businesses are Pacific Coast Packaging, Sun-Empire Foods, Schaad Family Almonds, Bianchi Winery, Mariani Raisin Company, KBC Trading and Processing Company, and Helena Chemical Company.

Caruthers

William "Billy" Caruthers was born in Vermont in 1840. He came west to California and settled in the Liberty area near present-day Riverdale. He purchased three and one-quarter sections of desert land from the state of California for $1.25 an acre. At first he raised sheep, then in 1888, he began to raise cattle and grain.

In 1888 the Southern Pacific Railroad began grading a line from Kerman south. Caruthers, realizing that the railroad would provide a shipping point for him and other farmers in the area, offered the railroad a half-section of his land. He suggested the property would be a good location for a station and a town site. In exchange, he asked the railroad to give him half of the proceeds from the sale of the town lots and name the town Caruthers. His proposal was accepted by the railroad owners. Two grain companies opened warehouses at the new townsite even before the railroad siding and switch were completed.

A branch of Valley Lumber Company of Fresno opened also. A school district and post office were established in 1892. The town began to grow. Grape vineyards and fruit orchards began to replace the grain fields. A high school was built and a number of businesses opened. In 1996 the population of Caruthers was about 900. The Caruthers District Fair, which was first held in 1923, is an event that draws many to the community each year.

Huron

In the mid-1870s, the Southern Pacific Railroad started to build a rail line west from Goshen that would extend through the southwest area of Fresno County to Tres Pinos in San Benito County. In 1877 the line was completed to a point just nine miles north of the Fresno County line. A station

The Kerman Inn as it looked in 1914

was built and a turntable was put in place so trains could turn around and head back to Goshen. A post office, called Huron, opened on June 18, 1877.

The area contained many sheep ranches and Huron became a shipping center for wool and sheep. From 1913-1915, more wool was shipped from Huron than from any other wool producing center in the country. Huron also became a shipping point for the other crops that were being farmed in the area. By 1890 the town had a population of 250. An 1892 fire destroyed many of the businesses in town. This was repeated on February 9, 1919, when fire once again hit the town. In 1916 the first deep irrigation well was dug in the area. Other wells were dug nearby at the Frank Diener ranch and the Jack O'Neill ranch. In the late 1920s, the first oil well in the Kettleman Oil fields came in. Huron became an oil well supply center.

After World War II, more fields were planted and crop production increased. On April 30, 1951, Huron was incorporated. Today, row crops including broccoli, asparagus, and tomatoes are being harvested in the fields around Huron. Lettuce is the main crop and Dole's Lettuce California and Fresh Express are the largest companies in the area. On December 31, 1998, Huron received the distinction of being designated an Enterprise Community. Only 20 cities in the country were granted this honor. Huron's population in 1990 was 4,766.

This 1918 photograph shows a street in Caruthers. The large wood-framed building was a hotel.

This photograph of the Coalinga oil fields in 1921 is a testament to the oil-producing activity in the Coalinga area.

Coalinga

The 1880s saw coal being mined in the hills of southwestern Fresno County. Eight years later, in 1888, the Southern Pacific Railroad extended its line from Huron to Alcalde. A spur line was built from the coal mine to the railroad. Coaling Stations B and C were located on the spur line. Coaling Station A was established at the point where it joined the rail line. The name was shortened to CoalingA and then to Coalinga. When a post office was opened at the station on July 22, 1889, it was given the name Coalinga.

The real growth of the town didn't begin until the first oil well was brought in 1896. A store and a saloon opened for business that year. In 1897 the Blue Goose well was drilled and oil began to flow — 500 to 1,000 barrels a day. Coalinga became a boom town, the only city in Fresno County with that distinction. By 1900 Coalinga was becoming a town and a rather free-wheeling one at that. Front Street, also called Whiskey Row, had 13 saloons and related businesses (gambling dens and bawdy houses) that all did a lively business. Water was brought by train from Tulare then hauled into town by horse-drawn wagon.

In spite of its boom town flavor, Coalinga also had churches, an active literary society, many businesses and a growing population. Coalinga was incorporated on April 6, 1906. In 1912 colorful Whiskey Row was destroyed by fire. Seventy years later another disaster befell the city. The community was hit by a 6.7 earthquake on May 2, 1983. This was followed five minutes later by a 5.6 aftershock. The quake caused more damage than any other quake in the more recent history of Fresno County. Coalinga suffered a tremendous amount of destruction to its buildings and residences. Although the oil boom is over, the Coalinga Oil Field continues to produce. It rates ninth among giant oil fields in California in terms of production in 1997. In that year, 9,626,000 barrels of oil came out of the Coalinga Oil Fields. Its cumulative production since inception totals 849,112,000 barrels of oil.

Mendota

In 1891 when the Southern Pacific Railroad was building a rail line from Los Banos to Armona near present-day Lemoore, they needed switching, storage and miscellaneous facilities at a midway point on the line. Firebaugh was in the perfect location but was ruled out because of its unstable reputation. The railroad decided to build a station nine miles southeast of Firebaugh and create a new town. It was named Mendota, according to William Bright in *1500 California Place Names*, possibly for a town in either Wisconsin or Minnesota — the reason for the naming has been lost.

The railroad built a large station, a roundhouse and warehouse. The site had an artesian well, a number of side tracks and a turntable. A saloon and hotel were built. On July 21, 1892, the post office opened. A school district was formed as the town began to grow. In 1903 the first irrigation well was dug. Gustave Herminghaus owned a huge ranch across the San Joaquin River from Mendota. He was a large factor in the economy of the town since his employees lived there and he was a major shipper on the railroad.

In 1910 the railroad tore down the roundhouse and removed many of the tracks. About this time Herminghaus sold his land. This had an impact on the town and slowed its growth. Irrigation made farming possible and as crop production increased, the town began to grow. Many farm workers made Mendota their home. In 1942 Mendota was incorporated. Today, the major crops grown in the Mendota area are cantaloupes, tomatoes, corn, cotton, broccoli and watermelons. The 1999 population was 7,689.

Tranquillity

The townsite of Tranquillity was once part of the Jefferson James Ranch, founded in 1857. Located near the Fresno Slough, during the rainy season the area became a vast tule swamp. It was in that condition when James arrived. He set about building a drainage system for the swamp land, thus reclaiming the land for agricultural use. He continued to add to his holdings. By 1890 he owned between 155,000 to 161,000 acres of land. He had 36 individual ranches. In 1908 he sold a portion of his ranch to colonists. His son-in-law Walker C. Graves was put in charge of handling the land transactions for the new colony that he named Tranquillity Colony. It was named in honor of his ancestral home in Lexington, Kentucky — a plantation named Tranquillity that was his birthplace.

Roads were laid out in the new colony, a one-room school was built and settlers began to arrive. In 1910 the townsite began to truly look like a town with a post office, a saloon, livery stable, blacksmith shop, general store and a hotel. In 1912 the first train came through Tranquillity. The area was suited to raising dairy cows and many fields were planted with alfalfa. A creamery was built in the town.

In 1929 the Tranquillity National Bank failed because the bank manager had embezzled funds. The Tranquillity Co-op Creamery owned the bank. It was a blow to the community — affecting almost every family in the town. Tranquillity was never incorporated. Its population in 1996 was 600. The crops grown nearby are alfalfa, sugar beets and cotton.

San Joaquin

In 1912 plans were under way for another community on the valley's west side. This time the planner envisioned a city that would be comparable to Fresno. A gentleman from Chicago, Benjamin F. Graham, purchased a portion of the old James Ranch for $3 million. He wanted to build a town named Grahamtown. Great care was spent in the planning of the new town — parks, roads and public buildings were all factored into the latest urban planning equation that would create a beautiful city.

On April 16, 1913, the post office opened — two days later the name of the new city was changed to San Joaquin. Graham lost controlling interest in the project that was now controlled by a group of Los Angeles capitalists. They wanted the new city to advertise its close proximity to the mightiest river in the valley — the San Joaquin. In 1920 the city of San Joaquin was incorporated. Although the city grew, it never became the large "city beautiful" that Benjamin Graham envisioned. It boasted a population in 1999 of

3,095. Cotton and melons are the major crops produced in the fields nearby. Most of the industry is ag-related.

Malaga

The town of Malaga, just south of Fresno, was platted about 1883. The last town to be established on the Central Pacific Railroad, it takes its name from a variety of grape. A school opened on May 4, 1885. Additions had to be made to the building within a few years — a testament to the growing town. Malaga and muscat grapes were planted in vineyards nearby. Orchard trees were planted also. John Cartwright opened a pruning shears shop and a post office was established — both in 1885. About 1900 many Mexican immigrants moved to the town as the need for field laborers grew. Today, industrial plants in south Fresno are encroaching on Malaga. The population in 1996 was 800 people.

Calwa

The California Wine Association started construction on a $2.5 million winery and distillery southeast of Fresno in 1896 — at that time, the largest facility of its kind in California. The Santa Fe Railroad tracks went through the area where this complex was located and it became the home to many of the employees of the railroad.

In March 1913, Speed B. Leas laid out the townsite between the Santa Fe tracks, Jensen, Vine and Cedar avenues. The new town became known as Calwa, taking its name from the California Wine Association. In 1916 a school district was established, which in 1948 became part of the Fresno City Schools. Because the community was in the county and the school was in the city, the school grounds could not be used for recreational programs after school — there was no joint use plan between the city and the county.

After many attempts to create a recreational center, the issue was put on the ballot. On March 1, 1955, the Calwa Park and Recreational District was created with five elected trustees to oversee its operations. The next step was to purchase land. The members of the Calwa Civic Betterment Association organized events to raise money for a park and went door-to-door asking for citizen involvement. The entire community got behind the project, which resulted ultimately in the opening of Calwa Park on March 8, 1958. The 25-acre park, located on Church Avenue between Cedar and Maple avenues, is still the center of recreational programs for the citizens of Calwa.

Biola

On December 1, 1912, it was announced that a new town was being laid out northwest of downtown Fresno by the James J. Murray Company, an agent for the Villa Land Company, which owned the property. An agreement had been made with the Fresno Traction Company which was to build a rail line to the townsite. The line was finished in 1913. The new town was named Biola by one of the owners of the San Joaquin Power Company, William D. Kerckhoff. Biola is an acronym for the Bible Institute of Los Angeles, Kerckhoff's favorite religious organization.

On December 1, 1913, the Southern Pacific Railroad began to lease the rail line — an arrangement that continued until they purchased the line on October 26, 1936. In the 1960s the line was discontinued. A grammar school was built in 1914. The town had several stores, including Belluomini Hardware which has been in business for 50 years. Biola is located just south of Shaw Avenue at Biola Avenue north and west of Fresno. Biola today has a population of about 800, although it varies because of the influx of migrant workers who help during the harvest season.

Several industries located in or near Biola are: Salwasser Dehydrator; Mariani Raisin Company; Actegro, a fertilizer manufacturer; Biola Recycling; and Sahatta Packing Company. The area is filled with vineyards and orchards. Peaches, almonds, apples, grapes and raisins are the major crops grown around Biola.

Each community of Fresno County's heartland has a unique flavor and has made significant contributions to the story of California's central valley. In the next chapter we will venture into the foothills and mountains of Fresno County and explore its towns and history.

Chapter 5

The foothill and mountain areas of Fresno County held treasures other than gold. Tucked away in the mountains of the Sierra Nevada were valleys of untold beauty, rugged peaks of ancient grandeur, groves of giant trees that stood like silent sentinels in the hushed forest, and high alpine meadows that, in spring, were carpeted with wildflowers. The Sierra boasts the highest mountain in the contiguous United States (Mount Whitney, 14,494 ft.), the biggest trees and the deepest valley. The Sierra forests provided a major industry; its rivers provided not only water to irrigate the valley, but also a source of power for the communities of the mountains, the valley and Southern California. This is their story.

Visitors to the Mountains

Joseph Rutherford Walker and John C. Fremont, two of the first white men to explore the valley floor, also ventured into the mountains and foothills of the Sierra. In the 1860s early cattle and sheep men drove their stock into the mountains staking out grazing lands near the San Joaquin and Kings rivers. Beginning in 1860 geologist Josiah Dwight Whitney led a team of men who conducted a

Unless otherwise noted all images this chapter courtesy Laval Historical Collection

The Sierra Communities, Forests and Rivers 5

California geological survey to find new mineral resources. In 1864, while exploring the south fork of the Kings River, members of the team discovered the upper Kings River Canyon — a valley of beauty and grandeur that reminded them of Yosemite Valley. Judge E.C. Winchell and Capt. John N. Appleton also explored the area in the late 1860s. In the 1870s Frank Dusy, a pioneer sheep man who ranged somewhere between 13,000 to 24,000 sheep in the hills and valleys of the Sierra, discovered Tehipite Valley. Dusy, whose summer home was at Dinkey Creek, conducted numerous trips and explorations of the mountains with William Faymonville, J.W. Ferguson, Gustav Eisen and others.

Late in 1877 W.A. Clark, William Hicks, William Hilton and L.M. Grover explored the upper Kings River Canyon. In 1879 Dusy undertook a project that had lasting significance — he began to record the Sierra through photographs. Some eight years later, Lilbourne Winchell photographed Tehipite Valley.

One of the most important outcomes of these early trips into the Sierra was evident many years later. Gustav Eisen, on his trip with Frank Dusy, was awed by the giant sequoia trees. He was called upon to testify in regard to the conservation of the redwood trees before a congressional committee. At the time, the committee was investigating the possibility of opening up the area to lumbering. His affecting testimony in favor of saving the trees persuaded the legislators to preserve them.

Northern Foothill Settlements

Academy

This settlement was first called Big Dry Creek. Its first residents, John Greenup Simpson, William Lewis Lovely Witt and William Harshfield, arrived in 1852. Simpson, a stock raiser, became one of the most influential citizens of the area. Over the years he added to his land holdings. Eventually they totaled almost eight sections of land. After the creation of Fresno County in 1856, Simpson served on the Board of Supervisors.

Others came into the area soon after. John Shaid, Lewis Stemder, Louis Henrici, William Adshead and Maj. Wyatt arrived engaging in stock raising, ranching or, in the case of Adshead, a brick and stone mason, setting up a business. The 1860s saw the arrival of Maj. Thomas P. Nelson, William Walter Shipp and David Cowan Sample, who brought their flocks of sheep with them. Other stock raisers came, too. Most notable among them was Jesse August Blasingame. Blasingame, who had first come to California in 1849 during the Gold Rush, first settled near Big Dry Creek in 1862. He and his wife, Mary, and their two sons returned to the South to settle an estate. On their return trip he brought 2,000 head of cattle, which he drove across the plains from Texas to Nevada. He then sent the cattle on a train to San Francisco, Sacramento and Colfax. He sold the stock for a good price and brought his family back to the Big Dry Creek area in the late 1860s. Blasingame began purchasing land. Eventually his holdings extended almost from Friant to Academy — a distance of nine miles and included 12,000 acres.

In 1868 Francisco Jensen moved to the area from Millerton and opened a store. On March 25, 1870, a post office was established in Jensen's store with Jensen serving as postmaster. A school district was formed in 1869 and reorganized in 1879. The 42 students were taught by William Long. A circuit rider served the area's religious needs. Many of the settlers were members of the Methodist Episcopal Church South. In 1865 the Rev. Joel Hedgpeth became their minister.

In 1869 the congregation built a church on land donated by John Simpson. Fresno County's first church is still in use today.

The settlers of the area were staunch believers in education. A group of the leading citizens of the district formed a committee to build a school. The school that resulted from its efforts had the highest academic standards in the county. James Darwin Collins and his wife, Ann, were the first teachers. The top students, upon reaching graduation, were qualified to become teachers or to go on to college. The school was called the Academy and was Fresno County's first secondary school. Unfortunately, the top level classes at the Academy were dropped after several years and the Academy became just an elementary school. So important was the Academy that the settlement of Big Dry Creek began to be called Academy. An Academy post office was established in 1877.

James Darwin Collins and his wife, Ann, served as the first teachers at the Academy. In 1898 he was elected sheriff of Fresno County, a post he held for eight years.
Catherine Rehart Collection

(Opposite page)
John Greenup Simpson arrived at Big Dry Creek in 1852. He was a strong supporter of the formation of the Academy.

(Chapter opening photo)
A man on horseback surveys the sweeping vista of the high peaks of the Sierra Nevada.

Auberry

Around 1860 Albert and Absolom Yarborough, miners from Tennessee, settled in a valley a few miles north of Academy. According to Charles W. Clough and William B. Secrest Jr. in their book, *Fresno County: The Pioneer Years,* "Through casual pronunciation the valley, named after the Yarboroughs, was unofficially christened Auberoy, Aubery, and finally Auberry." Others moved into the valley, primarily engaging in raising stock like the Yarboroughs. Other early settlers were J.A. Armstrong, Thomas Blair, Olive Childers and John and Jack Corlew. An Auberry post office was established on June 12, 1884, at the southern end of the valley. It was moved twice — the last time, in 1906, to the site of the present-day community of Auberry. In the 1890s a road was built that connected to Tollhouse Road at Pine Ridge. Lumber was becoming increasingly important. Local residents augmented their income by hauling lumber from the saw mills to valley towns. Many new settlers came to the area when the first hydroelectric project at Big Creek required the building of a railroad through Auberry. The Auberry Union (School) District was formed in 1947.

The Academy, Fresno County's first secondary school, gave its name to the community nearby.

PRATHER

This small community takes its named from Joseph E. Prather who never actually lived there, but rather, in 1909 or 1910, brought his family to the Old Lodge Ranch near the intersection of Lodge and Auberry roads. Prathers wife was the former Dr. Minerva Chapele from Fresno. Their three sons were born at the ranch. Before the Prathers arrived the post office and a store were on the site known as Lodge. Only the store remains. Prather planted orchards and opened a blacksmith shop. When the railroad was being built through the area, the railroad asked Prather for a right-of-way across his ranch. He agreed as long as a siding was built on the ranch. In 1914 a Prather post office opened at Lodge.

The building was later moved to the community of Prather.

TOLLHOUSE

The first settler in the area of the present-day community of Tollhouse was Elijah Sauvers. He arrived in the early 1860s. The mountain peak that towers over the settlement, although misspelled as "Sarvers," was named for him. The next arrivals were two brothers, J.H. and J.N. Woods. They were trappers, but turned to making shakes for a living. Once the shakes were made they were faced with the problem of how to transport them to the valley. There were no roads. In October 1866 they acquired a franchise to build a toll road. The rates for use of the road were set by the Board of Supervisors. They were assisted in building the road by John W. Humphreys, a pioneer millman from Mariposa, who had recently arrived in the area. Using Chinese laborers from Millerton, the road was finished in fall 1867. It was a passable road, but not for the faint of heart. It had a very steep, narrow, twisted grade that only a skilled teamster dare travel, and then only with a trained team of horses. However, it provided a route to bring passengers into the mountains and to take lumber out.

In 1868 C.A. Yancy opened a hotel at Tollhouse and Henry Glass set up a blacksmith shop. A store opened in 1874 and the first post office opened at Tollhouse on May 8, 1876. By 1882 triweekly mail service was provided courtesy of brothers A.T. and Clark Stevens, who brought the mail by stage from their Black Hawk Stables in Fresno. The road was improved somewhat in 1892 when the Fresno and Pine Ridge Toll Road Company built an easier road next to the original. This was sold to the county in 1896. Today a newer, improved road bypasses Tollhouse. However, the old road and the community that flanks it are still available for those who wish to taste a bit of the past.

John W. Humphreys was one of the first pioneers in the Pine Ridge area. *Catherine Rehart Collection*

PINE RIDGE

Although not a true community as such, but rather an area about eight miles east of Auberry, it is important enough to be considered. It was here that John W. Humphreys and Moses Mock built their first sawmill in 1866-67. Humphreys built a home for his family nearby. It was purchased in 1874 by August Beringhoff, who shortly after changed his name to Bering. Bering built a barn and a store on the property, which changed hands again in 1882. The new owner's wife started selling

A Star Car races up Tollhouse grade in 1925 when the road was still rather primitive.

meals to the teamsters and other visitors to the area. On April 19, 1892, the Pine Ridge post office was established. Two years later a school district was formed. Other stores opened, but lumber remained the major economic base for Pine Ridge. Paul A. Vandor thought that as many as 84 saw mills were in operation in the area. Today the name Pine Ridge can be found on the map of Fresno County not only at the site of the small settlement, but as the name of the general area as well.

Southern Sierra Communities

Dunlap

Dunlap was first called Mill Creek. It is located in Shipe's Valley, which was named for 1853 settler John Shipe. In the early 1870s homesteaders began moving into the area. The Mill Creek School District was established on May 3, 1875. In fall 1881 George Dunlap Moss arrived to become the teacher at the Mill Creek School. He started a debating club that became very popular with his students. Moss applied to the United States government asking it to establish a post office at Mill Creek. His request was turned down because there were too many communities in California with similar names. Moss applied again, this time submitting his middle name, Dunlap. His request was approved. On November 13, 1882, the Dunlap post office opened in the school building with Moss serving not only as teacher, but also as postmaster. Moss moved away from the area in 1883.

In the 1890s the community began to grow. A number of businesses, including a hotel, were opened. Dunlap became a regular stop on the stage line. Orchards and vineyards were planted in the area around Dunlap. Today the Mill Creek School is known as the Dunlap School and is part of the Kings Canyon Unified School District.

Millwood

Millwood was a 1890s lumber town located near Sequoia Lake. The lake was formed to provide water for the Sanger Lumber Company's flume that sent logs from Millwood to Sanger. The Millwood post office was founded on June 22, 1894. A number of businesses opened and the town grew quickly. Many valley residents found Millwood an ideal spot for a summer vacation. It boasted not only two fine hotels, but also a boisterous red light district about a mile south of the town — the entertainment offered there was popular with loggers and visitors alike. The lumber operations in the area suffered during an economic depression. The Sanger Lumber Company went bankrupt in 1897. A new management team took over the business, but in 1908 the head of the flume was moved to Hume Lake. In 1909 the post office closed. All that remains of Millwood today is a historic marker, erected by the fraternal organization E Clampus Vitus, and two graves. One of the graves is that of a courtesan named Ruby Ellington. Although she died in 1894 someone still remembers her because from time to time fresh flowers are placed on her grave.

Squaw Valley

Helen and Forest Clingan in their book, *From Oak to Pine to Timberline,* cite several possible tales that explain how Squaw Valley was named. The most credible version, according to them, is that the name came from a footprint. "On the west side of the valley, just off Ruth Hill Road, there is a depression that resembles the imprint of a woman's moccasin in a low, granite rock, and the print carries the Indian name of Wootona (woman's foot)....since it is pointing into the valley, it designates the entire valley as woman's land, giving Squaw Valley its name. Legend also warns that death will come to anyone who puts his foot into the rock print." Settlers began coming into the area in the 1860s. A Squaw Valley School District was formed in 1871. The post office came later — in 1879. Hay, wheat, barley, berries and root crops were being cultivated in the valley. A Sunday School held classes, but it was not until 1900 that a church was built. The community has continued to grow and today exists comfortably along Highway 180. Its school district is now part of Kings Canyon Unified School District.

Lumber Industry

The four stages of industrial development in Fresno County, mining, stock raising, grain cultivation

The sun shines through the trees in a Sierra forest.

and agriculture, were previously noted. To these must be added one more — lumber. While the former stages flowed one into the other in succession, the lumber industry began its development soon after the miners arrived and continued apace for many years. The settling of Fresno County required wood for homes and stores. The forests of the Sierra filled this need.

According to Paul Vandor in his *History of Fresno County, California,* the first sawmill in Fresno County was at Millerton. In the year 1851, when the Gold Rush was in full swing, John Dwyer brought lumber to the busy mining camp of Millerton from the nearby mountains. Working with Clark Hoxie, Peter Fink and George Newton, Dwyer used a regular cross-cut saw to cut the lumber to build the Fort Miller Blockhouse.

In 1852 John Harms set up a sawmill at Redwood Creek; James Hulse built his at Corlew Meadow. In 1854 Harms' mill was purchased by Charles Porter Converse and moved to Crane Valley. As the decade progressed, the lumber industry began to expand to meet the need for building materials in the new towns and mining camps in the foothills. As the railroad began its trek through the valley, even more lumber was needed for the new towns that were established along its path. The decade of the 1860s and well into the 1870s saw the Pine Ridge area emerge as a major lumber center. All the forest land was owned by the government. Until 1880 trees could be cut without charge and at will. The land itself, including trees, could be purchased for $2.50 an acre. Many names fill the annals of the time — Humphreys, Donahoo, Bretz, Musick, Ockenden, Ruth, Bennett, Cummings, Littlefield, Foster, Smythe, McCardle and others set up sawmills in the area. Lumber was hauled out in wagons drawn by five or six oxen with an experienced teamster at the helm. Even after the Tollhouse grade was improved, it was still a difficult trip. This was an expensive business. According to Clough and Secrest in *Fresno County: The Pioneer Years,* "Freighters charged forty dollars to carry a thousand board feet to the valley floor." This situation led to discussions about building a flume to the valley, but at this time it came to naught.

In the beginning logs were pulled along the ground by yoked oxen. Later logs were placed on an ox-drawn wagon like this one with wooden wheels.

In 1890 Stevenson Meadow became the site for a new operation. Here William Stephenson and C.M. Bennett built a steam-powered mill. For the next two years they logged 150 acres taking out 3 million board feet of lumber. Two years later their mill was purchased by the Fresno Flume and Irrigation Company, which was owned by a group of Fresno business professionals. The company, the largest to operate in the area, already owned 12,000 acres of timberland in the area of Stevenson Basin. Once again, talk of building a flume became a priority. Although there were differences of opinion among the company's directors, in 1892 construction of a U-shaped flume began. A number of nearby sawmills supplied the lumber needed to build the flume. Having the necessary lumber was one thing, building it was quite another. It took at least 10 days to build one mile of the flume and then only if the best conditions prevailed. In sections, the flume ran along sheer granite cliffs. Men had to be lowered in rope baskets to drill and blast footholds where they could stand. Even then, the men standing on the footholds had to use one hand to hold onto a rope while working with their one free hand. It was not a job for anyone afraid of heights.

Then another matter presented itself. Once the flume was built, it would need water to carry the logs to the valley. To provide that needed resource, an earthen dam was built across Stevenson Creek. The $16,000 project was washed away in a flash flood soon after it was finished. In addition to that were the problems of the flume itself — it leaked so much water it could not properly transport the lumber that was needed to complete it. Again, the directors of the company were put to the test. Salvation came in the form of two lumber men from Michigan — men of

(Far left)
Charles B. Shaver is shown here. Shaver Lake bears his name.
Catherine Rehart Collection

The Shaver Mill sits on the edge of the lake created to serve as a millpond — Shaver Lake.

experience who had logged a great portion of the timberlands of their home state — Charles B. Shaver and Lewis P. Swift.

The first step, after securing the rights of the original company, was to reorganize, which they did under the name of the Fresno Flume and Irrigation Company. Next they added to their timberland holdings. They hired John Eastwood, Fresno's first city engineer, to design a proper flume. His V-shaped flume would have two tiers — the top would carry the cut lumber; the lower tier would carry irrigation water that would be sold to ranchers. (This part of the operation would later prove unfeasible.) Then they moved their most essential employees and their families from Michigan to their site of operations. They built a rock-filled dam across Stevenson Creek creating a mill pond for logs. The new reservoir was called Shaver Lake. Railroad spur lines brought logs from the timber sites to the lake. From there the logs were cut at the mill. Then the lumber was sent down the new V-shaped flume that had its terminus in Clovis where a planing mill and box factory were constructed. It was a successful operation continuing even after the deaths of both Swift and Shaver. In 1919 the sawmill and the company's holdings were purchased while plans were made for expansion of the Big Creek hydroelectric project.

The flume ran from Shaver Lake through the mountains and foothills finally arriving on the valley floor.

Meanwhile, the lumber industry was also moving apace in the mountains southeast of Pine Ridge. By the 1860s a number of sawmills were being used along Mill Creek near the Kings River. Nearby was a large basin-like area filled with the largest stand of giant sequoia trees in the world. It was in this basin that Charles Porter Converse settled. The basin still bears his name. In 1876 Converse established the Kings

When the logs arrived in Clovis they had traveled on the flume for 48 miles.

It took many lumberjacks to fell the enormous Mark Twain Tree in Converse Basin in 1891 because the only tools they had were hand axes.

River Lumber Company. He hoped to take logs out of the areas of Converse Basin and Mill Creek and chute them into the waters of the Kings River, which would transport them to a saw mill. His operation failed.

The Mark Twain Tree falling to earth

Others came into the area, and in 1888 a new Kings River Lumber Company was formed by Austin D. Moore and Hiram C. Smith, two San Francisco businessmen. They planned to build a railroad to take logs to Centerville. This was deemed impractical, so they decided to build a flume instead. Where would the terminus for the flume be? Since Sanger offered the company 65 acres free of charge — a better deal than Fresno offered — the terminus for the flume was going to be in Sanger. They hired Chinese laborers to build a dam on Mill Flat Meadow. The completion of the dam resulted in the creation of Sequoia Lake. Two sawmills, the Sequoia and the Abbot, were finished in 1889 and construction began on the V-shaped flume. On September 3, 1890, the flume was completed to its terminus in Sanger where a finishing mill and box, window sash and door factory were built.

In 1894, after facing financial problems and strikes, the company reorganized as the Sanger Lumber Company. The operation, which resulted in the destruction of the sequoias in Converse Basin, met with more difficulties. As the forests were decimated, logging had to take place farther and farther away from the center of operations, costing the company more money. Production slowed. In 1897 the company filed for bankruptcy. In 1905 the company was sold to Ira Bennet and Thomas Hume. The new Hume-Bennet Company picked Long Meadow as its base. The two men hired John Eastwood to design and direct the building of a dam, sawmill and drying kilns. They also extended the flume up the Kings River Canyon and Ten Mile Creek to the site. Now the flume, stretching a total distance

The lumberjacks who brought the Mark Twain Tree down pose on its stump.

of 59 miles, was the longest flume in the world. In 1909 the Hume Lake Dam and mill were completed. In 1912 Bennet was forced out of the company that now was run by Thomas Hume's son, George. In 1917 the company became known as the Sanger Lumber Company. A series of events over the next several years, including a fire that destroyed the mill and another fire that destroyed part of the flume, brought an end to logging operations. In 1935 20,000 acres of mountain property, including Converse Basin and Hume Lake, were sold to the U.S. Forest Service. Today they are part of Sequoia National Park.

Mention must also be made of the Sugar Pine Lumber Company of Pinedale. Though it was only in operation from 1921-1933, it had an average annual output of over 100 million board feet. Its sawmill was one of the most modern in the country at the time. The operation had the Sugar Pine Lumber Company rail line that connected logging branch lines to the Minarets and Western Railroad, a line that extended 56 miles from Bass Lake to Pinedale. The scheme was the brainchild of Elmer Cox, who developed the Madera Sugar Pine Company. Investors Arthur Fleming and Robert C. Gillis lent money to the project. Although the production figures were impressive, the venture had lost money since its inception. Ultimately, in 1933 the company ceased operations and the rail line was discontinued.

National Parks

In the late 1880s, timberlands were increasingly threatened by two things: the developing logging industry and the effect of sheep grazing on the terrain. Sheep were eating plants right down to the ground. When heavy rains came, erosion was a problem. They also brought the seeds of Johnson Grass from the valley in their coats — introducing the problem weed to the mountain areas. A bill had been introduced in the Senate as early as 1881 to deal with these problems, but it failed. Later in the decade it was put forward again. On September 25, 1890, President Benjamin Harrison signed into law a bill that created Sequoia and General Grant National Parks. On October 1, 1890, Yosemite National Park was created. In 1891 the California Legislature urged Congress to authorize a forest reserve system to protect forest land. On February 14, 1893, President Harrison signed into law a bill that created the Sierra Forest Reserve, the largest such reserve in the nation. It was to be managed by the General Land Office under the Department of the Interior. Under this law, sheep grazing was almost completely prohibited within the reserve's boundaries. In

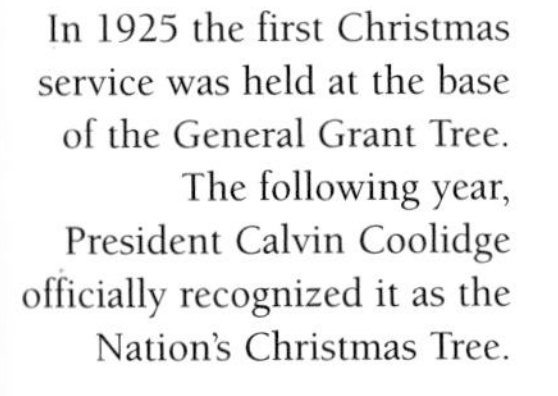

In 1925 the first Christmas service was held at the base of the General Grant Tree. The following year, President Calvin Coolidge officially recognized it as the Nation's Christmas Tree.

In 1896 water came to the San Joaquin Light and Power Company's Powerhouse I through a pipe that descended 1,410 feet down the mountain.

1905 administration of the reserve was transferred to the Department of Agriculture.

In 1908 it was renamed. The area south of the Kings River was called the Sequoia National Forest; the area north of the Kings River became the Sierra National Forest. In 1940, Kings Canyon became a national park.

In 1896 George W. Jewett served as foreman for Powerhouse I.

Water and Power

Any discussion of the harnessing of water to create electricity must begin with John Eastwood, the man whose genius paved the way for the development of hydroelectric power in the San Joaquin River.

John Eastwood was born in Scott County, Minnesota, in 1857. He graduated from State Normal School in Mankato in 1878 and was hired to work on the Minneapolis and St. Louis Railroad's Pacific extension line. In 1883 he brought his bride to Fresno and opened his own engineering office. He was hired in 1884 to survey a rail line down the Tollhouse grade bluff. A year later, after the incorporation of Fresno, the city hired him to do surveys and build streets and canals. He became Fresno's first city engineer. In addition, he kept his private business going. Among his clients was the Fresno Flume and Irrigation Company. According to Gene Rose in his book *Reflections of Shaver Lake,* "At that time, the enormous potential for electricity was virtually unknown. Yet Eastwood could see its potential for pumping water for the otherwise arid valley area. Remembering the deep canyons and cascading rivers he had seen en route to the Shaver mill, he began exploring the rugged canyon."

As Eastwood studied the area, he became more and more convinced that the rushing waters of the San Joaquin River held tremendous potential for a project of this kind. He presented his plan to a number of Fresno businessmen. One of them, John Seymour, president and major stockholder of the Fresno Water Company, believed in his idea. Together they created the San Joaquin Electric Company. Their first project was to build a powerhouse on the north fork of the San Joaquin River (present-day Willow Creek near Bass Lake) as it was called at that time. It was here that the river began a rapid descent — that rapid fall of water would be used to turn the turbines and generate power.

Work on San Joaquin Powerhouse No. 1 began April 1, 1895. Many were skeptical about the project. Some thought it was too far away to provide power for Fresno (37 miles). The skeptics were silenced a year later when the plant began to generate power. Mrs. Eastwood, at the substation in Fresno, was given the honor of pressing the button that started the machinery moving. At that time, the resulting transmission line was the longest in the world. However, problems did arise, most notably from the Fresno Gas and Electric Company, who hit them where it hurt most by filing riparian water claims and cutting off the water supply.

In 1899 the San Joaquin Electric Company filed bankruptcy papers. Eastwood, still believing in his project, headed for the mountains. With only his pack mule and horses for company, he spent months exploring the upper San Joaquin River surveying stream flows, and knowing now that to succeed any future projects had to depend upon stored water, looking for sites where dams could be built.

In 1902 William G. Kerckhoff and A.C. Balch purchased Eastwood's bankrupt company, adding it to a number of smaller companies they already owned. They incorporated the new company as the San Joaquin Power Company. In 1910 it became San Joaquin Light and Power Corporation, and in 1930 Pacific Gas and Electric Company. Kerckhoff was president; Balch, vice president and A.G. Wishon, manager of the company. Kerckhoff and Balch were already the partners of Henry Huntington, nephew of railroad owner Collis P. Huntington, in another venture — the Pacific Light and Power Company of Los Angeles, which is today the Southern California Edison Company.

In September 1902 two survey parties were sent out — one headed by Eastwood and one by Louie Manuel. According to David H. Redinger in *The Story of Big Creek,* the parties started at Shaver Lake and continued to present-day Huntington Lake "where lines and levels were run to determine quickly the available storage capacity of the reservoir, and where cross sections were taken of the proposed Dams 1 and 2. The surveys also included running a line over Kaiser Pass to determine the length of tunnel necessary to bring in the South Fork of the San Joaquin River." During his survey trip, Eastwood discovered a large gorge that dropped thousands of feet into the San Joaquin River. He applied the name Big Creek to this waterway because, even in late summer, it contained a large amount of water. Eastwood continued exploring the tributaries of Big Creek and filed water claims. According to William A. Myers in *Iron Men and Copper Wires,* Eastwood "located a powerhouse site near the junction of Big Creek and Pitman Creek, where Edison's Big Creek No. 1 plant now stands. He walked over Kaiser Pass running levels to show that additional water could be diverted from the upper San Joaquin River near Florence Lake into Big Creek's watershed. He also envisioned the storage of that water and natural runoff in a large reservoir in Big Creek Basin, today's Huntington Lake." His survey complete, Eastwood wrote Kerckhoff the following, "It gives me great pleasure to inform you that I have completed the surveys for a tunnel line to the junction of Pitman and Big Creeks, and I can place before you the most remarkable power project yet presented." Kerckhoff discussed Eastwood's report with Huntington, who was impressed with Eastwood's report. He hired Eastwood to prepare designs for the project, which he spent the next three years completing.

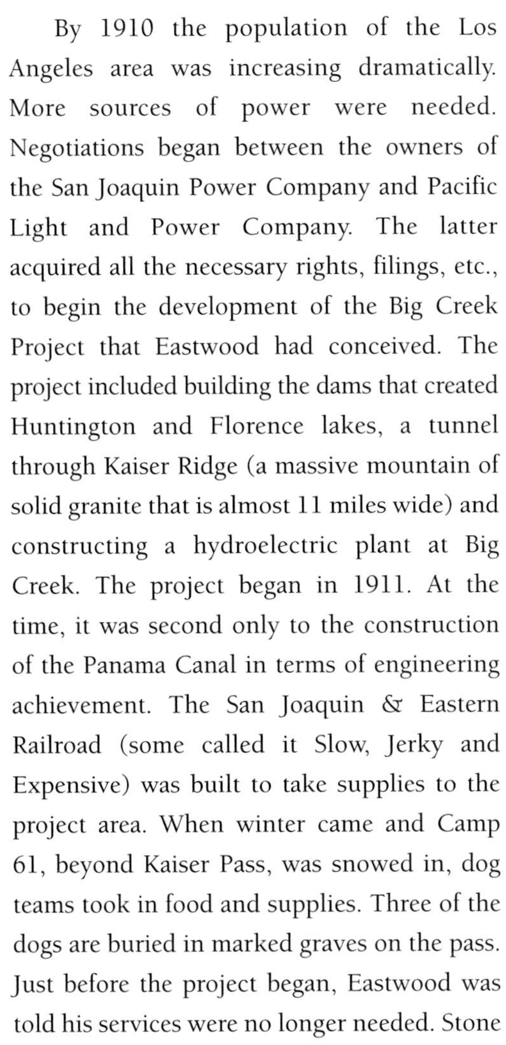

By 1910 the population of the Los Angeles area was increasing dramatically. More sources of power were needed. Negotiations began between the owners of the San Joaquin Power Company and Pacific Light and Power Company. The latter acquired all the necessary rights, filings, etc., to begin the development of the Big Creek Project that Eastwood had conceived. The project included building the dams that created Huntington and Florence lakes, a tunnel through Kaiser Ridge (a massive mountain of solid granite that is almost 11 miles wide) and constructing a hydroelectric plant at Big Creek. The project began in 1911. At the time, it was second only to the construction of the Panama Canal in terms of engineering achievement. The San Joaquin & Eastern Railroad (some called it Slow, Jerky and Expensive) was built to take supplies to the project area. When winter came and Camp 61, beyond Kaiser Pass, was snowed in, dog teams took in food and supplies. Three of the dogs are buried in marked graves on the pass. Just before the project began, Eastwood was told his services were no longer needed. Stone and Webster Engineering Corporation was hired to manage the project that Eastwood had conceived. He was given stock in the company, but as the project progressed, assessments were made against his holdings. He was left penniless. He went on to other projects designing dams in other states. In August 1924, at the age of 67, he drowned in the Kings River. Eastwood left a tremendous legacy to the people of Fresno County and, indeed, of California, yet his name has never graced a lake or dam that his genius made possible.

Construction of the Kerckhoff Powerhouse was completed in July 1920. It began operation on August 5, 1920.

In 1910 the San Joaquin Light and Power Company built the A.G. Wishon Powerhouse next to Eastwood's Powerhouse No. 1 on Willow Creek on the Madera County side of the San Joaquin River. In 1920 the Kerckhoff Powerhouse No. 1 was built on the Fresno County side about two miles downstream. At the same time, the Kerckhoff Reservoir was built. More recently, Kerckhoff Powerhouse No. 2 was built about two miles below No. 1. In 1927 attention turned to the north fork of the Kings River where two Balch Powerhouses were built. Then, in 1930 the company became part of Pacific Gas and Electric Company.

Today the Kings River network includes the Kings River Powerhouse, the Pine Flat Dam and Reservoir and the Haas Powerhouse in addition to the Balch Powerhouses. At the top of the network is Courtright Reservoir, Wishon Reservoir just below it, and Black Rock Reservoir just below Hass Powerhouse. All of these feed water to the generating plants that supply power and irrigation water to the Central Valley.

The resources of the mountains of the Sierra Nevada and the ingenuity of people have made it possible for many to live comfortably in California's Central Valley, an area that 135 years ago was a dry, dusty semiarid desert and home only to wild animals and native grasses.

CHAPTER 6

The last two decades of the 19th century had witnessed dramatic economic swings. The land boom of the 1880s was followed by a period of economic depression in the first five years of the 1890s. By the last half of the decade conditions began to improve. On January 1, 1900, Chester Harvey Rowell's editorial in the *Fresno Morning Republican* showed confidence in Fresno's future. He applauded the people of Fresno for their enlightened, energetic and enterprising spirit. Optimism was the byword for a new century.

As Fresno entered the 20th century, it could boast a population of 12,470. The city now encompassed 4.13 square miles. The next decade would see the city expand its boundaries as growth continued to the north and the east. Fresno was poised and ready to move forward on the path that would lead to the fulfillment of the vision Leland Stanford had seen for it — and for his railroad — on that November day in 1871. An optimistic spirit would lead the way.

Unless otherwise noted all images this chapter courtesy Laval Historical Collection

Fresno Comes of Age 6

The Reform Battle Rages On

The new century began with a new city charter, a new form of government and the first elected mayor in Fresno's history. Mayor Lewis Oliver Stephens, a leading Fresno undertaker, was a God-fearing, church-going, practical man who was determined to serve his city by being an independent mayor and moving forward with reform efforts. In this he was joined by the majority of the members of the newly elected Board of Trustees. A new police commission was put in place with W.T. Mattingly as chairman. He and Trustee John P. Strother, a respected attorney who was now the chairman of the police committee, began their job of trying to reform law enforcement. They also worked with the new mayor in leading the drive to suppress vice interests throughout Fresno and to license and regulate the saloons and related businesses. Even though they managed to bring a period of honest government to Fresno, their accomplishments were only a beginning. A law to close saloons for four hours a day still meant they could remain open for 20 hours. If a saloon had bartenders who acted as pimps or allowed gambling, the saloon was closed. Prostitution was not outlawed, but the open cribs next to the saloons were no longer allowed to exist. "Parlor houses" continued to operate in the tenderloin district. Although these were small steps, it still seemed like a revolution to many and managed to create unpopular feelings among many of the local business professionals who felt that the reformers were driving business away from Fresno. It was not long before saloon owners found ways to buy off the police and go back to their old ways of doing business. They just had to be more circumspect about it.

A number of significant additions to the city marked Stephens' term in office. In 1901 the horse car lines, which had provided colorful transportation for residents, were incorporated into a new system — an electrically powered street railway called the Fresno City Railway. The year 1902 brought two changes to Courthouse Park. A bandstand was built that would serve the city until its demolition in 1960. The members of the Fresno County Board of Supervisors decided that a new century meant progress and voted to install toilets in the Courthouse for the first time.

In 1895 Frederick C. Roeding offered the city 230 acres of land for a park with the provision that the city spend $1,500 per year for maintenance and plants. The offer was turned down. In 1903, during Stephens' term in office, the Roeding family again offered land for a park — this time 73 acres. This offer was accepted. Johannes Reimers, a noted landscape architect, was hired to design the park. Frederick's son, George, who was park commissioner, oversaw the planting and donated many trees and shrubs from his nursery to the park. Today Roeding Park is still one of Fresno's treasures.

Another park that was a haven for Fresnans began in 1900 when Leota Burnside married John Zapp. They moved to her father's ranch, which today would be approximately the southwest corner of Blackstone and Olive. Here they began to create a paradise. When completed, Zapp's Park had shallow lakes, trees, a dance pavilion, heated swimming pools, a bowling alley, covered boardwalks, a Ferris wheel, a small zoo and grassy picnic areas. It was enjoyed by Fresnans until about 1920 when the Zapps' deaths and development north caused the property to be subdivided.

As election time rolled around, the citizens of Fresno were not sure they wanted another four years of a dull, straight-laced, albeit honest regime. Reform was not much fun and, many thought, it wasn't helping business either. It was a threat to the "business as usual" saloon interests. Just to prove their point citizens elected into office the most colorful, controversial, fun-loving mayor in the history of Fresno — before or since. He possessed not only a joyous, devil-may-care personality, but he was supported by the vice interests of the tenderloin. "There was joy in the saloons last night and jubilation in the tenderloin. Booze flowed freely and likewise free," began the story in the *Fresno Morning Republican* the morning after the election of April 10, 1905 — the day W. Parker Lyon was elected mayor of Fresno. For the reformers, the election of Lyon was a total disaster. For the people of Fresno, it was a mixed blessing. For the next few years they would be treated to ongoing entertainment with a few solid accomplishments along the way.

A former fire insurance adjuster from Oakland, Lyon came to Fresno in 1892 and built up a successful used furniture business on I Street (Broadway). One of his marketing tools was his collection of chamber pots, which he once laid out in a serpentine fashion along the block leading customers to his store. He ran rather outrageous ads in the *Republican* on a regular basis, usually opposite Rowell's editorial page. Rowell, furious over Lyon's win, said he guessed it paid to advertise in his newspaper. Not surprisingly, the new laws that had been passed to govern the saloons were relaxed during Lyon's administration. Blessed with a glib, golden tongue, Lyon assured the populace, especially the church groups, that he was going to continue the reform efforts. At the same time he made sure that the saloon keepers and pimps knew that he was really their friend. Lyon fired Police Chief John J. White and replaced him with R.M. Devoe who was liked by the businessmen because he knew how the game was played.

(Opposite page, left)
Stephens & Bean's motorized hearse is shown parked in front of the Carnegie Library in 1904.

(Opposite page, right)
A trolley travels east on Mariposa Street toward the Courthouse in 1900.

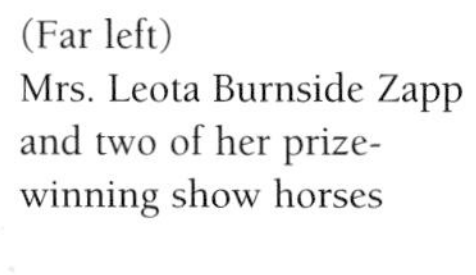

(Far left)
Mrs. Leota Burnside Zapp and two of her prize-winning show horses

These two Fresno matrons in their fashionable hats and gloves are about to ride the roller coaster at Zapp's Park.

The Ferris wheel was one of the many attractions at Zapp's Park.

Fresno's first true City Hall was built in 1907 and stood at the corner of Merced and Broadway streets.

In spite of this, Lyon really was committed to creating a better Fresno. He believed in the city's future and during his administration left some lasting achievements. Fresno's first City Hall building was constructed in 1907 at a cost of $75,000. A new sewer system, a concrete subway on Fresno Street, the paving of Tulare Street and a reduction in utility rates were accomplishments he could point to with pride. However, early in 1907 a story ran in the newspaper that told of Lyon selling furniture from his store to the madam who ran one of the largest brothels in the city.

Then, during an eight-month period in 1907, three police officers were killed while on duty. Crime was on the rise. People began to realize that while Lyon talked a good line, the criminal elements in the town were able to operate just as they had before Stephens' administration. That might have been all right in an earlier time, but Fresno was growing. It was not a small town anymore. Its citizens now wanted action, not words. The last straw occurred in July 1907.

Lyon and four of the trustees approved the opening of a new saloon in the 900 block of J Street (Fulton) although almost all the business professionals on both sides of the street disapproved. A story in the *Republican* charged that the mayor and one of his associates wanted to relocate the saloon so they could open a bank in its old location. This led the Rev. Dr. Thomas Boyd of the First Presbyterian Church to preach a sermon of the hellfire and brimstone variety dealing with the mayor who he declared was in league with the powers of darkness. Lyon tried to defend himself in letters to the *Republican* and the *Fresno Democrat,* Fresno's other newspaper. Other Protestant ministers took up the cause fueled by the flames of the increasingly popular temperance movement.

On March 10, 1908, a huge crowd gathered to hear speakers exhort the citizens to look at their city and the wide open vice interests that were allowed to operate because the city government was corrupt. A number of leading citizens spoke out siding with the Anti-Saloon League.

Lyon had enough. He resigned and headed with his family to Southern California. A wealthy man, he built a large home and a huge museum across the street from the Santa Anita racetrack.

He left his city a legacy of colorful stories. The following is one of the favorites. Just after the 1906 San Francisco earthquake, many of the "ladies" from the Barbary Coast came to Fresno. Their presence caused consternation among the local madams operating along I (Broadway) Street and in the tenderloin. The large number of newcomers brought unwanted competition.

The local madams took their cause to Mayor Lyon who promptly called his friends at the Southern Pacific Railroad and asked for a train to be placed at his disposal. Then he and the police chief marched through downtown rounding up the unwanted newcomers. They managed to round up a few upstanding citizens as well (members of the Baptist choir, a suffragist or two and a secretary) who had to be asked to step aside while the others were marched to the depot and put on the train.

The trip to Los Angeles was brightened with open bottles of champagne. One of the "ladies" was given a card to present to the mayor of Los Angeles. Signed by mayor W. Parker Lyon, it read, " I heard you were short of entertainment and we've got too much, so here's some." When the "ladies" arrived, the mayor of Los Angeles failed to see the humor in the situation.

Trustee Edward E. Bush, a planing mill operator, was appointed mayor to fill out the 13 months remaining of Lyon's term. Bush, an ally of Lyon's, did little to change the conditions in the city. The only real change was that the colorful fun that marked Lyon's tenure was replaced by a man who was dull in comparison. Bush's time in office appeared to be just holding on to the status quo until the next election.

Despite the battles over reform, the first decade of the 20th century was a period of economic growth. The city's boundaries were moving north and east. The crossing of Divisadero Street to create the new neighborhood of North Park caused the city to slightly shift the layout of the new streets so they would go directly north and south. (The downtown streets had been laid out parallel to the railroad.) Other neighborhoods began to develop north and east of downtown although they were yet to be incorporated into the city. The city was definitely on the move.

The decade also saw other changes. Horses were being replaced by automobiles. The Burnett Sanitarium, which Celia Burnett began in her boarding house, was incorporated. A new library was built with a $30,000 donation from Andrew Carnegie. New businesses opened, including a store owned by Emil Gottschalk in 1904. In 1905 the Fresno Musical Club, a group of musicians who sponsored a concert series that brought the leading musicians of the time to Fresno, was founded. Raisin Day was instituted in 1909 as an annual event to promote the raisin industry. In 1910 the first group to promote a local symphony was founded.

The reform efforts in Fresno were only part of a larger movement that was sweeping through California. The reform efforts statewide were rooted in a desire to free the California Republican Party from the control of the Southern Pacific Railroad's political hold. The desire for reform led to the creation of an insurgent movement within the party called the Lincoln-Roosevelt League. The league became, in effect, a third party and nominated its candidate, Hiram Johnson, for the office of governor. In 1910 Johnson was elected governor by the people of California. His win ended the political domination of the railroad over California politics. One of the leaders of the Lincoln-Roosevelt League was Chester Harvey Rowell, nephew of Dr. Chester Rowell and editor of the *Fresno Morning Republican*. His editorial page became a platform for the league's views. During the period from 1906-1910, the *Republican* grew in size and influence to become a leading newspaper in California. Other prominent Fresnans including J.C. Forkner joined the league. Their desire for reform statewide was echoed in their desire for local reform.

Mariposa Street in 1914 shows evidence of transition. Automobiles line the curbs and horse-drawn vehicles are still in use. The Grand Central Hotel is on the right.

Delivery boys lined the front of the newspaper office of the *Fresno Morning Republican* in 1913.

By 1910 the population of Fresno was 24,892, almost double the population in 1900. The downtown skyline remained unchanged. There were no high-rise buildings. This would soon change.

Growth, Temperance and War

The Fresno city election of April 12, 1909, brought Dr. Chester Rowell into the office of mayor. A referendum measure on the ballot that would abolish all the existing saloons in the city and allow liquor to be sold only in restaurants was passed by the voters. In

Dr. Chester Rowell

one of his first acts as mayor he vetoed the measure. Six votes of the trustees were needed to override his veto. Only five voted against the mayor. The measure failed. The reformers were horrified. Mayor Rowell said that the measure would not solve the problem and discriminated against the poor.

An interesting side note to this is that Dr. Rowell was still the owner of the *Republican*. Even though he sometimes disagreed with his nephew's editorial policy, he always was adamant in saying that his nephew was in control of the editorial page. The two men may have disagreed in print, but in private their relationship was strong.

Several weeks later a new ordinance was passed with the approval of Mayor Rowell. The new measure closed the licensed saloons, private clubs and cafes at midnight and all day Sunday. Editor Chester H. Rowell was delighted. This was not enough, however, for the prohibitionists. The Anti-Saloon League pressured the trustees until they voted for a prohibition ordinance that was later declared unconstitutional by the California Supreme Court.

Throughout his life in Fresno, Mayor Chester Rowell tried to do what was best for the people in his community. As a doctor, he tended the sick whether or not they had the ability to pay. As a state senator (he served two terms), he represented his community well. As mayor he continued to serve the community he had played such a strong role in building.

On May 23, 1912, he died while on a visit to Los Angeles. The outpouring of grief came from every quarter of the city. Flags were lowered to half-mast. Many buildings were draped in black. On May 26, at 2:00 p.m., the citizens of Fresno gathered in Courthouse Park for a memorial service. University of California President Benjamin Ide Wheeler gave one of the many eulogies. Many tears were shed as the people of Fresno remembered the many acts of kindness performed by this man. A statue of Dr. Rowell was erected at the Van Ness and Tulare entrance to Courthouse Park. The inscription reads, "Good Physician. Good Friend. Good Citizen."

Trustee Alva E. Snow, a strong supporter of Dr. Rowell's policies, was appointed to fill out his term. He did so admirably and was elected mayor in his own right in April 1913. Elected with him was a group of trustees who were well-qualified to serve. Snow's administration was overshadowed by the growing debate regarding prohibition. Although he was honest and progressive, the reformers felt his record regarding the saloons was not strong enough. He was defeated in the election of April 1917 by William F. Toomey.

Dr. Chester Rowell and his family on the porch of his Van Ness Avenue home — the future site of the Rowell building

(Far right) Mayor Toomey presents a $10,000 check to members of the YWCA for its building drive.

Fulton Street in 1917 shows the Griffith McKenzie Building dominating the skyline.

Toomey's administration began just as the United States became involved in World War I. Despite that, he presided over a period of steady population growth. The city had expanded far beyond its boundaries. Annexation was being considered. During these years, the face of downtown began to change. In 1913 the eight-story Hotel Fresno was the first of several tall buildings to be erected downtown. In 1914 the Griffith-McKenzie Building and the Helm Building were built. During the next six years, the Rowell Building, Mason Building, Mattei Building, T.W. Patterson Building, Pacific Southwest Building and San Joaquin Power Building all were built attesting not only to the prosperity of the time, but also to the optimism of Fresnans about the future of their city. The liquor issue that had dominated politics in Fresno for so long was briefly put on hold. On January 16, 1919, the prohibition amendment was ratified by Congress. By July the police chief was reporting that liquor arrests were down.

The Mattei Building at Fulton and Fresno streets under construction in 1920

The Administration Building of the Fresno Normal School under construction in 1915

The early years of the decade saw two important additions to the educational life of the Fresno community. In 1910 the first junior college in California began on the Fresno High School campus. A year later the Fresno Normal School was established on the same campus. Then, in 1913 Fresno Normal School moved to temporary buildings at Maroa and University avenues. Within three years a large brick building had been built at this location to house the new school. These two institutions, now called Fresno City College and California State University, Fresno, are regarded as important centers of higher learning in the Central Valley.

Between 1910 and 1914 two new subdivisions were built west and east of downtown Fresno. The Kearney Heights area and the Alta Vista tract are still neighborhoods that are vital and intact.

On April 6, 1917, the United States entered World War I. By June, Fresno men were registering for the draft. In the city alone, 3,710 men signed up. By summer local men were seeing duty at the European front. Their city stood behind them by donating clothing and shoes, volunteering for the Red Cross and purchasing war bonds. In 1919 a War History Committee was set up to record the events of the period. It became the Fresno Historical Society. On November 11, 1918, when the war ended, Mayor Toomey ordered all the church bells to be rung and the factory and railroad whistles to be sounded. People streamed from their homes and formed an impromptu parade that wound its way to Courthouse Park. There, on the steps of the historic Courthouse, a service of thanksgiving was held.

Charles Henry Cheney's vision for Fresno's Civic Center

In 1918 Charles Henry Cheney, a San Francisco architect and city planner, was hired to write a plan for Fresno. His "General Report on Progress of City Plan for Fresno" was filed with the city trustees and planning commission on May 31 of that year. Cheney's concepts for a civic center, streets, parks, railroad consolidation and downtown revitalization were considered progressive for the development of the young city. One of his suggestions was a parkway along the San Joaquin River. Although most of Cheney's ideas were not adopted, his plan is still considered a basic one for Fresno.

In 1919 J.C. Forkner and Wylie Giffen began developing a new tract on land north of Fresno. The name for the development was the Garden Home tract. Horace Cotton, a well-known landscape architect, was hired to design the landscaping. He planted deodar cedar trees along Van Ness Boulevard, the main street. Each street that intersected Van Ness was planted with a different variety of tree. The land was subdivided into parcels that were equal to 10 city lots and were sold for $1,250 to $1,500. The developers envisioned that each home would be situated amid 50 Kadota fig trees. The area today is called Old Fig Garden.

At the end of the decade and the beginning of 1920, Fresno's population stood at 45,080 and encompassed an area of 7.65 square miles.

Prohibition, Boom and Bust

The year 1920 was ushered in on the crest of an economic postwar boom. Raisin prices were 15-20 cents per pound and vineyards cost $1,000 per acre. Fresno was gaining a decidedly urban look with a vital downtown. More cars were on the streets and retail business was good. Chester H. Rowell sold his newspaper, the *Fresno Morning Republican,* for $1 million to George A. and Chase S. Osborn Jr. Twelve years later, it was purchased by *The Fresno Bee.*

The decade began with the drafting of a new city charter and a new form of government for Fresno. In July the citizens voted to accept it. Under the new system, the mayor and eight trustees would be replaced by a five-member commission that would have legislative and executive powers. The commissioner of public safety and welfare, the position with the most power since it would appoint the police and fire chiefs, would be the responsibility of the mayor. The mayor and the commissioners of finance and public works would serve full-time. The two remaining commissioners, who had only legislative powers and would be known as legislative commissioners, would serve in a part-time capacity.

The new governing body had problems from the beginning. In the city election of April 1921, Toomey ran against Truman G. Hart, one of Fresno's most regarded citizens, for the post of commissioner of public safety and welfare. Hart, who felt the new form of government had flaws that he would work hard to correct, won the top post. Charles Dillon won the finance post. Hart had believed for some time that a city manager, who was hired and was outside of politics, was needed to run the city. Events would soon prove him correct. In 1924 Dillon was convicted on 13 counts of misusing public funds and keeping false accounts of public expenditures. He went to prison where he served 18 months of a four-year sentence. Dillon was also sued by the city for $32,000 for which could not be accounted. His trials made newspaper headlines throughout the state. Mayor Hart tried to advance the idea of a city manager, but failed.

In the election of 1925 Hart chose not to run. Alpheus E. Sunderland, a fruit packer and merchant, became the next commissioner of public safety and welfare. He was joined by four other commissioners who vowed to work together for the good of the city.

Unfortunately, a short time later the Fresno County Grand Jury indicted a former acting police chief and 11 other police officials for conspiracy to violate the prohibition laws. They were accused of taking bribes from bootleggers and, in return for favors, letting local businesses who were selling liquor illegally know when police raids were going to take place. The former police chief testified that the mayor had told him vice was to be permitted. The mayor took the stand to defend himself, but a recall campaign nearly forced him out of office. He survived the recall election, but was defeated in the election of 1929.

The colorful boom period of the 1920s was evident during the first half of the decade. The Fresno Brewery changed from brewing beer to bottling soft drinks, but

(Far left)
The Fresno Brewery is shown here in 1919. The main building dates to 1889. Today it is the second oldest commercial building in Fresno.

On October 8, 1920, federal and local law enforcement officers dumped hundreds of gallons of outlawed liquor into Dry Creek.

harbored a speakeasy within its walls. Federal and local law enforcement officials broke open kegs of confiscated liquor, which they poured into Dry Creek. Fresno's second high school, Edison, was built. In 1921 the General Hospital of Fresno County (first called the County Hospital when it was established at Millerton and later moved to Fresno in 1874) was accredited for the first time. A school of nursing opened in the facility three years later. In 1922, KMJ, Fresno's first radio station, began broadcasting. In the same year *The Fresno Bee* newspaper began operation with Carlos McClatchy as editor and manager. Downtown continued to develop. Neighborhoods were created as the city continued its march north. Streets were paved and streetcar tracks were laid linking downtown to the new areas. The first junior high schools in Fresno, Washington and Longfellow, were built. The Pantages Theater (now Warnors) was opened in 1926. In 1927 the West Coast Relays track event was held for the first time. By 1925 the first signs of depression were evident as raisin prices collapsed. By 1929 half of Fresno County's farms faced foreclosure. In the same year the stock market crashed. The boom era was over.

In September 1929 St. Agnes Hospital was completed at its site on Fruit Avenue.

(Far right) Mayor "Zeke" Leymel dedicated the Belmont Avenue underpass on July 22, 1932.

Depression and New Beginnings

Although the city had grown in size during the decade of the 1920s, the population figures in 1930 showed less dramatic growth than during the era of the 1910s. In 1930 the number of people living in Fresno was 52,513 and the city encompassed 8.79 square miles.

As the new decade of the 1930s began, Fresno had a new mayor. Zygmunt "Zeke" S. Leymel, a very popular figure, was elected on April 15, 1929. A decorated veteran of the Spanish American War who served as Col. Theodore Roosevelt's personal orderly, Leymel was wounded in the battles of Bloody Creek and San Juan Hill. He also served in World War I. Leymel taught history and civics at Fresno High School and did a stint as football coach and vice principal. He left teaching in 1926, when he was elected the state assemblyman for the Fifty-first District. When elected mayor, he resigned from the state assembly.

No one since Dr. Chester Rowell had come to the office of mayor more prepared than Zeke Leymel. He had high hopes for making great contributions to his city. Unfortunately, just after he came into office, a gunman made two attempts on his life. The next day the stock market crashed. A few days later three west Fresnans were arrested on liquor conspiracy charges. It was said that members of the police department were also involved. The rest of Leymel's term, probably because the police department was being heavily investigated, was one in which the police department was fairly free of corruption.

Leymel achieved many good things for Fresno during his two terms in office. Chandler Field was completed. Fresno's water system was brought under the control of the city. The subway on Belmont Avenue

On July 7, 1931, Century Pacific Lines President O.R. Fuller assisted Elizabeth Chandler as she christened the airplane *Fresno* to launch air service at Chandler Field. Chandler is the granddaughter of W.F. Chandler, who donated the land for the airport.

Champion boxer Ralph Giordano "Young Corbett III" (right), and Walter Marty (left) who established a high jump record of 6 feet five-eighths inches, in the 1933 West Coast Relays.

was built with county, city and railroad money. Leymel also worked to bring many of the unincorporated neighborhoods into the city. Even though many were out of work and the Dust Bowl brought many people into the county from Oklahoma and Arkansas, new fortunes were being made in the Coalinga oil fields. The outward manifestation of this was a study in contrasts — soup kitchens and bread lines downtown, and lavish mansions rising up along Van Ness and Huntington boulevards. Several buildings were built in the developing civic center as part of the federal governments' project to put people back to work. With a combination of monies from a local bond election and from federal public works, the Fresno Memorial Auditorium was built. The Works Project Administration also built the Hall of Records (1937), the County Schools Building (1936) and the Federal Court Building and Post Office (1939). Although Leymel had led the city forward in many areas, he was voted out of office in 1937.

The new mayor was Frank Homan, the owner of the city's largest sporting goods store. Homan was one of the founders of the Sunnyside Country Club and a past president of the Fresno Rotary Club. He was well-liked, honest and had a reputation as a good team player. Homan's first accomplishment was to formulate a plan to build a new city hall. The facility would provide much needed office space for city staff. The commissioners voted to fund the project, which was completed in 1941. Built for $400,000, the new city hall, an ultramodern brick and glass structure designed by architect Ernest Kump Jr., won national recognition for its design. The building was constructed without asking the voters for bond approval. The modern design caused some consternation because the populace had not had an opportunity to give voice to their opinions about its design or its financing. During his administration Homan took credit for the creation of the Fresno Municipal Golf Course on the south bank of the San Joaquin River, new city parks, recreational centers and a new firehouse at E and Fresno streets.

On May 21, 1939, the last streetcar made its way north on Wishon Avenue. At a designated spot it met a motorized bus. A ceremony was held to mark the switch over from trolley cars to buses. By 1940 the trolley tracks had been taken up all over town. They were sent to smelters, melted down and turned into guns, tanks and warships.

In 1935 Ratcliffe Stadium is partially surrounded by farmland, and Blackstone Avenue is a two-lane road.

The Fresno Memorial Auditorium was dedicated on New Year's Eve 1936. It has been the site for important community activities ever since.

(Far left)
A view of the Fig Garden flood of 1938 from the air, looking north from Palm Avenue and the Santa Fe tracks

Looking north on Fulton Street in 1938

Two unidentified men are caught in the Fig Garden flood of 1938. The man on the left is sitting in a rowboat.

The decade held other achievements as well. In 1933, Ralph Giordano, known as Young Corbett III, won the World Welterweight Championship. He was given a hero's welcome in Courthouse Park. In 1937 three clergymen, Rabbi David L. Greenberg, Monsignor James Dowling and Episcopal Dean James M. Malloch, began a program on KMJ Radio called the "Forum For Better Understanding," in order to promote communication between people of the Central Valley. During World War II, their program was carried to Europe by Armed Forces Radio. A statue in their memory stands in Courthouse Park. In 1938 the neighborhood of Fig Garden was devastated by a massive flood. In 1939 construction began on Friant Dam and the Tower Theater opened. The neighborhood that had begun to grow north of downtown Fresno was developing a commercial district that would take its name from the new theater. Fresno was a growing, vital city once again. As the decade ended census figures showed its population to be 60,685 and its area encompassed 9.99 square miles.

War and Postwar Problems

Although the years of economic hardship seemed to be over, war clouds were looming on the horizon. Hitler's troops were making their way across Europe. In the election of 1941 Fresnans looked to a former war hero to lead the way. On April 14, 1941, Zeke Leymel was, once again, elected mayor of Fresno.

When Leymel took office he was faced with a city that had a rapidly expanding population — much of which was in unincorporated areas. Residents in these areas enjoyed city services, but did not pay city taxes. The boundaries of the city zigzagged all over the place. There were county islands everywhere. Many people did not know if they lived in the city or the county. The voters defeated all attempts to annex these areas. Fresno's historic cultural mix had been added to with several waves of new immigrant populations. Now the city had 65 identifiable ethnic groups within its boundaries. The new mayor was faced with an ongoing problem — the city was inefficiently run. It needed a manager at the helm who would administer the city's various departments. Since this situation was not going to change at present, Leymel used his experience and expertise to make the present system work.

Mayor Homan had been negotiating with the federal government about locating a major military air field in Fresno. It was decided to locate the field at

Clovis and Shields avenues. The city agreed to purchase the property and lease it to the military. The $2 million Hammer Field bomber base was open for operations by the end of 1941. At the height of the war, 60,000 people were stationed at Hammer Field or at Camp Pinedale at Herndon and Palm avenues. Entertainment was available for them at the USO clubs at 2136 Tulare Avenue and 457 H Street.

Less suitable entertainment could also be found in Fresno's red light district, which at the time was located mostly on Broadway just east of the Southern Pacific yard. The saloons and cribs of an earlier time that had accommodated miners and loggers had been replaced by bars and small hotels. The services they provided, however, were relatively unchanged. Fresno kept its reputation as a wide-open city. When the city offices moved to the new City Hall on Fresno Street, the police department moved into the old City Hall building on Broadway and Merced — right in the heart of all the action.

At the beginning of the 20th century, many Japanese immigrated to Fresno County because there was a great need for agricultural laborers. Later they established homes and engaged in farming. After the bombing of Pearl Harbor in 1941, a feeling of distrust and prejudice began to grow against them. Many of the newspapers in the communities around Fresno editorialized about the loyalty of Japanese Americans and warned against turning the actions of the Japanese government and military into discriminatory acts against American citizens. By 1942 public sentiment against Japanese Americans was growing all over the west. On February 19, 1942, President Franklin D. Roosevelt signed Executive Order 9066 that gave the military the authority to designate "military zones from which any or all persons may be excluded." In March citizens of Japanese descent were ordered to move to the eastern sections of Washington, Oregon and California. In Fresno County that translated into moving east of Highway 99. By April and May Japanese Americans living on the coast were evacuated to "assembly centers." Two centers were located in Fresno — at Camp Pinedale and at the Fresno Fairgrounds. In mid-July it was announced that all Japanese Americans living on the West Coast were to be moved first to assembly centers and then to "relocation centers" either at Tule Lake or Manzanar, California, or to centers outside California. When the

(Far right)
The First Christian Church at N and Tuolumne streets was built in 1912. Like many of Fresno's historic buildings it was torn down to make way for a newer building.

Mr. Nakamura and his son pose by the mailbox of their farm.

war ended many Japanese Americans returned to their homes and farms in Fresno County. In recent years efforts have been made to rectify the wrongs that were done to these citizens during the war years.

On May 8, 1945, the war in Europe ended. It was not until August 14 that the Japanese government surrendered and World War II was finally over. An

In the 1940s, Broadway was a bustling business district.

interdenominational service of thanksgiving was held at the First Christian Church. More than 18,000 men and women from Fresno County had served in the armed forces during the war. Some 550 did not come home, but paid the ultimate sacrifice for their country.

The city election of April 1945 pitted incumbent Republican Mayor Leymel against State Senator Hugh Burns, a Democrat. *The Fresno Bee,* which had always supported Leymel, turned its support to Burns. In spite of that Leymel captured 60 percent of the vote and was re-elected.

Leymel began his term by outlining a list of civic improvements that needed to be made. Included were expansion of the Chandler Field airport, a new sewage disposal plant, widening and rebuilding streets, completing the civic center, new public swimming pools, improvements to Roeding Park, and new firehouses and playgrounds. Before Leymel could complete his goals, he died following surgery for cancer in 1947. A funeral service with full military honors was held at the Fresno Memorial Auditorium. A huge crowd came to honor the man who had given so many years of his life to the betterment of Fresno. It was the largest public memorial since the funeral of Dr. Chester Rowell in 1912.

Just before Leymel's death, the citizens of Fresno voted to approve bond measures, which totaled $7,525,000, for new schools, sewers and work on the civic center. Glenn M. DeVore, who had three weeks earlier completed his term as a legislative commissioner, was appointed to finish out Leymel's term of office. DeVore, an ally of Leymel, began to try to complete the program outlined by him.

The skyline of Fresno at mid-century

A highlight of DeVore's administration was the city's acquisition of the old Hammer Field bomber base. Chandler Field was determined to be too small for the new aircraft that was being developed. The new Fresno Air Terminal, at the Hammer Field site, saw the first commercial flights take off on October 1, 1947.

Two problems, however, plagued DeVore's two years in office. One was housing, the other was crime. Thousands of veterans and their families, and seasonal agricultural laborers flooded the community needing shelter. This, combined with shortages of building materials, created a problem. The state and federal governments required veterans and facilities for the health and safety of the community to be given priority. Other building plans had to be shelved for the time being. At the same time, crime in West Fresno and downtown was worse than ever. The mayor was blamed for the situation.

The election of 1949 brought a new face to Fresno politics. Gordon G. Dunn, a former Stanford University track star, ran with a promise to clean up the vice and corruption in the wide-open town — and, in particular, the graft-ridden police department. Dunn beat DeVore and another candidate, Lewis C. Marley. A new era was about to begin.

In 1945 the Burnett Sanitarium was purchased by a nonprofit corporation and became Fresno Community Hospital. The Fresno Arts Center was incorporated on March 15, 1949. In 1949 the Fresno Zoological Society was incorporated and began to build the Roeding Park Zoo. A group of volunteers began to raise money to buy a baby elephant for the zoo. The school children of the Central Valley took up the cause and began to hold backyard carnivals, set up lemonade stands and found all sorts of imaginative ways to raise money. They brought their nickels, dimes and quarters to school where they were placed in special collection boxes. When the goal of $3,750 was reached, the baby elephant was purchased. A contest was held to choose the elephant's name. Roselene Swensen of Orosi, who submitted the name "Nosey," won. Nosey's arrival in Fresno was a tremendous day for the community. She appeared in the September 12, 1949, Fresno Police 49 Days Rodeo Parade. The streets were lined with delighted school children and their parents. Nosey became a dearly loved member of the Fresno community. On her last birthday, July 17, 1993, 3,926 people came to her public birthday party. She died on November 14 of that same year. It was a day of mourning for the Central Valley.

In 1950 Fresno's population had soared to 91,669. The city now stretched to cover 9.99 square miles.

Cleanup and Growth

True to his word, Mayor Gordon G. Dunn began his term in office doing exactly what he said he would — he demanded the resignations of Police Chief Raymond T. Wallace and Fire Chief L.A. Moore. The charge was that they had seriously mismanaged their departments. A few days later he appointed new men to the posts: I.M. Baylis as police chief and Gayle V. Coger as fire chief. Dunn then asked the state attorney general's office to investigate the corruption that he alleged permeated both departments. This drew the attention of Washington columnist Drew Pearson. His column soon exposed that the Fresno police chief had been accepting payoffs. The Internal Revenue Service found that information fascinating and began its own investigation. Ultimately, former Police Chief Wallace was convicted of income tax evasion, fined $10,000 and sentenced to two years in prison. However, it was never proven that he had been involved in graft.

Next on Dunn's list were the brothels and bars. Columnist Pearson was more than a little interested in this turn of events — so much so that he ran a list of Fresno's bawdy houses in his column. *The Fresno Bee* picked up the story listing all the establishments plus their addresses. Most were on Broadway and Tulare, but a few were located on H Street or in West Fresno. The mayor ordered raids on these businesses effectively shutting them down. He ordered the police to conduct regular inspections to make sure the businesses operating at these locations were respectable. In an article in the January 16, 1950, issue of *The Fresno Bee,* the West Fresno Chamber of Commerce commended Dunn for "making an earnest effort to give to Fresno a civic government of the highest type, free of all political influence. While this may not be the opinion of certain elements, it is the consensus of decent, law abiding people." Not everyone was so sure. The police department did not have enough manpower and resources to get rid of all the vice. In actuality, some of the businesses later reopened after things cooled down; others moved their operations to other parts of the city. As a result of this effort to clean up Fresno, the mayor was given the nickname, "No Fun Dunn."

One problem the mayor still faced was finances. The city budget was stretched thin by rapid growth, which, in turn, demanded more city services and improvements. This led to an increase in the city property tax rate — not a popular move. The city commission also added tax to hotel rooms and tobacco. The issue of providing public housing for the poor came to the fore once again with no action being taken.

In the campaign of 1953 Dunn ran on his record of reform against antireform forces made up of real estate and vice interests. These groups mounted a well-financed radio and newspaper advertising campaign that took their message into all the homes of Fresno. In spite of that, Dunn won the election by a margin of 2 to 1. The voters did reject a bond proposal that would have provided money for a new jail, police headquarters and an emergency hospital. One of the items on the ballot was a new city charter that would end the commission form of government and replace it with a strong mayor. A board of freeholders was also elected. It was charged with planning the new form of government. A year later in a special election, the voters rejected the plan the freeholders drew up, but they did approve enlarging, by two, the membership of the city commission.

The city at mid-decade entered a period of tremendous growth. Fresno's downtown, which had always been a vital center of retail business, banking and culture, was threatened by a new enemy — development. The site of the Melcon Markarian ranch, where figs and raisins had been cultivated, was now being turned into Fresno's first large shopping mall named Manchester Center. Several downtown businesses, including Sears, Roebuck and Company, left downtown for the new mall. It was a portent of things to come. The members of the city commission rolled up their sleeves and began to consider how to fight to save downtown.

They formed a Redevelopment Agency that would designate blighted areas that would be eligible for redevelopment and rehabilitation. Federal urban renewal funds were available as part of a federal postwar redevelopment program for cities. What it amounted to was using government power of imminent domain to sweep away slums and encourage private developers to move into the area and rebuild. A Downtown Association was formed to work with the city's planning department to save downtown. Victor Gruen Associates of Beverly Hills, an architectural firm, was hired to devise a plan for downtown. It conceived an idea for an open-air mall on Fulton Street that would be comprised of an 85 acre superblock with plazas, trees, fountains, art work — a pedestrian's dream.

In 1955 the city limits of Fresno and the city limits of Clovis met for the first time. In 1956 another shopping center opened at Palm and Shaw avenues — Fig Garden Village.

Mayor Dunn had been making efforts to strengthen his support on the commission. In 1954 Legislative Commissioner Chester H. Cary died. Ted C. Wills, a man with strong union connections, was appointed to fill out his term. In the city election of 1955, three new commissioners were elected. J.D. Stephens, a close friend of Dunn's and a grandson of L.O. Stephens, was elected. J.O. Thorpe, another friend of Dunn's and the vice chairman of the planning board, and Hattie May Hammat, a retired school principal, also won commission posts. Hammat was the first female to be elected to city office in Fresno. All three of the new commissioners were progressive and supportive of Dunn's programs. Ted C. Wills won his first election, thus retaining his position on the commission.

The commission began to discuss a new city charter. Fresno was the only city in California still operating under the commission system. Rather than have elected freeholders work out the system of government in the traditional way, it employed attorneys Harold V. Thompson and Chalmers E. Lones to work out the details. The completed plan was approved by the commission and presented to the voters in the election of April 1957. It provided for a six-member council and ceremonial presiding mayor with a full-time city administrator who would be appointed by the council. The voters approved the new charter, which would go into effect in 1958; but they did not favor Mayor Dunn so kindly. He was replaced by C. Cal Evans, a realtor.

Mayor Evans began his term by trying to fire Police Chief Henry R. Morton and Fire Chief Gayle V. Coger, both of whom were appointed by Gordon Dunn. Protected by civil service, they both refused to resign. The situation with Morton turned into a major confrontation, but Morton had many friends in the community and Evans was forced to back down. He charged Morton with the duty of cracking down on all the vice operations, including gambling and prostitution. Morton said he was doing the best he could given the resources he had. He later accused the mayor of interfering with the way he operated the police force. The battle between the two men ended only with the defeat of Evans in the city elections in April 1958.

A number of significant events occurred in the sporting world during the 1950s. Three World Amateur Softball Association championships were won by the Fresno Rockets softball team in 1953, 1954 and 1957. Champion auto racer Billy Vukovich won the Indianapolis 500 in 1953 and 1954. He was leading in the 1955 Indianapolis 500 race when he was tragically killed.

In 1949 five women, Patty Randall, Carolyn Peck, Gail Goodwin, Agnes Crockett and Helen Maupin Ross, decided they wanted to establish a hospital in Fresno just for children. Their dream was realized when Valley Children's Hospital and Guidance Clinic opened its doors on October 26, 1952. Almost 50 years later the hospital moved to its new facility on the Madera County bluffs overlooking the San Joaquin River.

In 1953 television arrived in Fresno. Station KMJ carried programs from all three major networks. Several months later ABC affiliate KJEO began broadcasting and in 1956 CBS affiliate KFRE went on the air. KMJ retained all the NBC programming.

On July 10, 1953, downtown Fresno was hit by a series of arson fires. The venerable Hughes Hotel was the first to be torched so thoroughly that it had to be torn down. Other downtown hotels, the Californian, the Adams, the Mission, the Gold and the Roslyn were all set on fire. Gottschalk's Department Store, JCPenney, the First Christian Church and the Brix Apartments also became targets of the arsonist. All these fires occurred within the space of four hours. First aid stations and food lines were set up in Courthouse Park for the weary firefighters. As they heard the news, people poured out of theaters and stores because they were afraid to be inside any building in case it, too, would begin to burn. It was a terrifying afternoon in the history of downtown Fresno. The arsonist was never caught.

In 1954 the Fresno Rotary clubs donated $76,000 to build Playland in Roeding Park. In 1958 Fresno was named one of the 10 best cities in the nation by a Columbia University survey. Also in 1958 the Fresno County Free Library moved into a new building on Mariposa Street and the Fresno State College campus moved north to Cedar and Shaw avenues.

Looking south on the newly completed Fulton Mall in 1965

The election of 1958 brought a new face to city hall. Investment broker Arthur L. Selland easily defeated his opponents to become the first mayor under the council-administrator charter. The new six-member city council comprised five of the incumbent commissioners and a newcomer, Wallace D. Henderson. Robert N. Klein was hired as the city's first chief administrative officer (CAO). The major task of Selland's first term was to work on plans for revitalizing downtown Fresno. The year 1960 saw the addition of two new buildings to the Civic Center — the state and federal buildings. Selland was easily elected to a second term in 1961.

As the city entered the 1960s, the population of 133,929 people lived within 28.64 square miles.

Demolition and the All-American City

Mayor Arthur Selland's second term began with attempts to get voters to approve a bond issue to finance the purchase of land and the building of a convention center. The voters turned it down. The promoters of the convention center solved the problem by coming up with a financial plan that would allow them to go ahead with the project without asking for voter approval. The City Council voted to join with the county under the state Joint Exercise of Powers Act in the creation of a City and County Convention Center Authority. The authority had the power to issue $8.5 million in revenue bonds to finance the project.

It was now 1963. The Gruen Plan for the Fulton Mall had been accepted and was ready to get under way. The convention center project also began. CAO Robert Klein resigned his post to go into private business. Henry Kennedy Hunter, the city manager of Riverside, was appointed Fresno's new CAO.

On the night of December 5, 1963, Mayor Selland and Herbert N. Ferguson, president of the Fresno County and City Chamber of Commerce, were killed in an automobile collision south of Fresno. The city went into mourning. Once again, a huge public memorial service was held at the Fresno Memorial Auditorium. With Selland's death, Councilman Wallace

D. Henderson, a strong supporter of Selland's projects, became mayor of Fresno.

In March 1964 work crews began tearing up Fulton Street. The building of the mall was underway. Other things were happening, too. Buildings that had graced the streets of the city since the 19th century were considered blighted or did not meet earthquake standards and were torn down. Ultimately, the face of downtown Fresno changed. What remained of the Victorian city quickly disappeared. In its place was a downtown mall with sculptures, fountains and trees that was designed for pedestrians. It was supposed to be the salvation of downtown Fresno. Soon after it was completed in September 1964, it was felt that it had stabilized downtown's businesses. About the time the mall project began, the 22-story Del Webb Towne House was built, changing the skyline of Fresno. It was now the tallest building in the city.

There was another issue in 1964 that made startling headlines. Chief Administrative Officer Hunter fired Police Chief Henry Morton for insubordination. Morton was a popular and politically well-connected police chief who was not about to leave his position. He appealed to the civil service board, which reinstated him. The council was split over the issue — should it agree with the board or with its city manager? After much heated debate, it voted to reinstate Chief Morton.

The city elections of 1965 brought a newcomer into the mayor's office — attorney Floyd H. Hyde. Two members of the city council who had supported Hunter were defeated in the election. Leland Scott and Robert B. Moore's council seats would now be held by Elvin C. Bell and Pat J. Camaroda. The power struggle, however, was still waging at city hall. Hunter refused to cooperate with the Morton supporters who felt Hunter had overstepped his authority by firing the police chief. Hunter, in turn, felt it was part of his job to maintain control over the city's various departments. Finally, the council met in executive session. It reappeared in the council chambers and voted unanimously to fire Hunter. Chief Morton, who many felt was the most politically powerful man in Fresno, was secure in the knowledge that he had won the fight.

Meanwhile, another storm had been brewing. In spring 1962 the members of the Board of Supervisors began to consider tearing down the Fresno County Courthouse that had stood at the center of the governmental and social life of the community since 1874. Some of the board members wanted to build a new structure rather than rehabilitate the old building. Many Fresnans were aghast. The board of directors of the Fresno City and County Historical Society issued a resolution stating that "No more beautiful, stately and historic building exists in the county. It represents

The historic Fresno County Courthouse embodied the heart of the Fresno community. Its demise in 1966 dealt downtown Fresno a stunning blow from which it has yet to recover.

the very heart and personality of Fresno and represents a tie with Fresno pioneer days. It is more significant and cherished than any museum or gallery could be." Other organizations and businesses, including *The Fresno Bee*, the San Joaquin Chapter of the American Institute of Architects and The Fresno County Bar Association, joined in the fight to save the historic building. On July 24, 1963, it was announced that Fresno County would receive $1,949,300 in federal grant monies for a new courthouse building provided the work would begin within 120 days. A citizens' group led by Edward Vagim was formed to fight the proposed demolition of the historic building. It gathered signatures on petitions in order to place the issue before the voters. The Fifth District Court of Appeals ruled that the supervisors had the right to make the decision. No election would be held. The site work on the new courthouse began. The new building began to take shape on land right in front of the historic structure. The contrast between the two buildings was startling. On February 12, 1966, furniture and items were moved from the old building to the new. On March 7 an auction of items from the Courthouse was held — 2,000 items were sold to people who wanted to own a piece of history. Then, on March 15 the cupola was taken down from the top of the dome. The statues of the two Goddesses of Justice and the statue of Liberty were removed from the roof top. On March 23 demolition began. First the two wings of the building were torn down and on April 7 the dome was scheduled to be toppled. The old building, however, did not go down without a fight. Even though it was considered too fragile to withstand an earthquake, the building put up a fight worthy of a champion. It took nine hours to bring down the dome and, with its toppling, the very heart of the city, indeed of the county, was torn apart — lying amid the ruins of the grand old building that, at its dedication, was prophesied to last for 1,000 years. The venerable building was gone. Out of its destruction something else was born. Fresnans opened their eyes and looked around and began to see for the first time that they were losing their city's architectural heritage. It was then that the first stirrings of a preservation movement were felt. It would not take full root until the 1970s, but it had begun, if only in the minds and hearts of those who watched on that April day when the dome of the Courthouse came crashing down.

Another blow to the architectural heritage of Fresno came in the early 1960s when the completion of the new Highway 99 resulted in the demolition of a major portion of historic West Fresno. Designated as a blighted area, building after building came down and neighborhoods were emotionally torn apart as the new freeway cut a swath across West Fresno. The result was to separate the area even more from the rest of the city. Some buildings remained, but much of the flavor of historic Chinatown was lost forever. The city learned one lesson — tearing out blighted areas did not solve social problems. New slums quickly replaced old ones.

The mid-1960s saw the first real test of the council's ability to hold to planning decisions. The council had stood behind the city's general plan and college community plan. They had been adopted in 1958 and 1961 and updated in the mid-1960s. The general plan called for controlled growth and encouraged developers to build downtown; the college community plan was aimed at keeping the area around Fresno State College residential and neighborhood/commercial. Regional shopping centers were only going to be allowed on Blackstone Avenue. In November 1965 Gordon L. MacDonald Investments Ltd. of Santa Barbara purchased 58 acres of land on Shaw Avenue between Fresno and First streets. It told the city it wanted to build a regional shopping center on the land provided the city would change the zoning. Although there was an outcry from the public and the planning department recommended that the council adhere to the plan in place, the Planning Commission voted to recommend the zoning change. The City Council, however, voted to adhere to the plan and not grant the change. Throughout 1966 there was a great deal of pressure on the council to reconsider. A failed attempt by another developer to put in a shopping center on Blackstone, made a majority of the council members, including Mayor Hyde, feel that they better let MacDonald build his shopping center on Shaw Avenue. On December 2, 1966, the council voted to approve the rezoning and the shopping center. In return, the developer agreed to bring new commercial development projects to downtown. Only Councilmen Ted C. Wills and Elvin Bell voted no. In 1970 the center, called Fashion Fair, opened. Not only did Fashion Fair have a negative impact on the downtown retail businesses, but it also changed the character of Shaw Avenue. A footnote to this story is that the developer did not keep his promise to the council about promoting downtown commercial development.

The mid-1960s saw the development of another city park. Ralph W. Woodward, son of O.J. Woodward, left a large part of his $1.6 million estate to the city of Fresno for a public park and bird sanctuary. Woodward Park opened to the public on November 5, 1970.

On March 21, 1968, Fresno was named an "All-American City" by the National Municipal League and *Look* magazine, the sponsors of the contest. Fresno won because of the involvement of its citizens working together to solve the problems of urban life, especially Fresno's preventive programs for youth problems. Other community accomplishments during the 1960s were the opening of Storyland in Roeding Park and the development of 235-acre Woodward Park. In 1965 the $10 million convention center complex was completed. The main arena was named for Mayor Selland.

During this turbulent decade the Fresno community, like the rest of the country, focused on such issues as civil rights, poverty and the Vietnam War. In 1964 Dr. Martin Luther King Jr. led a civil rights rally at Ratcliff Stadium.

A building under construction was a typical sight on the Fresno landscape as development moved north.

The end of the decade saw two changes in governmental life. Mayor Hyde resigned in January 1969 to accept the post of an assistant secretary of Housing and Urban Development in the Nixon administration. Councilman Ted C. Wills, the mayor pro-tempore, was appointed to fill out his term. Elma Sterling was appointed to fill out Wills' council term. Sterling, an African American, became the first minority to serve on the council. Neil Goedhard accepted the job of city manager, replacing John Taylor who resigned to accept a position in Kansas City, Missouri. In the city election of April 1969, Wills won a four-year term as mayor. Ted C. Wills was a strong union man. He had been a business agent and was the secretary-treasurer of the local Creamery Workers Union. His involvement with the union began in 1937. He had a reputation as a skilled negotiator. By now he was a real veteran of City Hall having served on the commission and council since 1954.

The city approached 1970 with a population of 165,655 living within the 41.8-square-mile area that comprised the city limits. The population of the metropolitan area was estimated at 413,000 people.

Northward Growth and Preservation Efforts

The sudden death in 1970 of 44-year-old City Manager Neil Goedhard was a shock to Fresnans. His assistant, John M. Simmons, was appointed to serve until a replacement could be found. In March 1971 Bruce J. Reiss, a deputy chief administrative officer for the city of Fresno, was hired as the new city manager. The council members' votes were split over the hiring, but the majority prevailed. They felt that one of Reiss' strengths was, as a native of Fresno, that he had a knowledge and understanding of local problems.

By 1970 Fresno was definitely a city on the move. The city was moving north toward the San Joaquin River at an amazing speed. An abundance of inexpensive, flat land that could be easily developed proved irresistible to promoters. The new subdivisions and shopping centers were causing the city to have to allocate more resources to these new areas at the expense of the inner city. Downtown was barely alive — kept that way only by federal money and redevelopment projects. Businesses were leaving the downtown mall and finding new life in the shopping centers of north Fresno.

The election of 1971 saw Al Villa, an attorney of Hispanic descent, become the first minority member to be elected to the City Council. The election also returned Melvin Bell to the council, and Paul G. Wasemiller, who had served on the council for 10 years, was re-elected to his post. Both received strong support from real estate developers.

Also in 1971 the federal government announced that Fresno was one of 20 "Planned Variation" cities chosen to receive monies for federally financed projects. The initial $5 million Fresno received was to be spent in neighborhoods outside West Fresno. The program required that elected neighborhood councils be set up. A newly formed Community Development Commission reviewed recommendations sent to it by the neighborhood councils and then sent a list of priorities to the City Council. Unfortunately, problems developed among the neighborhood groups — everyone felt their needs should be met first. Mayor Wills had to step in and mediate. Eventually, the councils were able to work together and the majority of the Planned Variation programs were completed.

The late 1970s and early 1980s would see Model Cities money used in West Fresno to build schools, housing projects, industrial and business developments and parks.

In early spring 1973 the planning commission and the City Council approved the site plan for a new St. Agnes Hospital that would be located on Herndon Avenue. These blessings were given in spite of efforts by the Citizens Against Urban Sprawl Environments and the Millbrook Committee for Better Planning.

The April 1973 election saw Mayor Ted C. Wills re-elected again. A reform group that urged more responsible planning and citizen participation in government, called the Committee for Responsible Government (CRG), supported three of the candidates who won seats on the council. Marc Stefano, who won re-election; Dale Doig, a high school government teacher; and Linda Mack, president of CRG. On election night Stefano announced that those elected would join with Councilman Villa to create a voting block on the council to stop leap-frog development and urban sprawl.

A few months after the election City Manager Bruce Reiss resigned. He was soon replaced by Ralph W. Hanley, deputy city manager for San Jose.

The early 1970s saw major campaigns to annex county islands — areas that were within the city boundaries. Mayor Wills urged residents of these county pockets to vote themselves into the city. Efforts were made to annex industrial fringe areas. Arguments were made that city services were enjoyed by people in these areas with the Fresno taxpayers footing the bill.

The election of April 1975 brought into office the youngest person ever to serve on the City Council. At age 26, Daniel Keenan Whitehurst, a lawyer and the son of a prominent funeral director, easily won the seat vacated by Paul Wasemiller, who had decided to retire. Whitehurst's easy charm and obvious intelligence seemed to energize the council — he certainly managed to captivate the community. He soon became a major voice on the council. Two years later, in March 1977, Whitehurst won the race for mayor defeating

The historic Grandlefider home in downtown Fresno was restored in the 1970s and continues to be a family residence.
Photo by Schyler Rehart

The convention business is an important part of Fresno's economy. The Fresno Convention Center complex includes the Saroyan Theater, Selland Arena, Exhibit Hall, Ballroom and Schoettler Conference Center. *Photo by Stephen L. Brown*

Ted C. Wills by 114 votes. Not only did voters elect Whitehurst, the youngest mayor in Fresno's history, but they also voted into office Joe Williams, the first African American elected to serve on Fresno's City Council. Linda Mack and Dale Doig won second terms. Shortly after the election, Councilman Al Villa was appointed a Fresno Municipal Court judge. His resignation from the council was followed by a special election in June. Joel Crosby, a Presbyterian minister who had been a candidate in the March election, won Villa's seat on the council. Also on the ballot was a charter amendment. Under this amendment the city would be divided into six geographical districts. Each district would have a representative to the council who lived in that district, but each would be voted on by the city at large. The mayor could live anywhere in the city and would be voted on by all the people. The amendment won. It was up to the council to decide on the new district boundaries, keeping in mind that they each had to have an equal population.

In November 1977 another special election was held to fill the seat left vacant when Whitehurst won the mayor's post. Ted C. Wills ran for that council seat and won, thereby setting up a confrontation in the next election with Crosby who lived in the same district. With Wills, who had years of experience in city government and was still on the council, and a young mayor who had a different governing style at the helm, the stage was set for confrontations. Whitehurst was cautious, urging the council to discuss matters thoroughly before making decisions — keeping long-range goals firmly in mind. Wills called Whitehurst indecisive and inexperienced. Wills also believed the council should govern the city, not the city manager.

Two months earlier, in September, City Manager Ralph Hanley fired Police Chief Harold E. Britton for refusing to support the city manager's plan for the police department's reorganization. Hanley said he had submitted the plan in an effort to combat rising crime in Fresno. Wills was angry, saying the city manager had overstepped his authority. Whitehurst and the majority of the council called it an act of courage. The civil service board reviewed the case and voted to reinstate Britton. The council majority fired the board and appointed a new one. According to the mayor, the old board had been biased. He said that the new board was selected with great care to ensure that the members were "independent and fair-minded." In spite of a failed recall attempt against the mayor and his council supporters, the council held tight. The new civil service board voted to uphold the firing of the police chief. In spite of this, a few months later the council voted to fire Hanley. The only opposing votes were Whitehurst's and Mack's. Assistant City Manager James E. Aldredge was appointed to fill in until a new city manager could be appointed.

On July 8, 1978, Gerald Newfarmer, city manager of Oakland, was chosen as Fresno's new city manager. As events would show, he turned out to be an even-handed negotiator who administered the city well. His first order of business was to find someone who could head the police department. On January 15, 1979, George K. Hansen was hired as chief of police. He served until April 6, 1983, when he died of a heart attack. His term in office was a crucial one and he is remembered as one of the most respected police chiefs in Fresno history.

The 1970s were marked by efforts to control urban sprawl. In 1976 the council adopted the Urban Growth Management (UGM) program that was touted as a program that would point the way to orderly growth. UGM called for developers to pay for bringing city services to their land. It was hoped this would encourage developers to build within the city rather than leapfrogging out into farmlands. This became a major political "hot potato" during the city elections of 1979. In this election, Ted Wills beat out Crosby for the District 1 seat. Joe Reich Jr. and Leonel Alvarado won the District 3 and 5 seats respectively.

Other issues and events made the headlines during the 1970s. An energy crisis brought high gasoline prices and utility rates. Fresno schools were desegregated with mandatory busing. Construction began on State Highway 41 that would eventually add impetus to the city's northward growth. The middle of the decade witnessed the first migration of Hmong and Vietnamese immigrants to Fresno.

One happy event was the celebration of the country's bicentennial in 1976. Many cities throughout the country had special projects during that year. Fresno's was the restoration of the historic Meux Home. It was a project that brought out the best in the community. Local businesses contributed labor and materials and citizens donated antique furniture, china, linens and money toward the preservation of this local treasure. When the restoration was complete, the Meux Home was listed in the National Register of Historic Places and opened to the public as a museum. Another project that received recognition by the Fresno Regional Bicentennial Commission was undertaken by the Historic Homes Committee of the Fresno Branch of the American Association of University Women. The committee, chaired by Valerie Comegys, published a book entitled, *Heritage Fresno Homes and People*. The book contained photos, descriptions and historical information about 93 homes in Fresno and seven nearby communities. The book was so popular it went into a second printing.

Meanwhile, the germ of an idea was making itself known at City Hall. During discussions of the general plan for the city, it was decided that a historic preservation element should be included in the general plan. In 1975 a Historic Preservation Committee was formed with Rosellen Kershaw as chair. The commission was charged with the duty of writing the preservation plans. Out of this would come the creation of a Historic Preservation Commission for the city of Fresno. The committee worked for two years. In 1977 it had fulfilled its duties and the committee disbanded. The Historic Preservation Commission for the city of Fresno was now in place. The first meeting of the new commission was in September 1977. Its mandated responsibilities were outlined in a memo sent by Al Solis, the secretary to the commission, to Assistant City Manager Sam McMurry. They were as follows: to "recommend designation of historic sites and districts; serve as the review board for regulated permits and demolition permits; and develop a historic districts and structures plan to be used in implementing the regulatory aspects of the ordinance." The Historic Preservation Ordinance for the City of Fresno, as it would be known, was still being drafted. It was approved by the commission on March 2, 1979, and received the approval of the City Council on April 24, 1979. In 1977 architect William E. Patnaude had been hired as a consultant by the city to survey 200 buildings that were in the older parts of the city, were at least 50 years old and were the best examples of different styles of architecture. The survey was complete in 1978. The ordinance had been approved along with its review criteria for determining whether or not a building was qualified for placement on a historic list. Now the mechanism was in place to begin the commission's mandated purpose. The Historic Preservation

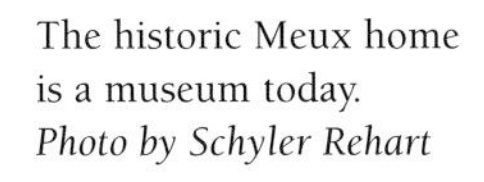

The historic Meux home is a museum today.
Photo by Schyler Rehart

Commission, meeting monthly, began the process of reviewing, one by one, the structures on the survey. When a building was deemed to meet one or more of the following conditions, as stated in Section 13-407 of the ordinance: historical and cultural significance; historic, architectural and engineering significance; and neighborhood and geographic setting, it was approved and sent to the City Council. If the council approved, the building was placed on the city's Local Official Register of Historic Resources. By the time the commission completed the process, over 140 buildings had been placed on the list. Once on the list, these structures could not be demolished without notice to the commission. Then, according to the terms of the ordinance, a 180-day waiting period went into effect during which time the commission and the city could work with the owner to try to find alternatives to demolition. The commission had other duties beyond those outlined in the ordinance. It also advised on the allocation of Community Development Block Grant funds. Al Solis, the present director of the Development Department for the city of Fresno, had been one of those who watched the dome of the historic Courthouse topple. He asked to serve as the staff's secretary to the commission — a post he held through most of this period. In 1981 the city budget did not include funding for the commission's staff. The commission's duties were transferred to the planning commission. A beginning had been made. The historic preservation story would not end here.

In 1980 Fresno's population had reached 218,202. The city now encompassed 68 square miles.

The interchange linking state highways 41, 168 and 180 is one more sign of Fresno's growth. Ultimately, these roads will provide easier and faster access to the mountain communities and national parks of Fresno, Madera, Mariposa and Tulare counties. *Photo by Stephen L. Brown*

The City Turns 100

The beginning of the 1980s brought another turning point for downtown. Since 1978 the council had been trying to convince Macy's department store to build in downtown instead of near Fashion Fair as it requested. In 1980 the council, under intense pressure from the community, gave in and approved a rezoning request that allowed Macy's to build just west of Fashion Fair. Some 65 other new stores were added and made part of an air-conditioned mall linking Macy's to the rest of Fashion Fair. Manchester Center underwent major expansion, too. Many businesses left downtown and relocated to north Fresno. Downtown was fast becoming strictly a government and financial center.

In the city election of 1981 voters returned Dan Whitehurst to office. Joe Williams and Dale Doig were also re-elected along with a newcomer Karen Humphrey, a local television reporter and anchorwoman.

During the next few years a number of buildings were constructed downtown. Another important project was the expansion of Selland Arena. Plans were also underway for a new Holiday Inn that would be located just west of the convention center. Whitehurst continued his efforts to contain urban sprawl and to annex new areas into the city.

The election of 1983 saw the re-election of Ted C. Wills and two newcomers — both political activists. Les Kimber and Chris Peterson would bring new perspectives to the City Council. In May of that same year City Manager Gerald Newfarmer resigned to become city manager of San Jose. He was replaced by Robert M. Christofferson in November.

On January 26, 1985, just a few weeks before the city election, Mayor Whitehurst resigned to accept a four-month fellowship at the John F. Kennedy School of Government at Harvard University. Whitehurst, in his final State of the City address, listed among his accomplishments that, as a result of his annexation program, 34,000 new residents were brought into the city. However, he felt his most important contribution was to bring a feeling of integrity to the office of mayor. Mayor Pro Tempore Dale Doig was appointed to serve as mayor until the March 1985 election, when he was elected in his own right to serve the people of

Fresno in that office. Karen Humphrey was re-elected to her council post and two new faces were elected to council positions — Rod Anaforian and Thomas A. MacMichael.

The first year of Dale Doig's term as mayor was marked by one of the great events in the history of Fresno — the celebration of 100 years of history. Fresno's birthday was October 27, 1985. Beginning in July, the city began to celebrate. The centennial events included walking tours of downtown with historical figures, a centennial pageant, publication of a centennial book, coronation of the centennial queen and king, a Fresno trivia contest, a dinner honoring businesses 85 years or older, the Fabulous Fresnans dinner, a centennial parade, band concerts, sporting events, photo exhibits, theatrical presentations, the Founder's Day dinner, religious ceremonies, a centennial festival and a dinner honoring the pioneer families. Linda Mack was chair and Kristine Procter was vice chair of the Centennial Coordinating Committee.

In 1986 another kind of event took place in the heart of the city. Camera crews and movie stars set up shop near the Water Tower for three days of filming a made-for-television miniseries. Entitled *Fresno,* with the captivating subtitle, *the Power, the Passion, the Produce,* the movie was planned as a spoof on the popular prime-time soap operas "Dallas" and "Dynasty." The story line focused on two feuding raisin families, the Canes and the Kensingtons, who were fighting for control of the raisin cartel. On the hot summer morning of July 15, Carol Burnett, who was playing Charlotte Kensington, stepped from her trailer and, at the request of onlookers, let forth her fabled ape call. Shooting that day centered around the Water Tower. Charles Grodin, playing Cane Kensington, was chased around the second story of that structure with two thugs and his brother in hot pursuit. Other sites used in the film were the Quist Dairy and Kearney Boulevard. When the miniseries premiered in November, parties were held all over the city. On the final night of the series, Fresnans saw their mayor, Dale Doig, in the film. In his role as the mayor of Fresno, he was holding court at a Raisin Ball dressed as the King of Siam. During that week, the country's eyes focused on Fresno. They found out that Fresnans were good sports and had a great sense of fun.

On July 23, 1986, the City Council voted 6-1 to accept the resignation of City Manager Robert M. Christofferson. In a closed-door meeting the day before, the council had requested Christofferson's resignation. Only three years before, in a rare moment of City Council solidarity, his hiring had been unanimously approved. Privately members of the council cited problems with his handling of economic development projects, but the last straw seemed to be Christofferson's refusal to blame members of city staff for the fact that a new downtown parking garage had to be closed because of serious defects. Once again, Assistant City Manager James E. Aldredge stepped in to serve as acting city manager until the council appointed someone to fill the position. On December 23, after reviewing a list of potential candidates for the city manager job, the council appointed James E. Aldredge to the position. Aldredge, who had worked 27 years for the city, was a graduate of Fresno State College and held a doctorate in public administration. He possessed an excellent background in urban geography and regional planning.

Mayor Doig's first two years in office were marred by a grand jury investigation stemming from his association with a convicted cocaine dealer. His preoccupation

The Galleria in downtown Fresno is the centerpiece of Civic Center Square. An example of adaptive reuse, the building that was once Fresno's first postal substation now houses shops and restaurants.
Photo by Stephen L. Brown

with this matter derailed his intended plans for the city. As outlined in his campaign material, plans included affordable housing, safe neighborhoods, clean air and water, good transportation and top-notch schools. In a *Fresno Bee* article by reporter Royal Calkins, dated December 21, 1986, "his colleagues and others in Fresno politics generally agree he is a mayor without a mission and that he has forfeited much of his power in City Hall." However, Councilman Chris Peterson felt he was learning the job and becoming "more of a team leader, pulling the council together." The city election of 1987 brought a major change on the council. Ted C. Wills, who had served the city for 33 years, lost his council post to Craig Scharton.

The later years of Doig's four-year term saw plans approved for a new, state-of-the-art City Hall. Arthur Erickson, the winner of the prestigious Gold Medal of the American Institute of Architects in 1986, was selected as the principal design architect for the new building. The local firm of Allen Y. Lew and William E. Patnaude Inc. was also selected for the project. Patnaude developed the working drawings and oversaw the project. Construction began in September 1989. The new City Hall was going to make a unique design statement. Its steel and glass facade with a large, sloping roof would be unlike any other building in Fresno.

On December 27, 1988, Dale Doig announced that he would not seek a second term in office and was returning to teaching. That left the field open for Councilwoman Karen Humphrey, attorney Anthony Capozzi and six others in the 1989 race for mayor.

The decade of the 1980s witnessed a number of important events. In 1981 William Saroyan, noted author and native son, died in Fresno. His writing conveyed the Armenian experience as lived in Fresno and shared it with the world. The well-known, cherished figure who bicycled through the streets of the city wearing his crushed-fedora hat was mourned by one and all.

The Fresno Brewery, listed in the National Register of Historic Places, dates to 1889. It is the second-oldest commercial building in Fresno. *Photo by Schyler Rehart*

The expansion of the Fresno Arts Center was completed in 1983. In 1984 the Fresno Metropolitan Museum of Art, History and Science opened. It was housed in the historic Fresno Bee Building that is listed in the National Register of Historic Places. Two exciting sports events took place during the decade. In 1983 the Bulldog basketball team of California State University, Fresno, won the National Invitational Tournament Championship in New York. The following year the Bulldog football team won the California Bowl.

State Highway 41 was completed to Bullard Avenue in 1982 and to Herndon Avenue in 1989. It was only one indicator of the growth of the city. Woodward Lake, a man-made lake, was the centerpiece of a large development north of Fresno that attracted not only residents who wanted to be part of the northward expansion of the city, but other new development projects in the area. Businesses were fleeing the Fulton Mall in greater numbers to find more attractive sites in north Fresno. Some of Fresno's oldest businesses — Gottschalk's, Warner Co., Hodge & Sons, Berkeley's and Walter Smith's — made the move during the decade. A few new commitments were made to downtown, however. The Galleria project showed an innovative use for a historic building by converting Fresno's first postal substation into a mall with restaurants and businesses. The Ringside Youth Center on Van Ness Avenue, a boxing club, also opened for business.

In 1984 the Preservation Committee of the Fresno City and County Historical Society was formed. In the absence of a city Preservation Commission, this committee became a grassroots activist group for historic preservation. One of the many contributions the committee made was to petition the city to reactivate the Historic Preservation Commission. The driving force behind this effort was Russ Fey, a professor of urban planning at California State University, Fresno, and a Preservation Committee member who served as

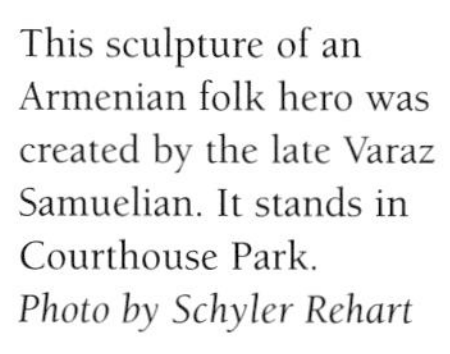

This sculpture of an Armenian folk hero was created by the late Varaz Samuelian. It stands in Courthouse Park.
Photo by Schyler Rehart

the first chairman of the newly formed commission when it was re-established in the late 1980s. The new commission continued the mandate outlined by the ordinance. To date, 228 buildings have been placed on the list of Historic Resources. The ordinance has been recently modified. The 180-day waiting period before demolition can take place has been removed. In its place is a new requirement — an Environmental Impact Report (EIR) is required by the California Environmental Quality Act (CEQA) before determination is made. This gives more strength to the ordinance. Another provision provides the mechanism for establishing historic districts.

In 1985 a group called Tree Fresno was formed. Its goals were to plant trees on busy streets and in neighborhoods and to initiate tree education programs. In the intervening years it has brought about a greening of Fresno and its efforts have greatly enhanced the environment and the beauty of the city.

In the mid-1980s a meeting was called by residents of the Tower District. The people who filled Roger Rocka's Music Hall on Wishon Avenue that Saturday morning wanted two things: a plan for their neighborhood and a course of action that would not be related to redevelopment. Councilman Craig Scharton, who represented this district, became a major force in developing a plan for the Tower District. The Historical Society's Preservation Committee also became involved. The city contracted with Wallace Roberts & Todd, Robert Bruce Anderson and TJKM to write the Tower District Specific Plan. It was adopted by the City Council on March 26, 1991. In December of that year the Tower District Design Review Committee, a volunteer group, was created. It continues to meet regularly and sees to it that the design standards set in place are maintained. According to Al Solis, the former director of the city's Development Department, the Tower District Specific Plan has been the "most low profile major change in the community." It has set a standard for future neighborhood plans.

In 1987 the City Council voted to support a proposed $5 million state bond issue that would be used to acquire land in San Joaquin River bottom between Friant Dam and State Highway 99.

According to an article in *The Fresno Bee* entitled, "Decade Delivers Growth, Grime to Valley," Fresno had one of the highest growth rates in California during the 1980s. This was due, in part, to migration from the Bay Area and Southern California, but also to the huge influx of Southeast Asian immigrants to the valley. Almost 40,000 refugees came to Fresno County, most of them Hmong from the mountains of Laos. The article also cited the growing environmental problems Fresno County faced in terms of water quality and clean air.

At the end of the 1980s, the population within Fresno's city limits stood at 317,000. The metropolitan area totaled 450,200 people.

Before the decade ended, however, history was made. In March 1989 a city election took place and the office of mayor of Fresno was won, for the first time in the city's history, by a female. Karen Humphrey, who 19 years before had opened another door for Fresno women by becoming Fresno's first female television newscaster, defeated seven other candidates to win an easy victory. Campaigning on a platform of revitalizing downtown, solving environmental problems, implementing responsible land-use planning, creating safe neighborhoods and creating jobs, Humphrey believed in involving people in the process of solving community problems.

Other election results that year showed Tom Bohigian winning a council seat for the first time. Tom MacMichael and Rod Anaforian were re-elected for another term.

New Beginnings as the Century Ends

On November 7, 1990, Michael Bierman became the new city manager. James Aldredge resigned in order to teach at California State University, Fresno.

In the city elections of 1991 Brian Setencich won a council seat, ousting Craig Scharton. Two council seats were not decided until the November run-off election. At that time Esther Padilla and Robert Smith won.

In 1991 the Little Hoover Commission was created by the City Council. The commission, consisting of nine private citizens (selected by an independent five-member group of community leaders to prevent political interference), was given the charge to study city government operations and return to the City Council within a year with recommendations for improvement. When the commissioners filed their report in March 1992, Commission Chairman James E. Shekoyan told the council that the nine committee members had spent 9,000 hours working on this project. He also said that 150 Fresnans serving on 14 task forces — each studying one of the 14 city departments — spent thousands of additional hours, along with individual commission members, interviewing city staff members and private experts. The final report of the commission offered 294 recommendations. One of the recommendations was to appoint a Charter Review Committee to study the structure of Fresno's city government at that time.

A number of accomplishments can be pointed to during Humphrey's administration. A plan for downtown was completed; the construction of a new 5th District Court of Appeals building and a new building for Pacific Gas & Electric Company — both at downtown sites; landscaping and painting projects enhanced the Fulton Mall; the construction of the new City Hall; the San Joaquin River Parkway became a reality; the Fresno Compact, a collaborative effort between education and business was formed; and the community-based policing program continued to be promoted and expanded. On February 17, 1992, the new City Hall was dedicated.

Her critics said that her consensus-building process took too much time — that more action and decision making was needed. According to an article in *The Fresno Bee* on April 22, 1990, Mayor Humphrey is quoted as responding: "I'm finding that the more effective kind of leadership is that which can bring people together because that is what produces lasting results."

In the city election of 1993, Fresno's first female mayor, Karen Humphrey, lost her re-election bid to Jim Patterson.

Also on the ballot was an amendment to the city charter. This amendment came from the Charter Review Committee that had been set up at the recommendation of the Little Hoover Commission. In approving the amendment, the citizens of Fresno brought about major changes in their city's government. According to the City Clerk for the City of Fresno Rebecca Klish, the new system worked in the following manner. The mayor was no longer a member of the City Council. The post would be considered the executive branch of city government. The mayor would have no vote, but veto power over the following: legislative acts, policy decisions, land-use decisions, issues involving taxes, any changes in the budget and any ballot measures proposed by the council. A majority of the council could override the mayor's veto. The mayor also would develop the city budget. The council would study, negotiate and vote on the budget. The mayor would have the power to use the line item veto, then the measure would go back to the council. Since budget issues would be at stake, five votes would be required to override the mayor's veto. The mayor would hire the city manager who would oversee all the other city employees. In addition, the mayor could only serve for two consecutive four-year terms.

The other part of the charter amendment pertained to the City Council. A seventh council district was created so there would be an odd number of council posts. The council members would be elected to four-year terms and limited to serving two consecutive terms. They would have to file their nomination papers 88 to 113 days before the March election. The day they would be first allowed to file would be the first day they could solicit or accept campaign contributions. They could continue to accept contributions until the end of the calendar year in which the election was held. Run-off elections would be held in November. One member of the council would be voted president of the council. The council would hire the city attorney, the city clerk and its own council assistants.

Jim Patterson was re-elected mayor in 1997, thus becoming the first strong mayor in the newly structured city government.

A Look Toward the Future

Looking back over the last 40 years of Fresno's history, one of the main issues has been the revitalization of downtown Fresno. Many plans have been achieved, many committees have been formed and still the question remains of how to revitalize downtown Fresno. Here, vision comes into play. It is important to consider how the historic core of the city is envisioned in this new century. Will downtown Fresno remain strictly a financial district and center for government or will it be a center for culture and the arts? Will good stores, restaurants and housing be in the future for this innermost part of the city? Something is stirring in downtown Fresno. The Civic Center Square complex has brought beauty and people downtown. The Crescent Building, the new additions to the convention center, the $100 million federal courthouse that will be built, a baseball stadium, a proposed development in old Armenian Town, the new Kearney Palms shopping center in West Fresno, a proposed large medical center complex — these projects and others point the way to a new life for downtown. The phrase, "If you build it, they will come" may sound trite, but people will come downtown if there is a reason to — if there is something for them to do. Projects such as these point the way to a renaissance for Fresno's central core.

Another bright spot for the inner city is the Center City Development Committee. They are studying how to develop 23 miles of the inner city by building homes and schools. The challenges are endless, but the rewards could be also — not just for Fresnans, but for all the residents of the Central Valley. And in June 2000, Fresno was once again named an all-American city.

As the century moves forward, it is tempting to look back to the beginnings of the city of Fresno. The first meeting of the Board of Trustees took place around a table in a real estate office. There was very little money in the city's coffers. The six paid city employees included three police officers. Out of this tiny village nucleus grew a large city. Now, at the beginning of the 21st century, the City Council meets in a large, modern City Hall. The city's operating budget is $617 million with its net budget at $589 million. The city employs between 3,000 and 3,500 people. The city has a population of 415,400. It is a complex operation serving a uniquely cosmopolitan collection of communities that add up to a city proud of its past, appreciative of its ethnically diverse makeup, cognizant of its agricultural base, and aware of its problems and willing to work to resolve them — a city facing a future bright with promise.

Fresno's 1990 steel-and-glass City Hall adds a futuristic component to the downtown skyline and, at night, shimmers with jewel-like brilliance.
William E. Patnaude, FAIA

PARTNERS IN FRESNO

Table of Contents

AGRIBUSINESS

MANUFACTURING & DISTRIBUTION

MARKETPLACE

PROFESSIONAL SERVICES

QUALITY OF LIFE

TECHNOLOGY

PATRONS

American Transfer Company, Inc.
BSK
Wild Water Adventures

George Salwasser and Family

Biola has always been home to George Salwasser. In 1905 George's grandparents immigrated to the small farming community from the Volga River basin in Russia. They were of German ancestry and settled on a farm only a mile or so from where George was born in 1950 to Walter and Lillian Salwasser. The fourth and last son, George grew up within a few miles of his home and business today. After graduating from Central High School, he worked for his dad and saved his money. At 19, he got his business license, bought a tractor and spray rig, and began commercial crop spraying. Unbeknownst to him at the time, George was taking the first of many steps toward realizing the American Dream.

The next major development occurred in 1971. George was having a cup of coffee with a local farmer he had known since his childhood. The farmer realized George's dedication to hard work and honest professionalism, even as a young adult, and offered to sell his farm to George.

Charlotte and George Salwasser

George continued commercial crop spraying while starting to harvest grapes on his newly acquired farm. As a result of his hard work and drive to succeed, the Salwasser farm grew in acreage. Realizing that diversification was critical to the success of his business, George not only grew Thompson seedless grapes, but also set aside land to harvest varieties for the wine industry. The additional acreage also allowed George to begin a dehydration business. Though he dehydrated his own grapes by more traditional means, George bought impressive quantities of grapes from local farmers and used large-scale electric dehydrators that could complete the drying process within a matter of hours. These dehydrators also made it possible to produce raisins even during the rainy autumn and winter months, making George's farm highly productive and operational year-round.

George's wife, Charlotte, also contributes to all aspects of the business. Though she swore she'd never marry a farmer, Charlotte grew up on a nearby farm and understands the agriculture industry well. It only seemed natural that she should take on the responsibilities of various aspects of the Salwasser operation. As the Salwasser family has grown, George and Charlotte's children, George Jr. and Keri, have helped with the family business as well. George's "extended family," as he affectionately likes to call his employees, also have grown up locally and have an extensive background in farming as well as the raisin industry. Together, the combined talent produces a knowledgeable team, always ready to address the issues and trends of the local and wide-scale agriculture market.

In more recent years, Salwasser Inc. has partnered with the Mariani family of San Jose in a joint venture — The Mariani Raisin Company — to process, pack and distribute raisins. George had realized the growth potential that could result from packing, marketing and distributing his own product under his own label. Approaching the Mariani family, which excelled in marketing and distribution, to form a partnership seemed like the best way to make this plan profitable. As a result of the partnership, a state-of-the-art packing facility was incorporated into Salwasser's farming

George J. Salwasser Sr.'s newly constructed office complex is located on his farm near Kerman, California.

operations, and today the company is one of the largest raisin processors in the industry. Although the merger was only launched in 1993, Mariani raisins are already sold to 35 countries.

As his wholesale business was growing, George also saw the potential of a retail market. Named for his daughter, who had been seeking various means to more fully participate in the family business, Keri's Kountry Store opened in 1994. The store sells everything from crafts made by local artisans to beautifully packaged dried fruits from the packing house. In its rural setting, George did not anticipate extensive walk-in traffic, and encouraged his children to develop marketing strategies for the store. He believed their participation would foster a sense of pride and ownership in the family business. And with this encouragement, a mail-order business, "Build Your Own Basket," was developed that markets holiday and gift-giving specialties.

GEORGE WANTS HIS CONTRIBUTIONS TO THE COMMUNITY AND HIS VARIOUS BUSINESS VENTURES TO REFLECT HIS STEADFAST, HEARTFELT APPROACH TO LIFE. HE CONSTANTLY ACKNOWLEDGES HIS HUMBLE BEGINNINGS AND RESPECTS HARD WORK.

George has also had the foresight to use the Internet to further this venture. The "Build Your Own Basket" Web site allows consumers to purchase attractive gift baskets with customized combinations of fruits. Mariani premium produce is offered, as well as specialty raisins, natural sun-dried raisins and nuts. Capitalizing on the San Joaquin Valley's reputation for sunny weather, rich soil and quality fruit, the offering of locally dried fruits and nuts has wide appeal. Most recently, soups, pastas, coffees and teas have been added to the online selection of products available for the gift baskets. The idea has taken off, and the Salwassers are shipping the baskets all over the United States.

George and his family also believe in giving back to the community that has supported them through the years. Not only has he served on the Raisin Administrative Board, but the Salwassers also support youth groups and sponsor Little League teams. George wants his contributions to the community and his various business ventures to reflect his steadfast, heartfelt approach to life. He constantly acknowledges his humble beginnings and respects hard work. He believes this work ethic has helped to bring him success, and knows that it will be a positive influence in the lives of others as well.

Alexius International, Inc.

Alexius International, Inc. was established in Fresno, California, in 1980 as an engineering company specializing in dried fruit processing machinery projects to serve the needs of the agro-industries in the San Joaquin Valley and Middle Eastern countries. The founder of Alexius, engineer Hassan Dwidar, received his master's degree in food technology engineering from Alexandria University in Egypt, where he was born. After graduation he was a manager for the KAHA Company in Alexandria, Egypt. During the 70s he joined the United Nations Industrial Development Organization (UNIDO) as an international expert in the field of agro-industrial operations. In 1980 he emigrated to the United States. Considering his background and past experience on the international level, it was natural that he desired to establish an international company in the United States, serving the great need for the advancing technology in food processing in developing nations, particularly since he had already established the contacts needed for introducing his new ideas and machinery to these nations during his international services with UNIDO.

ALEXIUS IS A CO-PACKER FOR POWERBAR AND SUNDATE OF COACHELLA.

Along the way Dwidar, through Alexius International, Inc., has offered consulting services to well-known companies including FMC; Bektel, in the United States; Technipetrol, in Italy; EMBRAPA, in Brazil; the Private Department for His Highness the President and Crown Prince of the United Arab Emirates; and the Ministry of Agriculture, in Oman.

SINCE 1983 ALEXIUS HAS EMERGED AS A TURNKEY PROJECT SUPPLIER FOR FOOD PROCESSING PROJECTS IN THE MIDDLE EAST AND GULF COUNTRIES.

Since 1983 Alexius International, Inc. has emerged as a turnkey project supplier for many processing projects in the Middle East and Gulf countries.

Most recently, Alexius introduced newly developed technology and machinery for the production of natural candy bars from fruit with no added sugar or preservatives. Alexius has been working recently in conjunction with American companies as copacker for PowerBar, Sundate of Coachella and Sierra Nut House. Alexius has also taken action to diversify its activities by creating valuable products from the surpluses of the agro-industrial products, beginning with production of energy bars and high-fiber fruit bars from the surplus of fresh and dried fruit. These current products represent a valuable development to the San Joaquin Valley as value-added products, which will increase the profitability of local food industries.

ALEXIUS IS CREATING VALUABLE PRODUCTS FROM THE SURPLUSES OF THE AGRI-INDUSTRIAL PRODUCTS, BEGINNING WITH PRODUCTION OF ENERGY BARS AND HIGH-FIBER FRUIT BARS FROM THE SURPLUS OF FRESH AND DRIED FRUIT.

Alexius began its operation with one person in 1980 and it has been steadily growing, increasing employment opportunities and exporting its machinery internationally. It began with $5,000 in capital and is now valued at over $5 million in net worth.

Expectations for the future include expanding the natural candy bar lines and copacking activities, using the natural resources of the San Joaquin Valley.

Dwidar believes as technology continues to advance and new value-added products are developed, Alexius' role in the San Joaquin Valley will expand and the company will contribute more products and services to the local and international communities.

Central California Hispanic Chamber of Commerce

wThe Central California Hispanic Chamber of Commerce was created in 1984 by local community leaders who recognized the need for an organization that represented the Latino-based businesses of the area. The Mexican-American community of the San Joaquin Valley had come through a very significant era of its history. The decades of the 50s, 60s and 70s saw a dramatic increase in college-educated Hispanics as evidenced in the fields of medicine, law and business. By the mid-70s, San Joaquin Valley's elected ranks contained over 50 of Mexican descent, affirming the confidence and respect citizens of the area held for these officials. It was a time of political, social and economic growth. It was also a time of local population growth with the arrival of many immigrants as well as Mexican-Americans from Texas and Arizona.

Years before, immigrants from Mexico were employed as agricultural workers in the San Joaquin Valley. After World War II, the area's agricultural growth slowed and mechanization cut employment opportunities. To compound the situation, displaced laborers from other states as well as Mexico moved into the valley in search of work. As a consequence, seasonal unemployment intensified and, to make matters worse, retraining programs were scarce. These conditions motivated many farmworkers to move to the cities to find work. The gains, even so, for the Mexican-American population in general was impressive due to its uncompromising commitment to succeed. Steadier jobs were found, children obtained better education and went on to accomplish feats uncommon to earlier generations. Throughout the valley, Mexican-Americans bettered themselves as a result of attending public schools, gaining a command of the English language and going on to higher education.

Current CCHCC President Gilbert Servin

After fighting in World War II and the Korean War, Mexican-Americans were much less tolerant of bigotry, and organized to augment their potential political power and exercise their civil rights. The 50s had forged an activism that precipitated the formation of new organizations, which had a sense of collective purpose and a determination to end discrimination. By 1960, over 55 percent of the Mexican-American population in Fresno County worked in jobs outside agriculture. Two decades later, when the Hispanic Chamber was formed, only 30 percent remained tied to agriculture, with the number of professionals doubling. The earnings of families increased dramatically in spite of many poor, under-educated newcomers. In two decades, the Latino community had made important strides, and the time had come for those in white-collar professions and business owners to band together to assist others in achieving similar goals.

Currently, the Central California Hispanic Chamber of Commerce is very involved in addressing the quality of life in the Mexican-American community. Through the chamber and its supporters, more and more Latinos have access to local government, lending institutions and corporate America. The struggle against poverty persists, but as the record shows, a proud heritage points to the ongoing success of the Mexican-American people of the valley.

Fresno attorney Ed Valdez addressing the first Spanish speaking-only workshop sponsored by the Central California Hispanic Chamber of Commerce

Producers Dairy Foods

Treating people fairly and honestly, as his parents had taught him back when he was riding a horse five miles each way to school in the mining camps of Pleasant Valley, California, has always been important to Larry Shehadey, chairman of Producers Dairy Foods.

Shehadey is quick to credit his considerable success to that honest work ethic, the contributions of others and fate. He hadn't planned on coming to Fresno or on buying a business in the city. Although fate may have brought Larry Shehadey to Fresno, it was his dedication to honesty and quality that not only built one of the most successful dairy food operations in the western United States, but also established a personal reputation of the highest order.

Producers Dairy Foods headquarters in Fresno, California

He had gone to work for Par Soap in 1930 and over the years rose from salesman to vice president. Shehadey has always been open-minded and eager to learn. While sales manager for Par Soap, and traveling 11 western states, he was learning constantly about the different aspects of business — and the differing attitudes of people. He enjoyed meeting people in the various regions he covered. He was always receptive to a good idea or a better way of doing business, but values were always the one common denominator for Shehadey. He credits his boss at Par Soap for helping to strengthen his good ethics and positive attitude.

Safeway, Inc. bought out Par Soap in 1948 and wanted Shehadey to stay on, but he made use of his sales skills and many contacts in the wholesale and retail industries elsewhere. He worked as an independent promotional representative and helped to introduce a new whipped topping, RediWhip, to the market.

While promoting RediWhip in Fresno, he became acquainted with two of the owners of Producers Dairy Foods, which had been founded in 1932. The partners each held 25 percent of the company. When the other 50 percent became available, they asked Shehadey to purchase it.

Larry Shehadey bought half of Producers Dairy in 1949 and soon afterward became its general manager. Motivated to provide customers with the highest quality products possible, Shehadey installed the most modern packaging equipment available during his first year. By 1951 he had made Producers the first dairy in the state to have a completely refrigerated delivery fleet.

By 1955 Shehadey owned 100 percent of Producers Dairy, and it has been family owned and operated ever since. His commitment to quality prompted Shehadey to establish his own dairy herd in 1959. Nearly 35 percent of the milk processed by Producers Dairy Foods comes from Shehadey's own Bar 20 dairy herds.

Owning its own herds helps Producers Dairy to maintain very strict quality standards. The California Department of Agriculture allows milk to contain up to 50,000 parts of bacteria per million, but Producers Dairy adheres to its own standard of just 10,000 parts per million. Not only does Shehadey's own dairy farm achieve this low bacteria level, but Producers demands that dairies from which it purchases milk also meet this stringent requirement. In addition, to ensure that customers get the finest dairy products, the processing

Larry (left) and Richard Shehadey continue the Producers Dairy tradition of personal attention to quality products.

plant has been continually upgraded with the most modern processing and sanitizing equipment.

Modern equipment and scrupulous standards are vital aspects of Producers' dedication to quality, but Larry Shehadey also wants employees to understand that they have a responsibility to the public to produce the freshest product possible. He tells them that babies drink Producers Milk. If that milk is sour or off flavor and the baby starts crying the mother may not know why, and the baby can't tell her. Shehadey's sense of accountability has permeated the company.

Concern for children prompted Shehadey to arrange for cowboy star Hopalong Cassidy's picture, along with that of his horse, Topper, to appear on Producers milk cartons in the early 1950s. "He was healthy, strong, reliable — the qualities I wanted to convey," says Larry Shehadey. Cassidy, who became Larry Shehadey's good friend, appeared at the opening of Shehadey's dairy farm to thousands of fans' delight. To Shehadey's delight, the Hopalong Cassidy advertising campaign doubled sales in just two years. Hopalong's picture still appears on cartons of Producers Dairy milk.

A founding member of the All Star Dairy Association and past president of Dairy Institute of California, Shehadey has served on many dairy boards, including the Dairy Council of California and California Growers Association. In 1999, after celebrating 50 years at Producers Dairy Foods, Larry Shehadey became chairman and his son, Richard, took over as general manager. His other son, John, is in charge of a chain of family-owned convenience stores.

Larry Shehadey still runs the Bar 20 dairy farm with the help of General Manager Corky Bloise. Shehadey praises Bloise very highly, and says he could never repay all that he has done for him.

Shehadey lavishes praise generously and credits the help he's received from many people. Producers Dairy has also been a generous contributor to worthy causes. Larry Shehadey is a member of many organizations, including the California State University, Fresno, Family Business Council, the Fresno Chamber of Commerce and the Police Activities League. He has supported the Boy Scouts, Big Brothers and Big Sisters. Shehadey has funded scholarships for hundreds of students at Fresno City College and sponsors numerous sporting events including the annual Producers Dairy Jr. Football Bowl, and is a founding sponsor and member of the Fresno Athletic Hall of Fame. In 1999 Larry Shehadey was a recipient of the prestigious Leon S. Peters Award, which honors a business professional for devotion to improving life in Fresno and the Central Valley.

Hopalong Cassidy's picture is on the milk cartons because good guys drink milk. In the case of Producers, good guys make milk, too. It may have been fate that brought Larry Shehadey to Fresno. Still, it is evident to all who meet him that his success in producing healthy, wholesome dairy foods is the result of his healthy values and wholesome life.

Producers Dairy Foods Bar 20 dairy farm

Tri-Tech Graphics, Inc.

In today's fast-paced world people no longer have the time or patience for lengthy passages of text in an advertising message. Catching the consumer's attention now requires an easily remembered, immediately recognizable image that instantly communicates an idea and creates an indelible impression. In other words, graphic identification — a unique commodity that Tri-Tech Graphics, Inc. provides for such household names as Coca-Cola, Pepsi Cola, Anheuser-Busch, Enterprise Rent-A-Car, Chanel, Vendo Company, Orchard Supply Hardware and the Pierre Smirnoff Company. Years of ingenuity and commitment to quality have earned Tri-Tech Graphics the privilege of being the exclusive international supplier of graphic images to corporations like Evian Natural Spring Water and Triarc Beverage Group's RC Cola.

Not only have the creative geniuses at work behind Tri-Tech Graphics helped to put Fresno, California, on the map, they've done it with a larger-than-life three-dimensional look and feel. Creators of backlit 3-D animated signs, Tri-Tech Graphics, Inc. has been the recipient of numerous coveted awards, a list that includes bringing home to Fresno top honors in the 26th annual Key Awards for work on the Universal Pictures film *The Frighteners*, a science fiction thriller starring Michael J. Fox.

Graphic for outdoor bus shelter

Outdoor vending display

Standing five-and-a-half feet tall, this animated three-dimensional display box was the first of its kind to be used for in-house promotion of movies in theaters. It was so imposing that one theater owner in Los Angeles decided it was too frighteningly effective and declined the opportunity to use it.

Tri-Tech Graphics is currently the only commercial screen printer utilizing the screen printing process on lenticular plastic sheeting, the material responsible for the 3-D look that gives Tri-Tech Graphics the capability of producing such large scale 3-D animation. Tri-Tech Graphics' founder Richard Guest began his experiments with screen printing on lenticular material in the early 1990s, confident that he could create a high demand for these large-format signs for entertainment, advertising and promotion. The hunch paid off.

Following close on the heels of *The Frighteners* display was a joint promotion with Smirnoff for the James Bond film, *Tomorrow Never Dies*, featuring a three-foot-high 3-D martini glass. Floating lemon peels spelled out "007" when viewed from different angles. Promotional copy for the film, embedded in the image, appeared or disappeared depending on the angle from which it was viewed.

Tri-Tech Graphics also created a display for the film *Species II* that incorporated a human image that "morphed" into a life-size, 3-D version of the film's alien.

In addition to creating 3-D display images for movie promotions and vending machines, the graphics experts at Tri-Tech work with four-color process printing to produce signs, labels, point-of-purchase displays, transit markings, visual merchandising and a variety of other printed materials for customers, all having one thing in common — bold, eye-catching colors and memorable images.

Now a member of the Sanden Group of companies, Tri-Tech Graphics, Inc. got its start in October 1984 with four employees, a number that included original owners Richard Guest and Lloyd Anderson.

Occupying 30,000 square feet, they went to work with only one arm press and two semiautomatic presses, catering primarily to the soft drink industry by creating appealing displays for vending machines.

By its 15th year in business, Tri-Tech Graphics had grown to 84 employees, sharing more than 70,000 square feet of space with 10 presses and a warehousing facility from which Tri-Tech Graphics ships signs, banners and captivating graphic images to stops all over the world.

With its roots in the beverage industry and known for demanding exceptionally high standards of its graphic images, Tri-Tech Graphics insists on quality workmanship. While these high standards seem to have fallen by the wayside industrywide, Tri-Tech Graphics makes a point of maintaining the kind of exceptional quality upon which its foundations were built. Each piece that comes off of one of its presses is placed on a lightbox and inspected for color and sharpness of image.

Colors chosen for each project are continually monitored throughout the printing process by a sophisticated color-matching computer system that assures the color of the finished piece is exactly the color the customer requested. Color density is measured and matched on each job during proofing, then logged into the computer for future customer reference.

An in-house computerized system is used to test the durability of materials. The accelerated weathering system can simulate different lighting, temperatures and moisture conditions to allow a long-range look at environmental effects in a very compressed amount of time. One hundred days in the simulator can approximate three to four years of wear.

Screen printing has been looked upon as an art, due largely to the many variables in the process. The industry at large, and Tri-Tech in particular, is working to achieve more scientific control over the process through computerization, digital technology and state-of-the-art equipment, with an eye toward improving the consistency of the process.

Tri-Tech Graphics' corporate leaders see their employees as another strong factor in achieving quality assurance. Their philosophy of quality extends to include a higher quality of life for its people. Since employees work long days at the facility, steps are taken throughout to ensure their comfort and to provide a relaxed, friendly atmosphere that fosters the kind of creativity that has made the company so strong.

Another Tri-Tech commitment to quality that strongly impacts the community of Fresno is its contribution to higher environmental standards. The plant uses UV-curing inks on its products instead of water- or solvent-based inks, eliminating volatile organic compound (VOC) by-products.

Keeping an evervigilant eye on the future, Tri-Tech Graphics looks not only to continue expanding its international boundaries by creating powerful images for companies around the globe, but also to expanding its horizons locally by doing more work in the county.

Tri-Tech Graphics headquarters in Fresno, California

UpRight, Inc.

INNOVATION KEEPS UPRIGHT GROWING

It's another example of necessity giving rise to an important invention. In 1946 a mechanical engineer living in Berkeley, California, needed to paint his two-story house. Frustrated by conventional scaffolding that would not accommodate the uneven terrain surrounding his home, Wallace Johnson came up with aluminum scaffolding with adjustable legs. His invention provided him with a convenient, level surface to work.

The inventor also recognized the commercial promise of his scaffolding in the construction and maintenance industries. In 1947 he founded Up-Right Scaffolds, forerunner of UpRight, Inc., making the world's first line of aluminum scaffolding with adjustable legs.

(Far right) Scissor lifts are generally known for the steel supports that fold out in accordion fashion as the machines elevate. Some scissors, such as this LX41, come with spacious platforms capable of supporting sizeable loads of workers and materials.

An UpRight SB80 telescopic boom lift helped architects take a close look at the Fresno Water Tower before finalizing plans to renovate the historic structure into a visitors center.

For its first 15 years, Johnson's company primarily made aluminum scaffolding. Though as technology evolved, the company expanded the product line. UpRight ventured into powered elevating work platforms known as push-arounds for use in schools, hospitals, universities and other high-maintenance structures. Later, elevating platforms propelled by gasoline, propane, diesel or electric engines were introduced. Diesel-driven equipment hit a chord in Europe where gasoline is expensive. The electric-powered lifts have a worldwide appeal for indoor use because no exhaust fumes are generated.

Scissor lifts, identified mainly for a cross-bracing of steel supporting a platform, grew to be the company's main revenue source. Boom lifts, known primarily for their ability to telescope beyond the footprint of supporting chassis, also figure heavily in the company's growth. Telehandlers, capable of lifting thousands of pounds of construction and other materials, make up the newest product line. That moves UpRight from simply moving people close to the task at hand to positioning heavy loads of building supplies where they need to be.

UpRight sells its products through a worldwide network of dealers who sell or rent the equipment mainly to construction, industrial, institutional and commercial clients.

Many UpRight scaffolds are custom-made. Examples include a 131-foot-tall structure for scientific observation of the flora and fauna of the Malaysian rainforest. UpRight scaffolding also was used to assist in restoration of the Jefferson Memorial in Washington, D.C., and Michaelangelo's paintings at the Sistine Chapel in Italy. The company also has built many special scaffolds for the National Aeronautics and Space Administration (NASA) and the military for uses ranging from satellite construction to portable ramps used to load injured personnel onto airplanes.

UpRight equipment recently played a role in the renovation of a century-old landmark in Fresno that is on the National Registry of Historic Places. With the help of government and philanthropic organizations, the Fresno Water Tower was transformed into a visitors center. Architects used an UpRight SB80 telescopic boom lift to visually inspect the structure prior to the main construction phase.

During his lifetime, Johnson became the mayor of Berkeley and was widely recognized for his inventions. Working with the University of California, Davis, Johnson developed a grape harvester. The main users of the harvesting machines were farmers in the Central San Joaquin Valley. So, in 1972, Johnson opened a factory on Todd Street in Selma, the "Raisin Capital of the World," to make the harvesters. Two years later, UpRight opened its Park Street complex in Selma, consolidating its U.S. operations there during the 1980s.

In 1998 another UpRight factory opened in Madera, just 40 miles north of Selma. Sitting on 40 acres, the complex quickly grew to more than 300,000 square feet of manufacturing and office space. The Madera plant specializes in making boom lifts and telehandlers.

Wallace "Wally" Johnson: An imaginative spirit marked the career of this inventor, entrepreneur and politician. Johnson founded Up-Right Scaffolds, forerunner of UpRight, Inc.

The headquarters complex in Selma has more than 330,000 square feet of manufacturing and office buildings. The factory's emphasis is on the production of scissor lifts. The company's research and development, marketing and a number of other key departments also are located in Selma.

UpRight employs more than 650 people in Selma and Madera, underscoring its importance to the economies of both towns. Add to that plans to hire an additional 300 workers by 2001. Worldwide revenues for UpRight exceed $200 million.

The company also has a third factory in Ireland at Dun Laoire, just outside Dublin. The plant makes scaffolding and trailer-mounted aerial lifts. A warehouse, service and distribution center for Europe is located at Rotterdam in the Netherlands.

It's difficult to say if Johnson was a visionary or simply practical, but global marketing has helped UpRight prosper amid economic downturns in individual countries. The international thrust began with sales in the United Kingdom and France, and expanded worldwide later. For many years UpRight was the only U.S. access-equipment manufacturer tapping markets in many foreign lands.

When Johnson died in 1980, UpRight, Inc. was sold. The business remains privately held, and operates with the same inventive sprit. An example is boom lifts. UpRight added them in the mid-1990s after forging a solid reputation with scaffolding, push-arounds and scissor lifts. By early 1999, the diverse lineup of self-propelled lifts ranged in maximum working heights from 18 to 86 feet. Telehandlers were added as the calendar flipped over to 2000.

A custom-made UpRight scaffold helped restoration specialists return the paintings of Michaelangelo inside Italy's Sistine Chapel to their former glory.

Today UpRight has hundreds of distributors in the United States, Europe, South America, the Pacific Rim, the Middle East, Australia and other locations. Some of those dealers have more than 200 outlets.

The company's proud past seems destined to serve as a foundation for a powerful future. Providing on-the-job access solutions involving personnel and materials will undoubtedly spur innovation that enhances operator safety and productivity.

The Vendo Company

For over 60 years The Vendo Company of Fresno, California, has helped quench the world's thirst — keeping beverages cold and readily available for consumers not only where they live, but where they work, play, shop, travel and relax.

The beverage-vending machine, so universally recognized today, traces its roots back to the 1930s. The first machines were not coin-operated, but simple coolers packed with ice and bottles of soda and run on the honor system. When the first coin-operated machines appeared, they worked poorly, jamming frequently and accepting almost any kind of slug.

Enlisted men enjoying a cold beverage from a Vendo Coke machine, c. 1950

Brothers Elmer F. and John T. Pierson changed all that. The Piersons purchased a patent for a simple, inexpensive and reliable vending lid. This lid could be locked on top of the Westinghouse and Frigidaire chest coolers already present in service stations and grocery stores, thereby converting them into vending machines. With $3,000 in start-up capital, the brothers started The Vendo Company in 1937 in Kansas City, Missouri. Joined by J.E. Hagstrom and his company, they developed the first truly workable vending system — a lid called "The Red Top."

The Red Top moved the delivery opening to the next bottle in the chest, rather than moving bottles through the ice. This innovation eliminated the jamming problem and made the machine simple and practical. It virtually created a major market and changed the world of beverage retailing.

The 1941 attack on Pearl Harbor curtailed Vendo's production, like that of most other peacetime industries. Despite severe wartime restrictions, soft drinks were classified as "essential for soldier morale" by the U.S. War Department, and Vendo was authorized to produce 5,000 Red Tops for military training camps and war plants. Vendo further supported the nation's war effort by producing radar detection systems and associated electronic equipment. The company earned an impressive seven Army-Navy "E" awards for excellence in fulfilling Army and Navy production contracts.

The end of the war brought about a prosperous new era for America and for the vending industry. In the 50s the industry "exploded" both in geography and in scope. As more Americans began to move to the suburbs, soft drink bottlers rushed to extend their vending operations. Vending also began to expand internationally, with Vendo products being shipped to 20 different countries by 1956.

Beverage vending machines had a new look in the 50s — upright, streamlined units with round-cornered cabinets. Vendo built a giant new plant during this decade and introduced vending machines to support multiple products. These machines brought more variety to the public and allowed bottlers to significantly increase their volume.

Vendo diversified its production in the 50s, developing machines to sell packaged snacks, fresh foods, coffee, milk and ice cream. The company tested automated convenience stores, restaurants and drive-in refreshment stations serviced totally by vending machines.

Vendo first established itself in Fresno in 1956 by merging with its former rival, the Vendorlator Manufacturing Company. Like Vendo, Vendorlator had been in business since 1937. The company was founded as a copartnership by Harry S. Childers and Howard M. Tripp. While Vendo had mainly served Coca-Cola bottlers before the merger, Vendorlator counted Pepsi-Cola and Royal Crown among its principal customers. After the merger, the combined companies became a major supplier for the entire soft drink industry.

The Vendo Company went public in 1956, and company stock began trading on the New York Stock Exchange in 1961, where it remained for over 20 years. The 60s were a time of worldwide expansion for Vendo. Mitsubishi Heavy Industries began manufacturing Vendo beverage coolers in Japan in 1962. Vendo's international division also had licensed manufacturing operations in England and Mexico. In 1964 it began new subsidiaries and contract manufacturing facilities in Belgium, Australia, Italy, Germany, France and Canada.

Always the industry pioneer, in the late 60s Vendo was one of the first to introduce vending machines for canned beverages. These machines were a great advantage for bottlers, who could fit nearly twice as many cans as bottles in a machine of the same size.

The energy crisis of the 70s struck a blow to many American industries, and vending was no exception. Vending machines were considered nonessential and many companies cut back on their purchases. Also, due to the oil crisis and many factory closings, fewer machines were placed in factories and gas stations. In the mid-70s Vendo left Kansas City and sold its snack machine division. Retaining only its cold drink machine line, the company split its operations between the Fresno plant and a new facility in Corinth, Mississippi.

In 1981 Vendo concentrated all of its domestic manufacturing and administrative offices in Fresno and, in 1988, was acquired by the Sanden Corporation, Japan. For more than 50 years Sanden has been a leading manufacturer of automotive air-conditioning compressers and systems, vending machines, commercial freezers and refrigerated showcases. The company has infused Vendo with superior technology, state-of-the-art equipment and research facilities.

The 80s and 90s have brought continued technological innovation and global expansion for Vendo. Some of these advances include programmable electronic vending machines, high-capacity machines that accommodate plastic bottles in a wide variety of sizes and shapes, and machines that accept debit cards and "smart cards."

Pepsi machine, c. 1955-1960

Today Vendo employs almost 800 people in Fresno and works with numerous Vendo sales, service and manufacturing operations throughout the world. Vendo continues to expand its reach into markets such as Africa, the Middle East, Latin America and Eastern Europe.

Vendo strives for global excellence, fostering cooperation among all Sanden/Vendo operations worldwide to actualize the best concepts in vending equipment. In 1999, Vendo achieved ISO 9001 certification and will continue to pursue several other quality initiatives.

From the Red Top affixed to a simple cooler filled with ice and bottles of soda to the electronically controlled, high-capacity, multiproduct vending machines of today, Vendo continues to blaze trails in innovation, design, technology, manufacturing and service.

A Vendo production worker attaches a door guard to the cabinet of a Pepsi vending machine on the Fresno assembly line.

Gottschalks, Inc.

It may have been Fresno's first traffic jam. Hours before Gottschalks' grand opening on September 17, 1904, horse-drawn streetcars and buggies had to contend with thousands of Fresno's citizens, including many of its most fashionable, who lined the streets admiring the fine merchandise through the new store's wide show windows. Since its inception, Gottschalks has strived to give customers the best shopping experience possible.

Founder Emil Gottschalk, 1861-1939

Chairman Joe Levy sees the success of Gottschalks, now the largest independent department store chain based in California, as rooted in two precepts: keep it simple and take care of the customer. Those two elements of Gottschalks' golden rule are legacies from the firm's founder, Emil Gottschalk, Levy's great-uncle.

Service has been a Gottschalks' byword since the beginning, when the company's horse and carriage delivery service would often make a special run with just a few yards of material or a 5 cent spool of thread. Today Gottschalks continues that tradition of service in a fashion that would be sure to please Emil Gottschalk.

Joe Levy recounts the situation where not long ago a woman called him. She had bought a wedding gown at one of Gottschalks' competitors. Unfortunately the lady's marriage plans had fallen apart. To make matters worse, although the expensive bridal gown was still new and had never been worn, the store where she bought it would not take it back or give her any credit.

Joe told her to bring it over. Gottschalks hadn't sold her the dress, but took it in and gave her credit. That's how Gottschalks keeps customers coming back, generation after generation, to their hometown store.

Gottschalks strives to be the hometown store in every city it serves throughout the western United States — not by just calling itself the hometown store, but by acting that way.

Gottschalks Dollar Days, 1912

Emil Gottschalk spent his life learning how to care for the needs of the customer. Born in Muhlhausen Saxony, West Germany, he immigrated as a youth with his family to New York City. After graduating from high school at 16, he attended Columbia University part time while working in sales to support himself.

When Emil had graduated from college and was working full time, a manufacturer's representative who admired Gottschalk's talents as a salesman, and knew of his desire to move west, secured him a job with Weinstock Lubin, a Sacramento department store. Gotttschalk went to work for the company, gaining valuable experience in retail, the business he loved. Emil moved up through the ranks, and through his ample ability became the store's manager by the age of 29.

His position required considerable travel, and it was during one of his business trips that Emil Gottschalk met and fell in love with Dora Korn. A few years later they were married. Dora's father was part-owner of Kutner-Goldstein, a Fresno dry goods business, and they persuaded Emil to join the firm.

In 1894, just nine years after the city had incorporated, Emil Gottschalk and his new bride, Dora, settled in Fresno. Gottschalk started at Kutner-Goldstein as the merchandise manager, but through his considerable experience and talent he soon advanced to general manager.

Gottschalk worked a decade for the company and became respected in the industry for his ability and integrity. He was also well known and liked throughout the Fresno community. Things had been going well. Kutner-Goldstein had told Gottschalk that after working there 10 years it would give him a stock option to buy an interest in the business. When 10 years passed, however, and the firm had failed to make good on its promise, a disappointed Gottschalk quit in disgust and began to think about opening his own business.

Then Emil Gottschalk's fate changed in the Forsythe Barber Shop. While getting his daily shave, he was seated next to T.W. Patterson, who happened to be seeking a tenant for the ground floor of the four-story building he was constructing at the corner of J and Tulare streets.

Patterson had long been an admirer of Emil's business ability and having heard about Gottschalk's desire to be on his own, he leaned over and said, "Emil, if you are still interested in going into business for yourself, I would like to build you a store in my building."

Seeing the chance to pursue his dream, Gottschalk didn't hesitate. He signed a lease with Patterson. He then asked his brother-in-law, Henry Korn, who was employed at Farmer's Bank, to join him. With the help of other family members, he raised the capital to make his start.

Emil held a meeting in the apartment of Zelda Kredo, then a buyer at Kutner-Goldstein, to discuss his plans. Five of his department managers and nine other Kutner-Goldstein employees agreed to join in his new venture. Zelda Kredo was to remain with Gottschalks for 50 years.

Emil Gottschalk had a vision of creating a successful department store. He believed that he could profit fairly by giving San Joaquin Valley customers the same high-fashion, quality merchandise then only found in New York, Europe and San Francisco. He also believed that service should show respect for the customer and provide convenience and satisfaction without question. At the age of 43, with 25 years in retailing and 28 employees, Emil Gottschalk was ready to pursue his dream.

Gottschalks, Fulton and Kern streets, 1926

Gottschalk's elegant store opened to great fanfare. With his vision, talent for creative retailing and dedication to service, it was an immediate success.

Emil Gottschalk welcomed success and made plans to grow. His vision, after all, was not just for a dry goods store but a true department store serving the entire valley. His courage was also immense. He immediately began to set aside part of each year's profits for expansion. He sold stock to manufacturers and other investors to raise additional money. In 1914 Gottschalk began construction on a new two-story department store comprising an unheard of 100,000 square feet, nearly four times the space he then occupied.

The new location was a great success. Gottschalks continued to provide the best in merchandise and service. The store offered fabulous imported items Emil Gottschalk found on his buying trips to Europe: Belgian lace, Swiss handkerchiefs, European

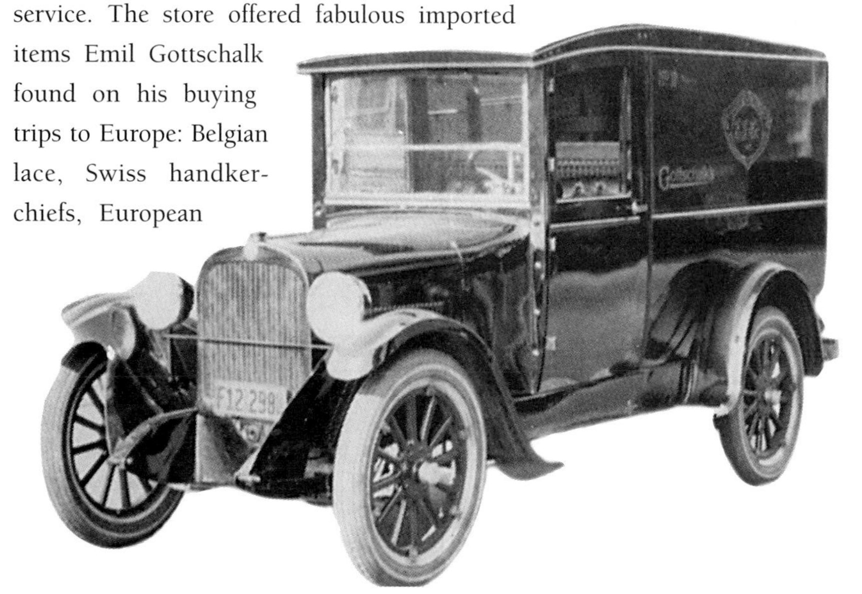
Gottschalks' furniture delivery truck during the 1920s

Outside Gottschalks' downtown store the day after Thanksgiving, November 22, 1940, traditionally the busiest day of the year

toys and Christmas ornaments, items that in those days were not available in this country. It featured a "Brightlight Basement" with a soda fountain, candy, manicurists, hairdressers, toys and large household goods. It embraced innovative advertising and marketing techniques, gave out coupons, offered free delivery by parcel post within 150 miles and had a liberal money-back policy.

The store was the first in the valley to have air conditioning. Gottschalks was also the first in Fresno to have a five-day work week, one of the first large toy departments, was the first in the valley to offer charge accounts and the first to have a U.S. Post Office in a retail store. In 1976 Gottschalks was among the first retailers in the United States to use IBM computer terminals. The company continues to implement new technology, update the appearance of the stores and enhance the merchandise mix to improve its performance for customers and stockholders alike.

Corporate offices, Fresno, California

From the beginning Gottschalks was a family business. Abe Blum, Emil's young nephew, came west to join his uncle's small store in 1908. A graduate of Rutger's University, Blum started in the shipping room and advanced to sales and administrative positions. He became president in 1955.

In 1920 Irving W. Levy, a nephew of Dora Gottschalk, Emil's wife, joined the business. He too worked his way up through many positions. After years as general merchandise manager, he was elected president in 1960.

Gerald Blum, Abe's son, joined the company in 1951, and Irving W. Levy's son, Joe Levy, came to work for Gottschalks in 1956. I.W. Levy died in 1982, and Joe Levy, who had been serving as executive vice president, was elected chairman and CEO. That same year Gerald Blum became president and COO. Gerald Blum retired as vice chairman and still serves as a consultant. James Famalette became president and chief operating officer in 1997.

Gottschalks, Inc. went public in 1986 and is listed on the New York Stock Exchange. It is following the board of directors' direction to pursue an aggressive growth pattern through carefully planned expansion.

After Emil Gottschalk's 1914 move to the 100,000-square-foot location, the company did not open any new stores until 1961 when Gottschalks opened its first branch in Merced, California. Under Joe Levy's stewardship, the company today has more than 40 Gottschalks department stores and 20 Village East specialty stores in the western United States. Sales have steadily increased, hitting the $500 million mark in fiscal 1998.

Yes, things have changed since Emil Gottschalk first brought hard-to-get merchandise to the San Joaquin Valley. Quality goods are now more widely available, but Gottschalks' well-stocked stores serve small to midsize markets with national brand merchandise, often offering residents choices not otherwise available; its sales associates are well trained, knowledgeable and dedicated to their customers. Gottschalks' customer service is still the envy of the industry.

The firm has maintained its commitment to giving customers the best overall value, a combination of service, high-quality brand-name merchandise and competitive prices. It continues to gain customer loyalty and has earned the allegiance of four generations of customers by providing the best shopping experience possible. Incidents such as the one Joe Levy tells about the wedding gown may be rare in any industry, but that degree of customer care is what Gottschalks delivers every day.

Gottschalks' reputation as the hometown store is reflected not only in personal and attentive customer service, but in its high level of commitment to the community. It holds "charity days" events before the grand openings of all new Gottschalks' stores to raise funds for local charities. It contributes nearly 5 percent of net earnings to local nonprofit organizations. Gottschalks is a major contributor and supporter of California State University, Fresno; Fresno Metropolitan Museum; Fresno Art Center; American Heart Association; Arte Americas; Tree Fresno; NAACP; Marjaree Mason Center; Big Brothers Big Sisters; Fresno Philharmonic Orchestra; Combined Health Appeal of Central California; and United Way among many others.

Enthusiasm for Gottschalks' community involvement, its history, traditions and business, permeates the company. As Joe Levy says, "It's so darn exciting! When you get into retail, when you catch it, it's so exciting." After all these years in the business, he still gets excited when an item catches on — when people like it and buy it.

He likes to tell a story about a candle. It was in November. Joe walked into a Gottschalks store and was talking with sales associates. One of them showed him a large scented candle that was selling for $9.95. The associate told Joe, "We just got 48 of these in and I've sold 36 in the last hour." Joe got excited.

Levy bought a candle and took it back to the corporate office. He started inquiring about the product and how many Gottschalks had bought. They told him the company had purchased a container load, about 4,000 candles, and the buyer thought that was marvelous.

Visalia storefront

Joe knew they should have 20 containers. He jumped into action. The store ended up selling more than 100,000 candles. If he hadn't walked in and bought that candle, the one full container would have been sold, and as Levy said, "everyone would have been happy." Instead everyone got a lot happier when Gottschalks sold more than $1 million worth of candles.

The retail business involves many elements: picking the item, advertising, monitoring public acceptance, correct ordering and logistics. Still, in the end everything hinges on the customer's satisfaction with the shopping experience. For Gottschalks, guided by the spirit of Emil Gottschalk's dedication to service, it's simple: make it the best.

Piccadilly Inn Hotels

Piccadilly Inn Hotels are the fulfillment of a dream D. Paul Fansler had for his beloved town of Fresno. A man of great vision and determination, Fansler was a business pioneer in the Central Valley. Born on August 24, 1927, he faced his first challenge at age 6 when his father passed away. As the only son with two older sisters, his mother told him that he was now the man of the family. He took this new role very seriously, doing any odd jobs he could find to help augment his mother's salary as a waitress. Through his mother's example, he developed a respect and admiration for all men and women working in service industries. This appreciation stayed with him his entire life and influenced all his future business transactions.

The Piccadilly Inn Shaw, the company's flagship hotel, offers unique dining amongst its lush, park-like grounds.

After graduating from Roosevelt High School he joined the Merchant Marines. When his tour of duty ended he returned to Fresno to pursue his dream of becoming a successful life insurance salesman. Because of his young age, life insurance companies were reluctant to give him an opportunity in sales. Determined to follow his dream, Fansler tried for eight months to convince them to hire him and, finally, Bankers Life Nebraska recognized that he was a highly motivated and gifted young man and offered him a job. Although he didn't receive a traditional college education, he set about to obtain the best training available in the life insurance profession. Through a two-year correspondence program offered by Purdue University, he became a Chartered Life Underwriter, the highest professional designation in life insurance.

The Piccadilly Inn Airport provides many amenities for business travelers.

Fansler had such a strong belief in the city of Fresno that he wanted to be part of its future development. In 1963 he pioneered West Shaw Avenue by purchasing land and erecting the first office building in that area, overseeing every aspect of construction himself. Because of his great respect for the working man and woman, he made sure that building contractors were paid immediately after completing each job. People knew that his word was as good as his signature. Some of his first office tenants agreed to rental terms with only a handshake. One tenant in this new office building never had a signed lease in the 14 years that he rented from Fansler.

In 1968 Fansler expanded his development of West Shaw Avenue by purchasing a 40-acre fig orchard and building the small, specialty-minded Piccadilly Square Shopping Center on this site in 1971. Immediately he began investigating the possibility of building his first hotel across the street. Whenever he started a new project, he did his own feasibility study and this hotel venture was no exception. As a life insurance salesman, Fansler traveled extensively, gaining hotel knowledge by asking questions, taking notes and pictures, and incorporating the best ideas in his own hotel designs. He found that the majority of hotels wouldn't honor a guest's request if it wasn't part of their policy. From this experience, he vowed to build hotels that catered to the needs of each guest. Thus the slogan, "We are a hotel for guests, not for staff," was born.

With Fansler overseeing the construction of the hotel, Piccadilly Inn Shaw opened in 1973. The target date for opening was June 30th, but construction problems delayed the opening for 10 days. True to his nature of turning a problem into an opportunity, Fansler had the Piccadilly Inn marquee read "Grand Opening June 40th."

At the time of the hotel's opening, development on West Shaw Avenue was sparse. He knew if they were going to get people to come to his hotel and shopping center, he was going to have to provide transportation. In keeping with the Piccadilly theme, Fansler bought a double-decker English bus that picked people up in the more populated sections of town and delivered them to his businesses. Employees, dressed in period English costumes, accompanied the bus and escorted guests to the hotel.

Development of clientele for the Piccadilly Inn Shaw was slow because early customers were mainly travelers coming off Interstate 99. To further enhance early business he personally called on local businesses, as well as companies frequently traveling to the Fresno area, to introduce the amenities of his new facility. Fansler helped with any work that was needed to get his new project off the ground. He was not above making a bed or cleaning a room, if that's what needed to be done.

In 1980 he acquired Piccadilly Inn Airport near today's Fresno Yosemite International Airport. Again he was faced with turning a problem into an opportunity. On February 19, 1980, a freak tornado came through the Fresno area and hit Piccadilly Inn Airport, damaging the lobby's ceiling. Large laundry carts were brought in to capture the leakage, but the hotel stayed open, offering for dinner that night "Tornadoes of Beef" as its main course.

The fall of 1984 saw the opening of Piccadilly's third hotel, Piccadilly Inn University, across Shaw Avenue from California State University, Fresno. While Fansler concentrated on acquiring his latest project, Marlene Fansler used her unique creative talent to design and oversee its interior decoration. This gave the chain three full-service hotels, exactly five miles apart, targeting the three most vital areas of Fresno. Fansler's last development was the opening of Chateau Inn adjacent to Piccadilly Airport on July 5, 1989.

Each Piccadilly Inn Hotel has its own unique personality and function. Piccadilly Inn Shaw caters primarily to individual corporate travelers. Its lush park environment is fitting for Fansler's flagship hotel. Piccadilly Inn University plays host to many of the sports teams visiting Fresno. It also caters to the university's travelers and business groups. Piccadilly Inn Airport specializes in large corporate groups as well as individual business travelers. Chateau Inn is a lovely "rooms only" hotel catering to the more "rate sensitive" guest. Many leisure travelers stay here for wedding parties and reunions on the weekends.

Many wedding parties and reunions are accommodated a Piccadilly's Chateau Inn.

Fansler passed away in 1990. The hotel chain was sold in 1997 and continues to be named Piccadilly and managed by the same local professional team.

Always a community-minded person, Fansler developed a nonprofit charitable corporation, which carried on his work after his death on August 8, 1990. The hotels and staff are involved in providing rooms for the Miss California Pageant, participating in the national United Cerebral Palsy Respitality Program and funding many other worthy causes.

D. Paul Fansler's legacy of dedication to the Fresno community in both business and philanthropy will continue to impact the people of the Central Valley as they move farther into the 21st century.

Piccadilly Inn University offers a relaxing outdoor environment to the sports teams visiting Fresno.

Estrada's Spanish Kitchen

It's a family thing. They have always been welcome here, the bigger, the better. And some are now represented by their fourth and fifth generations — the "regulars" at Estrada's Spanish Kitchen.

When reminiscing about the joys of family, some of the warmest memories are of holiday feasts, and even those gatherings at Grandma's house for Sunday dinner. The food was hot, it was good, there was always plenty of it, and it was prepared the old-fashioned way — with love and care, using recipes handed down from mother to daughter since time immemorial. That same warm atmosphere prevails at Estrada's Spanish Kitchen, as well as the same strict adherence to family recipes that made dinner at Grandma's such an enticing and delicious experience.

1914 Bardo Lane in Visalia — the original Estrada's Spanish Kitchen

Upon entering Cruz Estrada's, customers are greeted by a sign that states, "This is not a 'fast food' restaurant." Indeed, this is anything but fast food; its preparation began nearly 150 years ago. In an age of shortcuts and substitutions, Cruz Estrada's is still preparing food like Grandma did — with fresh ingredients, time and care, using family recipes and secrets of culinary art that were brought to California from South America in the mid-1800s. The recipes traveled to America with the great-great-grandmother of Lou Ann Kirkham, one of the current owners of Cruz Estrada's.

The family's time-honored traditions of food preparation are key to the one-of-a-kind flavors that can be found at Cruz Estrada's. Costly spices and fresh ingredients such as garlic, cumin, oregano and chiles, along with a healthy dose of close attention, create truly discriminating dishes that make experiencing Estrada's food a must.

Some of the dishes first-timers will want to try at Estrada's, and some of the dishes for which the business has become famous, are Cruz's Tostada Compuesta, created in the early 1920s, and Estrada's unusual macaroni and cheese, which has been frozen, packed in dry ice and shipped as far away as Japan to former patrons who were in need of an "Estrada's fix."

The family business began in the early 1900s. The brainchild of Louisa Forquera Estrada, it was more a need for survival than an entrepreneurial concept. When her husband, Manuel, passed away, she was faced with finding a way to support her 10 children on her own. Using the family's cherished recipes, Louisa got started by making tamales and having the oldest children sell them to neighbors.

She then leased a large home on Main Street in Visalia and began what was to become a four-generation tradition of serving extraordinary homestyle cuisine to California residents. Eventually, Louisa's children would establish eight Estrada family restaurants in San Diego, Los Angeles, Bakersfield, Visalia, south San Francisco, Monterey and Fresno.

The Fresno eateries were founded by Cruz Estrada Dillard in 1914 with two locations, one on O Street and another on Van Ness Avenue. In 1925 Cruz and her husband purchased a home on North Blackstone that served as both family home and restaurant for more than 72 years.

Cruz, along with her sister, brother-in-law, Hubert, and Delores Forkel, developed a broad-based clientele from the citizens of Fresno and the surrounding areas. After World War II, her sons, Ralph and Tobe Dillard, joined forces with Cruz and the others to help serve the Estrada family cuisine to the community.

By the 1950s the Estrada family had four restaurants in operation. Louisa passed the original restaurant in Visalia to her son, Manuel "Bud" Estrada, and her daughter, Estephina "Tashie" Gonzales. They kept the business in the family home until the mid-1950s when it was relocated to Mooney Boulevard.

As with any venture, success did not come without strife. Over the years, the business had to survive the Great Depression, two World Wars, the Korean War, the Vietnam War and the rising costs of supplies and taxes.

Additional troubles came in the early 1950s when an earthquake destroyed the Bakersfield restaurant. The south San Francisco operation was sold in the mid-1970s and the original establishment in Visalia closed in January 1992, leaving Fresno as the main location for Estrada's Spanish Kitchen.

In the 1980s Ralph and his two sons, Randy and Matthew Dillard, took over the operation of the Fresno restaurant after the death of Ralph's mother, Cruz. The family remained in the Blackstone home until Ralph Dillard's death. The family closed the business there December 30, 1997, after 72 continuous years of service at this location. It was a sad farewell from the city of Fresno to this long-standing and much-loved institution.

The family tradition is being carried on today in the San Joaquin Valley by Ralph Dillard's son, Matthew, his daughter, Lou Ann, and her husband, Donald Kirkham. Their new restaurant is named after Matthew and Lou Ann's grandmother, Cruz Estrada Dillard. Cruz Estrada's Early California Cuisine opened March 13, 1998, in north Fresno, with reverent determination to honor the original family recipes brought to California so many years ago.

Lou Ann and her partners are looking forward to a long and prosperous future, which according to current planning, will feature larger-scale production and sales of famous Estrada's sauces and products, including prepared frozen dinners.

The Estrada family has always considered itself to be an integral part of a much larger family — the community it serves. It has contributed to the Poverello house, a local homeless shelter, auctions to benefit local activities such as the Fresno Metropolitan Museum, and has fed the homeless right out of the back door of the family restaurants, particularly during World War II and the Depression. Whether it's a longing for that old, warm family feeling, or just a hankering for good, hot, homestyle cuisine, Fresno-area families are still arriving in droves to the new Cruz Estrada's Early California Cuisine, where cooking up Sunday supper isn't just a business — it's a way of life that has tied the Estrada family to Fresno history for more than four generations.

370 N. Blackstone Avenue — the Fresno location of Estrada's Spanish Kitchen for more than 72 years

KERR RUG COMPANY

Kerr Rug Company is a Fresno landmark that holds a place not only in local history, but in world history as well. The broadloom tufting machine was invented and developed at Kerr Rug, an achievement that redesigned the interiors of homes and businesses forever as wall-to-wall carpeting became the industry standard.

Kerr Rug Company is family owned and operated, serving Fresno in the same location since the Kerr brothers opened the doors in 1912. Visitors to the downtown store can feel that sense of local history for the showroom has remained much the same through the years. Its corner location, just across the street from the railroad, offers a panoramic view of the city. Its water tower with the Kerr name emblazoned on it has been a landmark for years, especially when state Highway 99 was built through the downtown area. Inside, the early 20th century architecture of the original interior sets off a colorful display of carpeting from which to choose. The people at Kerr Rug have also remained much the same through the years, with third-generation employees there today. The knowledge and skill that come from working in a family business are passed along as benefits to the customer.

Employees' parents and grandparents at the original Kerr Rug Company building

After several decades the Kerr family sold the business to Phil Berven of Berven Carpet Mills. Located in Fresno, Berven was the largest carpet manufacturer west of the Mississippi and at the time was in a period of expansion. It opened Kerr retail stores in Visalia, Merced, Sacramento, Yuba City and a second location in Fresno. Berven, however, went out of business during the early 1970s. Kerr was then purchased by Neil Hatleli, Glenn Moran and Frank Robertson. After 10 years Robertson retired and sold his shares to Hatleli and Moran. By this time the Northern California stores had been closed, leaving the Visalia, Merced and Fresno stores. When Hatleli also retired, his son, Scott, who had been managing the Merced store, stepped into a company management position. After a two-year battle with cancer Moran passed away in December 1996, leaving Scott to single-handedly run Kerr Rug for about a year. In January1998 John Patrick joined Kerr Rug and its tradition of being a family owned and operated business. Today the company is headed by Scott Hatleli and John Patrick. Again a growing company, last year a retail store was opened in Oakhurst to serve the mountain community.

Perhaps the greatest accomplishment of Kerr Rug Company is the invention and development of the broadloom tufting machine at the main Fresno store. Prior to broadloom tufting, rugs were woven on a narrow loom only 27 inches wide. The wall-to-wall carpeting that is known today was nonexistent and a room-sized rug was expensive. The development of the 12-foot-wide broadloom made carpeting affordable for the everyday, average household because rugs could be made much faster. This lowered manufacturing costs and home decorating dramatically changed, with wall-to-wall carpeting rapidly being installed in homes across the nation. And it all began at Kerr Rug.

KERR RUG COMPANY IS FAMILY OWNED AND OPERATED, SERVING FRESNO IN THE SAME LOCATION SINCE THE KERR BROTHERS OPENED THE DOORS IN 1912.

For a time carpeting was actually manufactured in the downtown Fresno store. Some of the original machinery is still in the building. During the Berven years carpeting was produced in several locations around town — down the street near the current convention center, and in Pinedale, as well as other locations.

Kerr Rug has always been retail oriented, selling to the general public. At first only rugs were offered as a specialty, with other businesses doing carpeting and linoleum. Today Kerr not only maintains a well-stocked selection of carpeting, but an entire line of flooring products and services. Kerr provides and installs everything for floors, from hardwood and tile to sheet vinyl and aggregate. New floor products are continually coming on the market and Kerr Rug keeps in step with the latest industry developments.

THE BROADLOOM TUFTING MACHINE WAS INVENTED AND DEVELOPED AT KERR RUG, AN ACHIEVEMENT THAT REDESIGNED THE INTERIORS OF HOMES AND BUSINESSES FOREVER AS WALL-TO-WALL CARPETING BECAME THE INDUSTRY STANDARD.

The company has a commitment to meet the public's changing needs. This means Kerr offers a diverse line of products and services that include auto carpeting, ceramic tile and borders. Insets for hardwood floors are currently mass produced and Kerr offers this option as well.

Recently the company has migrated into commercial work as well as retail. Kerr Rug's commercial division has installed floors at assisted living complexes and apartment units. Renovation projects in the area include large scale work such as the old foundry in Fresno, which is being transformed into Valley Foundry Park, soon to be one of Fresno's largest industrial parks. Kerr is supplying this mammoth project with 10,000 square yards of carpeting. The Sports Café, owned by some members of the San Francisco 49ers, is one of its new commercial enterprises and boasts custom-made inlaid team logos. In addition, the Visalia store is involved with community self-help projects.

This aerial view of the Berven facility shows downtown Fresno in the background.

Kerr also offers custom services for businesses and organizations that want company logos woven into carpets. Today's methodology allows intricate carpeting insets that can be installed on site at a client's facility. This is accomplished by scaling a company logo to the exact size of the carpet inlay, then tracing it directly on the carpet and weaving it in place. In addition to this service, the artisans at Kerr design and make custom rugs for trade shows and other commercial displays.

Kerr Rug Company continues to serve its customers' needs by keeping costs down. For the commercial client as well as the retail customer, Kerr regularly makes special carpeting purchases in order to maintain a large carpet selection. Because of this, customers find a wide variety of products that are affordable and immediately available.

Kerr stocks many brands of carpets, but it is interesting to note that Berven carpets is one of the choices still available. Only a few years ago Kerr Rug Company developed the broadloom tufting machine that allowed Berven Carpet mills to manufacture its line. Berven then purchased Kerr, and today Kerr still offers the Berven line, thus completing the circle.

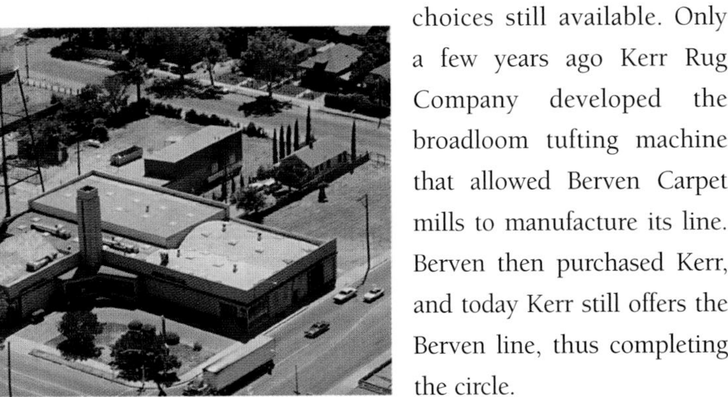

The downtown Fresno site today — the original building appears in the lower left.

Premier Management & Development Company

The firm gives employees extensive training, teaching the skills necessary to serve guests expertly and considerately.

Guests are prized at Premier Management & Development Company. The firm recognizes that the only indispensable people in its operation are the guests who stay in the hotel properties it owns and manages. The company's principals have learned from decades in the hospitality industry that the simple secret of success is to keep guests satisfied. Premier caters to guests' needs with attentive service, well-managed and maintained properties and the thoughtful extras that make its hotels an outstanding value.

Principal Amrit Patel serves on advisory panels for Holiday Inn Hotels and Super 8 Motels. With more than 26 years of hotel experience, he is a recipient of the prestigious "Distinguished Hotelier of the Year" award, presented by the Asian-American Hotel Owners Association. Principal Mukesh Desai, a certified hotel administrator, brings nearly 20 years of hotel management experience to the organization. District Manager Paul Adams is a certified hotel administrator with more than 30 years experience in full-service hotel management.

Experience has taught Premier's principals that a staff of dedicated employees underlies its goal of keeping guests happy. The company believes that while guests are indispensable, employees are the organization's most important asset. Staff members are considered partners in the operation and are treated accordingly. As a result, many employees have been with the company 10 years and some as long as 25 years.

The firm gives employees extensive training, teaching the skills necessary to serve guests expertly and considerately. Experience has also taught Premier the value of well-maintained properties. The company regularly replaces and maintains furnishings and fixtures at the properties to keep them aesthetically pleasing as well as functional.

Guests are sure to have a pleasing stay at any of Premier Management's three Fresno hotels, the Holiday Inn Express, Comfort Suites and Marriott Fairfield Inn. Whether in Fresno for pleasure, or to conduct business at one of the city's corporate, medical or educational facilities, the hotels all provide comfortable rooms in convenient, central locations.

Within a one-hour drive from Yosemite, Sequoia and Kings Canyon, Premier's Fresno properties provide perfect accommodations for those interested in visiting these magnificent national parks. Guests staying with Premier will find themselves well-situated to enjoy the famous Blossom Trail, tour nearby California wineries, or take in the San Joaquin Valley's other beautiful outdoor recreational areas. Sierra Summit and Badger Pass Ski Resort are just 40 and 70 miles away, respectively. Millerton Lake is less than a 10-mile trip. Golf courses, theaters, museums and shopping malls are all nearby and can be reached in just minutes.

Holiday Inn Express, Comfort Suites and the Marriott Fairfield Inn are located in central Fresno, just off State Highway 41, all within three miles of California State University, Fresno, and less than a mile from Saint Agnes Hospital, Kaiser Permanente Medical Center and Fresno Surgical Center. The properties all provide easy access to Valley Children's Hospital. Any of the three hotels are an ideal place to stay when conducting business at these institutions.

The three beautifully maintained properties offer complimentary continental breakfast and free local calls. The Comfort Suites and Marriott Fairfield Inn have indoor heated pools and indoor corridors. For those who prefer the convenience of parking at their room, the Holiday Inn Express has outdoor hallways, with easy access to vehicles from the comfortable rooms. Guests can swim under the clear blue Fresno skies in the Holiday Inn's full-size outdoor pool.

Guests at the distinctively designed Comfort Suites can wake up to freshly brewed in-room coffee before going down to enjoy their free continental

Guests are sure to have a pleasing stay at any of Premier Management's three Fresno hotels, the Holiday Inn Express, Comfort Suites and Marriott Fairfield Inn.

breakfast. The spacious, well-equipped rooms include microwave ovens, refrigerators, irons and ironing boards. Suites have relaxing in-room whirlpool baths. Most rooms include sleeper sofas. In addition to the luxurious indoor pool and Jacuzzi, the property offers a conference room and guest laundry. It's a great spot for an extended stay or a quick getaway.

With 24-hour facsimile service, spacious rooms and well-lit work areas, the Marriott Fairfield Inn is the perfect choice for business travelers. Road warriors can relax in comfortable beds while enjoying free cable on remote control televisions. Thoughtful amenities and Marriott's 70-year tradition of service assure guests that their stay will be a pleasurable one.

The only surprises at the Holiday Inn Express are pleasant ones, such as free HBO on remote control cable televisions, VCRs in some rooms, free local calls and complimentary continental breakfast. The property has a conference room available and guests can enjoy a refreshing dip in the full-size outdoor swimming pool. The centrally located property offers comfortable accommodations at very affordable rates.

Premier Management cordially welcomes all to beautiful Fresno. The company is very involved in community affairs, making every effort to keep the area a lovely place to live and visit. It contributes to many worthwhile organizations, including Tree Fresno, the American Heart Association and various youth sports activities.

The firm's Comfort Suites property presented "Over the River for Kids." Premier Management & Development Company, with other corporate sponsors, staged the noncompetitive community event to raise money for Valley Children's Hospital.

Community pride is also evident in the well-kept Premier properties. The management company is proud to welcome guests to Fresno, an outstanding community, and to their fine hotels, Comfort Suites, Holiday Inn Express and Marriott Fairfield Inn, all outstanding values.

Guests are well-situated to visit the famous Blossom Trail, wineries, Sierra Summit and Badger Pass Ski Resort.

Sam's Luggage

In 1917 Fresno was a small town. Like most small towns in the early 20th century, the bustle of business was in the center of the city. The concept of a mall was still decades away, so people traveled, usually on foot, from one store to the next acquiring staples, running errands or seeking repairs.

Often included on the itinerary was Sam's Re-Nu-All, a shoe repair shop that was established on a foundation of hope and that has endured for 80 years on a business plan drawn on family values. The first shoe repair store opened by Mugerdich Samuelian was tucked beneath the stairwell of a pool hall located in the Grand Central Hotel on Fulton Street. Young Samuelian opened the small business after being told that a long-promised vacation had to be postponed. Samuelian was a dedicated employee and probably wouldn't have minded taking his vacation at another time if the circumstances had been different. But this wasn't just any vacation; this was his honeymoon.

Mugerdich (Sam) Samuelian stands proudly in front of his selection of fine leather goods. *c. 1940*

Samuelian had plans to marry his sweetheart, Dovey, and when the store owner for whom he worked gave the ultimatum that the vacation was off or Sam would lose his job, Sam decided his bride was more important. The decision not only turned him into a married man, it transformed him into an independent business owner.

Although she was primarily a homemaker, Samuelian's new wife pitched in to provide a service that women of today will probably never be called on to perform. In the early 1920s women presented themselves in public wearing conservative attire and the glimpse of an uncovered ankle was considered provocative. To help women feel more comfortable about sitting in the shop without shoes while her husband made repairs, Dovey made coverlets for the women to drape over their feet. About the size of a pillow case and trimmed in satin, the coverlets became another reason that the shoe repair shop became a success.

Samuelian escaped a volatile era in the history of his native Armenia and arrived in the United States without money or a command of English. Although filled with hope and armed with diligence, there were times in America that were reminiscent of the turmoil and prejudice left behind in Armenia. Refugees were often unwelcome in America and for a time Samuelian endured broken windows and threats. His reaction to the prejudice was to tell his family to be patient. "They will come to know us in time," Samuelian assured his wife, "and when they know us they will love us." The wisdom proved sound, and after a time the same neighbors who hurled rocks and cruel words came to be patrons and friends of the Samuelian family.

The little shop gained a reputation for using the best leather in its repairs and for quickly repairing customers' shoes. This wasn't always easy. During World War II everything, including leather goods, was rationed. For a time the front of Sam's shoe repair store looked more like the entrance to a movie theater. People stood in long lines waiting to get shoes repaired, knowing that short supplies mandated a first come, first served policy.

In 1945 Sam's Re-Nu-All moved to its third location on Mariposa Street to accommodate a larger selection of merchandise.

The Mariposa location relieved traffic jams and welcomed the introduction of luggage into the new store.

While customers waited, Sam worked as fast as he could without sacrificing quality. When the war and rationing ended, customers were able once again to drop off their repairs without fear of losing their places in line, or being turned away because the ration of materials had been depleted. The end of the war also saw the return of Samuelian's three sons, Morris, Harold and Richard, who joined the family business.

Interestingly, while the conclusion of the war cured the long lines, a new challenge presented itself when the repair store was cited by the city for causing traffic jams. A steady stream of customers would double-park while dropping off their shoes and the city appealed to Sam to find some way to get his customers to stop tying up traffic. There wasn't much the family could do except tell customers about the city's reprimand. Eventually the problem was solved when the store moved to its present location where a large parking lot is available.

Over the years the small shoe repair shop has gone from a basement to a street front location, and finally to a stand-alone building. The business itself also evolved with the times, changing from little more than a simple cobbler's bench to a luggage showroom. Men and women still bring in their shoes, but the repairs now include purses, briefcases, suitcases and just about anything made of leather.

The small town of Fresno has grown into a metropolis of more than 700,000 people, but when asked, most of them know exactly where Sam's Luggage is located on Blackstone Avenue. The store has made a lasting impression on many people who have been just passing through as well. Sam's has come to the rescue of such famous visitors as Red Skelton, Victor Borge, Bob Hope and California Secretary of State Bill Jones. Once, the renowned trumpeter Dizzy Gillespie was in town to give a performance and he spent a whole evening with the Samuelian family while a piece of luggage was being repaired.

Even those who move away from the Fresno area continue to be patrons of Sam's. The store receives weekly packages containing merchandise in need of repair from such places as far away as Montana and Arizona.

As with most businesses, the store has adapted to better meet the needs of its customers. After introducing luggage, a natural progression was to begin carrying accessories such as travel clocks, passport holders and other conveniences for people on the move.

By the 1970s there were nine members of the Samuelian family working in the store. Even those who aren't directly related have been with the business long enough to be considered family, with one salesperson boasting 30 years and the current shoe cobbler having 42 years on the job. "This is a happy, joyous business," smiles the present manager of the store, Merlene Samuelian. "Our customers are loyal and it's still a family business."

(Left to right)
Brothers Richard, Morris and Harold Samuelian

Valley Lahvosh Baking Company

The story of Valley Lahvosh Baking Company began in the early 1900s when thousands of Armenians fled to America, seeking to escape massacre at the hands of the occupying Turkish forces. One of these Armenians was master baker Gazair Saghatelian who came to the United States in 1905 with only the shirt on his back, his recipes in his pocket, his life experience in his head and his young family in his heart. After several years of hard work and unflagging optimism he was able to buy a corner lot in the heart of Fresno's Armenian Town to begin his dream of opening a bakery. In February 1922 the warm fragrance of freshly baked Peda bread and Lahvosh crackerbread filled the neighborhood, signaling the opening of Gazair's new venture, which he named California Baking Company.

The bakers, drivers and delivery trucks in front of the bakery c. 1930

Gazair's signature bread was named Peda, a recipe he developed to mark the beginning of his new business in America. Starting with one of his old recipes, he formed each loaf by hand, adding milk wash to give the loaf gloss and finishing with a sprinkling of sesame seeds. At first the center of his new bread would rise too high, a problem solved by gently pressing a circular indentation in the center of each unbaked loaf of Peda. This signature characteristic survives to this day, and the center of each loaf of Peda remains everyone's favorite part of this truly original hearth bread.

Gazair Saghatelian was a dynamic man, full of energy and drive — a natural leader. He was constantly seeking ways to improve his business, and California Baking Company was one of the earliest local companies to put delivery trucks into service. By doing so, he was able to fulfill the demand for his fine breads.

Gazair was also a generous and giving man. During the Great Depression when everyone was struggling to make ends meet, Gazair would provide his bakers lunches of freshly cooked lamb and fresh Peda bread in addition to their wages. Many children were offered jobs at the bakery in exchange for 25 cents and two loaves of Peda, giving those youngsters a chance to help their families. To this day visitors stop by the bakery to tell stories of how Gazair left bread at the doorsteps of neighboring families during those difficult times.

Gazair and his wife, Haiganoush, raised six children in a house adjacent to the bakery. After Gazair's death in 1945 his eldest son, Samuel, took over the business, eventually renaming it Valley Bakery. Sam baked bread alongside his bakers every day of his life, passing on in 1982 at the age of 64. He maintained the traditions and baking techniques of his father, ensuring that each loaf was made by hand and using the finest ingredients.

Gazair's youngest daughter, Janet, has managed the bakery ever since. Janet has been working at the bakery since she was 10 years old, and has been working full time since the age of 12. Like the Saghatelians before her, Janet wanted to leave her own mark on the business, and decided that she wanted to expand the offerings of her bakery's crackerbread, known as Valley Lahvosh. After developing a wide array of new sizes, Janet hit on what would become her signature product — heart-shaped Lahvosh crackerbread called, naturally — Hearts! The development of a heart shape was a nod to Janet's longtime love of all things heart-shaped, stemming from her principle that one should always follow one's heart. Valley Lahvosh Hearts are now the flagship product baked by the family business that Janet renamed Valley Lahvosh Baking Company.

Armed with this and other new products, in the summer of 1982 Janet decided to take her family legacy on the road, "breaking bread" at food shows with chefs, caterers, food editors — anyone who valued a quality product. Janet received extensive media coverage in publications like the *Los Angeles Times* and *Better Homes and Gardens* for popularizing Armenian sandwiches known as Valley Wraps or caravans. *Sunset Magazine* ran a feature on Janet's recipe for Fresno's Super Sandwich, a family-sized sandwich using Peda bread, and *Victoria Magazine* featured Janet's Hearts.

Taking what she had learned on the road to heart, Janet next developed a soft, flexible, high-moisture variety of her Valley Lahvosh crackerbread called Valley Wraps. It is this innovative product that is credited with starting the very popular wrap-sandwich trend, and is among Valley Lahvosh Baking Company's most popular products.

Over the years Valley Lahvosh has achieved tremendous growth.

Gazair Saghatelian, the baker from Armenia who began this thriving business

Gazair's youngest daughter, Janet, pictured here in the retail store in the early 1960s, operates Valley Lahvosh Baking Company today.

Agnes C. Saghatelian, executive vice president and daughter of Janet, granddaughter of Gazair

The original corner bakery has expanded to occupy the entire block, but still sits on the same property, still features its corner store and still uses some of the original equipment that started a family legacy. The overhead proofer that Gazair installed in 1932 is still used daily as the bread rises on its way to the ovens.

Today Janet is still active in the company, but day-to-day responsibilities have been assumed by her daughter, Agnes. Born in 1969, Agnes graduated from California State University, Fresno, with a degree in business. True to the family tradition, Agnes has been working at the bakery since she was a young girl of 14. She continues to gain experience and knowledge, carrying on her grandfather's legacy by committing herself to the family business, anxious to make her mark in the years ahead.

Having won many awards over the years for its quality products, Valley Lahvosh ended the 20th century with the honor of receiving the American Tasting Institute's (ATI) Best of Show Award for its entire product line. The company received two of ATI's highest honors, having both its Valley Lahvosh crackerbread and Valley Wrap flatbread declared the finest made in America.

BennettFrost Personnel Services

BennettFrost Personnel Services has been an asset to the greater Fresno business community since its establishment in 1992. From its beginning, the company philosophy has been to be honest, treat people with respect and meet the staffing needs of the business community it serves. BennettFrost has been so successful with this concept it was granted Fresno Compact's Outstanding Business/School Partnership Award in 1999. The Fresno Compact Award, sponsored by *The Fresno Bee*, honors companies for preparing students for the increasing demands of society and the workplace. Much of this success is a result of the dynamic and effective team that has been put together by owner Cathy Bennett Frost.

The staff at the Fresno office of BennettFrost Personnel Services is shown in its recently expanded facilities.

Cathy established her company with a staff of two, and now has 25 full-time employees at four locations. The main office in Fresno has outgrown its facilities three times, and the company has expanded to offices in Visalia and Clovis. BennettFrost has an on-site management agreement with the newly built Valley Children's Hospital in Madera County. Hundreds of people are placed annually in clerical, administrative, medical, industrial and manufacturing positions. As a service business dedicated to solving clients' problems, BennettFrost is held in the highest regard among employers. BennettFrost is noted for treating both business clients and field associates in a fair and professional manner.

The company has consistently expanded the number and kinds of services offered. BennettFrost began with placement of temporary workers to fill a need for well-screened and well-tested clerical office personnel. This was followed quickly with the same caliber of medical office personnel. From initially providing temporary workers and temp-to-hire services, the company has expanded to also provide direct-hire personnel, payroll services, credit and background checks as well as applicant screening and testing. It has recently added permanent-placement service to its temporary personnel placement and is able to match employees to job specifications for companies that want to hire permanent workers. Finding people with skills in computer-related fields continues to be a demand, and the company stays involved with schools to find the workers that are needed. The creation of partnerships with employers, including Valley Children's Hospital, benefits both the employer and BennettFrost. Having on-site offices at clients' businesses ensures that workers will be available when needed.

The staff in the Clovis office places people in manufacturing and light industrial positions.

High ethical standards and certification of staff members are part of the company's policy. Staff members are always encouraged to think creatively to find innovative solutions to clients' staffing needs. They are continually challenged to accept the next level of responsibility to improve customer service for both field associates and employer clients. The staff is the backbone of the company and is noted for going above and beyond the expected. The staff works as a team, respecting its diversity and strengths. Staff members receive training in upgrading skills and tuition reimbursement for pursuing related education.

Cathy Frost, president of BennettFrost Personnel Services

BennettFrost is a company where people who have difficulty finding jobs on their own can turn for a chance to become productive members of the community. The staff specializes in making people feel good about themselves and giving them a chance to succeed. In turn, the company has helped hundreds of businesses find temporary and permanent employees.

BennettFrost contributes to a number of community organizations including Fresno Rescue Mission. It assists graduates of the Probation Education and Employment Program in finding jobs. Cathy Frost is respected in the community as a person with high integrity and values. She has dedicated herself not only to her company and the businesses it serves, but also to the greater community. As the first female president of the Fresno Metropolitan Museum, and the vice chair of the New United Way campaign, she is esteemed as a benchmark of Fresno's women in business. Cathy Frost and her staff serve on many other community boards and committees, including State Center Community College District, KVPR (Valley Public Radio), Fresno Women's Network, Marjaree Mason Center and Area Agency on Aging. The company supports the River Parkway Trust, the renovation of the Coke Hollowell Education Center as well as the beautification of the highways.

The success of BennettFrost can be attributed to people — people with a vision for business, people growing through efforts of a service-oriented team, and people who serve valley employers with the skills and training needed for the jobs. People who need work are placed in good jobs. Companies needing trained personnel are receiving the best available. Cathy Bennett Frost has realized her vision of establishing a business serving the community by providing skilled workers and providing valley job seekers the opportunity to find employment.

The Visalia office staff shown here is a major part of the BennettFrost team.

Ivory Global Capital Group

In the blink of an eye the present becomes the past and the future becomes the present. Mankind has always been fascinated by thoughts of what that future holds. While the future remains impossible to predict, one can always plan for it. Helping people to shape the future is what Ivory Global Capital Group is all about.

With an in-depth analysis of a client's investment options, as well as a long, hard look at what that individual can expect to receive from company retirement pensions and social security benefits, Joe Rivera and Jimmy Wong can help determine what a client may require to meet their needs and maintain their lifestyle at retirement and provide a clearly defined plan to get them there.

While many people seem to think that financial planning is something they can't afford, Rivera and Wong are living proof that it's within anyone's reach. Both California State University, Fresno, alumni, they come from vastly differing backgrounds — with one thing in common — each has proven by example that it's possible to overcome diversity to shape their own destiny.

Joe Rivera, CFP, helps clients plan for the future.

Born in Hong Kong, Wong immigrated with his family to Fresno in 1969. His relatives referred to America as the "Mountain of Gold" — a land glimmering with opportunity and possibility.

Living the American dream, Wong enrolled in college, but he grew restless during undergraduate studies and quit college to go to work. After two years of intense work and little or no vacation time, he realized that his career path was not meeting his expectations. Tired and burned out, Wong purchased a $99 ticket to New York for a two-week break that would define his future.

An early fascination with the mysteries of the stock market led Wong to Wall Street. During the oil crisis of the early 70s, Wong had become mesmerized by the variety of world events that affected the wildly fluctuating oil prices. "I touched that stone wall in front of the New York Stock Exchange and everything changed in that moment," says Wong. Upon arriving home he gave two weeks notice at his job and embarked upon studies in finance. He has since earned the titles of certified financial planner and certified fund specialist.

For Rivera, becoming a certified financial planner not only meant a brighter future for himself, but the opportunity to help other Hispanics build a better tomorrow.

Born and raised in Delano, California, Rivera is a first-generation Mexican-American, the son of migrant farm workers who worked the fields from elementary school through high school. He realized early on that he wanted something more for the rest of his life and he knew that education was the way to get it.

When a family friend offered Rivera a job in a shoe store, he jumped at it. "Here was my chance to get out of the fields," he said, "to work in a business where I could wear a white shirt and tie." From there, he went into an area of business that he saw was vastly under-represented by Latinos, thriving on the challenge of succeeding in an area that is not common ground for his peers. He earned a bachelor's degree in marketing at California State University, Fresno, and earned his certification in certified financial planning through the University of Southern California.

The two met as co-workers at another company in 1985. However, with the unique ability that each has to envision a more valuable future, they saw a better possibility for themselves — a business of their own, providing advisory services that include asset allocation, estate planning, retirement planning, and managing pension funds for nonprofit organizations, corporations and municipalities, as well as for individuals.

In 1990 the two joined forces to form Ivory Global Capital Group, a Registered Investment Advisory firm offering a broad spectrum of financial planning and investment advisory services to individuals, corporations, municipalities, pension funds and small businesses, utilizing an approach that combines professional risk management with fundamental research and analysis. Investment portfolios are designed to strive to maximize growth during rising markets and strive to minimize the volatility of client assets during declining market situations.

Today's burgeoning Internet access has spawned a developing trend in do-it-yourself investing. Ivory Global feels one drawback to that approach is that most people lack the time and education to keep on

WHILE MANY PEOPLE SEEM TO THINK THAT FINANCIAL PLANNING IS SOMETHING THEY CAN'T AFFORD, RIVERA AND WONG ARE LIVING PROOF THAT IT'S WITHIN ANYONE'S REACH.

top of the field, not to mention a lack of objectivity. Truly keeping up with the markets and maintaining broad exposure to the variety of available options is a full-time job.

Investment planning is a very dynamic arena. An investment vehicle that was very popular a year ago may be more vulnerable in today's market. And because the stock market has climbed for several years straight doesn't mean it will continue. His job, says Wong, is to provide access to information his clients may not have, and to use his experience to

Jimmy Wong, CFP, provides access to information his clients may not have.

interpret what that information might mean to the client's future. In addition, a professional will bring to the table investment opportunities the client may not have considered.

Wong and Rivera constantly monitor and analyze the markets and trends, and clients' accounts are reviewed on a monthly basis and modified accordingly. They believe they are able to find an easier path to the goal because they're out there every day looking for opportunities and watching for danger signs.

Compared to those companies that work on a commission-only basis, Ivory Global Capital Group is able to maintain maximum objectivity and flexibility when devising an investment plan. Rivera's and Wong's salary is based on total assets managed, creating great incentive to perform for their clients.

It also means the universe of options doesn't shrink to only those products that will pay them a commission. They can make the best choices from all possible options, even keeping a client's money out of the market if it's the safest choice at the time. Rivera says it allows him to look out for his clients on a short-term, mid-term and long-term basis, rather than just trying to make a sale today.

The future is only a moment away. Ivory Global Capital Group is helping clients determine what the future will hold. Advisory services are offered through Ivory Global Capital Group. Securities are offered through the Mutual Services Corporation, a member of the NASD/SIPC.

Manco Abbott, Inc.

In an area where service is rendered, Manco Abbott has distinguished itself in the real estate management field. Maintaining its high level of community involvement, Manco continually endeavors to make central California a better place to live while it conducts business as the area's premier property management firm. The company, established in 1972 as Manco West, exhibits a genuinely caring attitude combined with corporate sophistication and professionalism. These elements combine to mark its accomplishments and relationships with many satisfied clients. The largest real estate management firm serving the San Joaquin Valley and central California coast has its headquarters in Fresno with branch offices in Bakersfield, Stockton and Carmel.

Manco Abbott, Inc. — established 1972

Manco Abbott's mission is to enhance the value of clients' real estate assets. It accomplishes this by providing a range of services tailored to a client's needs through an individualized management plan. The firm manages shopping centers, apartments, industrial complexes and office buildings. It handles day-to-day operation of the properties, provides high-quality maintenance supervision, expertly monitors the market to optimize rent levels and consults with owners on methods to increase income. Manco Abbott delivers more than just the standard in its proactive, problem-solving support for the highest level of quality services in central California.

Property managers are the everpresent caretakers, maintaining and cutting costs to defend a property's value. They are the evervigilant professionals seeking methods to stimulate income and increase asset value. In this often unheralded field, Manco Abbott has distinguished itself through its exceptional efforts and results. With three decades of experience, Manco Abbott knows and understands its business and marketplace and has the vision and professional expertise to make the difference.

In all accords dealing with this type of service, actions may speak louder than words, but results tell a story of success. When it took over the management of a drug-infested, run-down and bankrupt apartment complex in Tehachapi, the firm's creativity, expertise and hard work turned things around in an astonishing fashion. The occupancy rate rose from below 20 percent to above 80 percent, and the bank was able to sell the property for its intended asking price — all this in a relatively short span of time.

Manco Abbott achieved results of a similar nature when it took over management of one of the largest apartment complexes in Fresno. The property had fallen into foreclosure and was more than 25 percent vacant. Manco turned it around, bringing the occupancy rate up to more than 96 percent. The one-time problem property was sold for more than $18 million.

These turnarounds not only demonstrate the firm's ability to perform for its clients, they also improve the quality of life in the community. Manco Abbott took properties which were full of blight, contributing to neighborhood neglect and crime, and made them whole again, improving living conditions for the entire area.

The company's two principals bring varied yet complementary talents to the table. Hal Kissler, certified property manager (CPM), chief executive officer and the company's original founder, is a graduate of California State University, Fresno. Kissler has an extensive background in investment counseling, business and real estate management. He is a past president of the local chapter of the Institute of Real Estate Management(IREM). Hal has been a stalwart member of the local community for many years. His openhearted generosity and tremendous affection for the Fresno area have made an imprint on the firm's business philosophy.

Michael S. Goldfarb, CPM, chief operating officer, has decades of experience at the highest corporate level in property management. He is a past president of Security Management, one of the country's largest property management companies and also has served as president of Florida's largest multifamily housing developer. He is a past president of the Fresno IREM chapter and a past director of the California Apartment Association — Fresno.

Kissler and Goldfarb have both received CPM "Man of the Year," awards from the Institute of Real Estate Management. They both possess the expertise and experience to fully understand client needs and market fluctuations. Their management skill has kept Manco Abbott on track during its steady growth and has helped clients achieve their objectives.

Manco Abbott has gathered a top-flight group of professionals to round out the executive management team. Maureen Spenhoff, chief financial officer, has been with Manco for over 17 years; Gloria Schermerhorn, executive vice president, and Judy Russell, human resources manager, both have 20 plus years with the firm. In fact, employees at all levels have been with the company for decades. These include among others: Robyn Popp, assistant controller; Jamie Rohrer, assistant; and Valerie Hirning, manager. Tenure among these and other dedicated and valued individuals combine to demonstrate substantial stability and commitment to corporate objectives. Key players hold the prestigious designations of CPM, certified shopping center manager (CSM) and certified commercial investment manager (CCIM). Real estate managers administer clients' individualized management plans. They are supported by technical personnel in such areas as engineering, supervision, accounting, data processing and legal affairs.

Owners must be kept informed and their desires implemented effectively. Proper communication is essential. Manco Abbott provides monthly reports, statistical information and comparative studies on property operations, using state-of-the-art real estate management systems. The reports detail an analysis of each month's operation results, income and expense levels and budget variances. These key indicators focus on the progress of each investment as measured against the individualized management plan.

Manco Abbott counts as clients firms such as Ralph's Grocery Co., Bank of America, Lendlease, Wells Fargo Bank, Wilson Development, ICI Development, Koll Investment Management, Betty Galanté, Leeds & Strauss and many others. Manco Abbott is noted for its outstanding, personal service regardless of the size of the real estate investment managed.

Manco Abbott's civic involvement goes beyond sprucing up neighborhoods. Kissler feels very strongly about giving back to the community. The company has been very active in its support of worthwhile organizations and charitable endeavors.

The community achievement of which the firm is most proud is the Marjaree Mason Thrift Store. The company has adopted the struggling thrift shop. Every Manco Abbott employee was asked to work in the store a minimum of four hours on company time. The efforts from approximately 30 Fresno-area Manco Abbott employees contributed hundreds of hours. Their service, which varied from folding clothes to management duties, helped to transform the thrift shop from a financial drain to a moneymaker. It now generates revenue that helps the Marjaree Mason Center with clothing and other needs required of its domestic violence shelter's occupants. The positive results tell a wonderful story of caring and giving to a community it serves.

Manco Abbott strives to increase the value of its clients assets and the value of life in the community — making Fresno a better place to live and demonstrating that property management is more than just managing property.

Delivering the highest level of quality services

Fresno Metropolitan Museum of Art, History and Science

A new era in Fresno's cultural development began in 1976 when local visionary Lewis S. Eaton gathered a group of civic leaders to explore the possibility of creating a regional museum for the San Joaquin Valley. Although generations of valley residents had aspired to build a museum, this desire had never taken shape. Now, working from a needs assessment study, this committee concluded that a museum program in art, history and science was needed to fill the cultural void in the area.

When Eaton learned that the McClatchy Broadcasting Corporation was planning to demolish its 85,000-square-foot Fresno Bee newspaper building in downtown Fresno, he thought the building could be a suitable site for the new museum. He contacted C.K. McClatchy and asked him to postpone demolition until he could have the building inspected and the committee could test community support for the project. McClatchy agreed to postpone demolition while these investigations took place. Although some community leaders were concerned with the location of the building, most enthusiastically supported the plan. Recognizing the community support, McClatchy offered to donate the building and passed title to the Fresno Regional Foundation, a local philanthropic group.

The Fresno Bee, 1939

Constructed in 1922 for $1 million by George D. Hudnett, Inc. of Sacramento, the Fresno Bee building is designed in Italian Renaissance style. Its five-story brick structure is adorned with arched windows, terra-cotta ornaments and a recessed porch and balcony. The interior of the building was remodeled several times to suit the needs of the growing newspaper and the addition of KMJ Radio. Located on the southwest corner of Van Ness and Calaveras, this property was originally owned by Edward Schwarz, a German immigrant who moved to Fresno to establish a beer garden. When he decided to build his establishment at Fresno and Fulton streets, he sold the land to McClatchy Broadcasting Corp.

After the acquisition of the building, museum organization began. In June 1979 the museum was chartered as a nonprofit entity. A board of directors was seated in March 1980 with Eaton as its first president. The new board adopted a mission statement that defined the direction of the museum as a diverse educational institution preserving and exhibiting objects of art, history and science for the Central Valley. To fulfill the board's directive for preserving Fresno's history, the Fresno Historical Society became the overseer of the history division of the museum in 1981, adding its large collection of Fresno-area archives and artifacts to the growing museum collection. In April, title to the building was transferred to the board and in May, Donald Brewer, an experienced museum administrator, was hired as executive director.

The architectural firm of Allen Lew and William Patnaude, Inc. was hired to draw up renovation plans, with costs estimated at between $4 and $5 million. To pay for building expenses, the museum began a fund drive raising $5.5 million between 1981 and 1985. In 1982 the board of directors hired J.E. Ethridge Co. of Clovis to begin converting 30,000 square feet from newsroom into galleries, service facilities and storage rooms. During the renovation process, the museum board held open house tours for the public that proved to be both educational and useful in building community support for the project.

During this period, the acquisitions committee acquired the nucleus of the permanent collection. Oscar and Maria Salzer, Los Angeles art collectors who were friends of museum director Brewer, donated 60 European and American still life and trompe l'oeil paintings (17th to the 20th centuries). Michael and Jeanne Adams and Anne Adams Helms began the Met's photographic collection with an important selection of Ansel Adams prints. Other collections consisted of motorcycle, hot rod and racecar models and antique woodworking tools.

The Met Research Library's collection began at the same time with a 500-volume California history library donated by Virginia Best Adams, wife of Ansel Adams. In addition to their art donation, Oscar and Maria Salzer also gave 20 years of volumes of the finest art magazines published. Don and Polly Brewer donated their collection of 400 art exhibition catalogs, monographs on artists and their work, and books on modern and contemporary American and European art. Adding to this eclectic collection, the research library received the original historic books and records of the Fresno Musical Club and examples of women's period clothing from the 1870s through the 1920s, given by the Fresno Historical Society.

A grand opening of the Fresno Metropolitan Museum of Art, History and Science was held in 1984, with a gala celebration involving the citizens of Fresno. Opening exhibitions included objects from the permanent collection, as well as exhibits of jade pieces from the National Museum of History of the Republic of China, space exploration photographs from the National Aeronautics and Space Administration (NASA) and the *Spirit of Fresno* airplane, a predecessor to Lindbergh's *Spirit of St. Louis*.

The Met continues to expand its physical parameters, as well as the scope of its educational programs. Dedicated to serving the diverse population of the Central Valley, the museum board has formed a citizens' advisory committee for exhibitions and education, and a marketing and outreach committee that has several ethnic community leaders as members. It has earned an outstanding reputation for multicultural exhibitions and programs, bilingual docents and presentations that are not language-dependent. In addition, the Reeves Exploration Center in the Rotary Play Yard Science Gallery provides easy access to hands-on exhibitions that have inspired hundreds of visitors, including those who are partially sited, deaf, or who have difficulty walking.

The San Joaquin Valley has long been the leading agricultural region in the country. There has been strong support from the community for several years to develop a plan for an agricultural museum in Fresno. In 1995 the Met secured a $1 million grant from the California Department of Parks & Recreation to build the California State Agricultural Museum in collaboration with California State University, Fresno. The museum will focus on education and science and offer hands-on programs that bring a greater understanding of the role agriculture plays in the Central Valley's history, as well as its importance in the world today.

The Fresno Metropolitan Museum opened in 1984.

The Fresno Metropolitan Museum of Art, History and Science has evolved into a premier cultural institution for the Central Valley. In 1995, the Met won Northern California's Award for Excellence in nonprofit management from Chevron and The Management Center of San Francisco, the first organization outside of the Bay Area to be so honored. In the same year, the Met also received a Central California Excellence in Business Award from *The Fresno Bee*.

Dinosaur Exhibition at the Fresno Met

San Joaquin Memorial High School

San Joaquin Memorial High School is a Catholic, coeducational, four-year college-preparatory high school offering an excellent curriculum for holistic education. Its goal is to encourage and direct students to become responsible members of, and contributors to, family, church and society while developing an authentic self-image, a respect for learning and a sense of justice. Owned and operated by the Roman Catholic Diocese of Fresno, the school is grounded in building a community of faith and service.

San Joaquin Memorial High School was founded by the diocese in 1945, staffed by Sisters of the Holy Cross, the De La Salle Christian Brothers and lay faculty. The Christian Brothers operated the school until 1998. San Joaquin Memorial opened for the 1945-46 academic year with 270 students. Though the school was proud of its 30 students in the first graduating class, enrollment has grown steadily each year to the present.

The beautifully landscaped campus of tile-roofed buildings is located in central Fresno, with adjacent access to three freeways. Designed by architect David Horn, the original Spanish-Mission styling is set off by shade trees and wide expanses of lawn adorned with marble statuary. The mid-60s saw facility growth when a cafeteria and auditorium were added along with expansion of athletic facilities. Other additions occurred in the 1980s when the Mary Alice Diener Media Center and science wing were built to complete the campus as it stands today.

The entrance of San Joaquin Memorial High School attests to its early California architecture and beautiful landscaping.

The high school attracts students from as far away as Visalia, Coarsegold, Hanford and Dos Palos. Some of these commuters drive the hour or so to the campus, and others prefer the option of taking the train to Fresno.

The outstanding faculty and staff are dedicated to encouraging each student to grow in self-discipline within the learning environment. A tutoring program in mathematics and English skills helps each student achieve the highest levels of college preparatory education. The student body is relatively small, with a current enrollment of approximately 700 students. The 1999 senior class consisted of 162 graduates, 98 percent of whom enrolled in two-year or four-year colleges. This is indicative of the historical percentage of San Joaquin graduates who go on to higher education. A high number of alumni remain in the community, and many are working in the public school sector of the Central Valley.

Along with the basic curriculum focusing on mathematics, English, science and social science, classes in religion are also a requirement. The Religious Education Program encompasses all aspects of school life in a Roman Catholic environment. It is based on the belief that whatever is done for the advancement of civilization and culture is within the realm of the church. Every service San Joaquin Memorial offers is judged within the context of these criteria, and is designed with the cooperation of all families in mind. The intellectual development of a student's religious character is enhanced through the Religious Studies Department. Studies include: Jewish and Christian scripture, doctrine, the sacraments, morality and Christian action. Daily Masses are offered. The Music Department, which is currently expanding and growing, reaches out to many students with a wide variety of classes. The library houses computers and provides Internet access for students. In addition to honoring a valedictorian, achievement awards are granted to individuals in each graduating class. These include Christian Character Awards and Student Leadership Awards. The top academic award is for General Academic Excellence, given to the senior with the highest cumulative grade point average.

Sports are important components of a well-rounded student education.

Student activities are a vital part of the growth of the individual and approximately 80 percent of the student body is active in clubs and organizations. These groups include: the Art Club — offering art workshops, field trips and community service projects; Block M — comprised of students who have earned a varsity letter; the Drama Club — fostering theater crafts; the Foreign Language Club — promoting Spanish and French culture; the Forensics Club — assisting in public speaking and debate; the Key Club — encouraging community service projects; the Nature Club —providing hiking and outdoor recreation; the Red and Blue — providing opportunities to participate in the school newspaper; the Science Club — exploring the field of science; and Pep and Cheer — enhancing school spirit at athletic games.

Service clubs are but one way for the student to be involved. San Joaquin also offers a full athletic curriculum. The teams have won the league trophy for overall sports for several years, and dominate the area's sports in football, baseball and track, winning championships many times. The school believes athletic participation is critical in the development of teamwork, sportsmanship and the desire to win tempered with the ability to graciously deal with defeat. The desired result is the development of personal values and the ability to work well with others. The athletic program is backed by strong alumni loyalty.

The Guidance and Counseling Department provides individualized services, assisting students to deal effectively with the problems facing high school students in today's society, whether they are academic, personal, or related to college and career. Teen support groups discuss issues such as drug and alcohol abuse, divorce, death and grief. The department enables students to become more acutely aware of their self-worth, interests and abilities, and to realize their maximum potential.

As a school that is administered by the Diocese of Fresno, San Joaquin promotes itself as a witness to Christ, but admits students of any religious orientation. The mission statement of San Joaquin Memorial states that every student is a child of God and has equal dignity and an inalienable right to the best education possible. The school exists to support and complement parents in their primary responsibility of educating their children. The underlying philosophy of preparing the minds, hearts and hands of the students helps them live wisely and generously in a technologically complex and interdependent world.

State-of-the-art technology is readily available for all students.

San Joaquin Valley College

In April 1977 Robert and Shirley Perry became pioneers in the field of vocational career training for the San Joaquin Valley. With their goal of providing quality education to students from diverse ethnic, cultural and educational backgrounds, they developed short-term career training that qualifies graduates to enter their chosen vocations. As a result, they established the first campus of San Joaquin Valley College in Visalia, offering a medical assistant program that filled a critical need in the community. Enrollment and curriculum quickly expanded. Within a few months they added complete dental assistant and respiratory therapy technician programs and, after only two years, received national accreditation from the Accrediting Bureau of Health Education Schools.

Robert and Shirley Perry's desire to meet the needs of students and professionals in other areas of the valley led them to establish a Bakersfield campus in November 1981. Building on the college's ability to adjust rapidly to the changing needs of industry and the employment interests of students, this branch of San Joaquin Valley College began to offer programs in dental assisting, medical assisting, business administration and secretarial services.

Providing health, business and technical training programs for brighter futures

Expanding further to the greater Fresno area, they opened the Fresno campus in April 1985, offering health, business and technical courses. The immediate success of this campus caused it to quickly outgrow its capacity. In January 1996 the college moved into a new 36,000-square-foot site with over 200 parking spaces. This new expansion allowed the college to enhance its curriculum with programs such as electronics technology and network systems administration.

The desire to offer an even more diversified curriculum led the college to initiate the Aviation Branch campus, located at the Fresno Air Terminal. This FAA-approved airframe and power plant technician program started in a separate classroom, which became a branch campus in 1993.

In May 1995 the ownership of San Joaquin Valley College changed to a second generation of the Perry family when Mark and Mike Perry, sons of Robert and Shirley, purchased the college from their parents. Mark took over the duties of President, while Mike serves as CEO. Their continuing objective is to maintain excellence in education by improving classroom facilities, equipment, curriculum, faculty and staff. They are also committed to assisting graduates in obtaining satisfying and rewarding positions compatible with their selected career goals through a full-time Employment Services Department.

Sons of the educational community in which they grew up, Mark and Mike Perry desired to further expand the scope of San Joaquin Valley College. "It has been said, 'Nothing attracts students like quality,' and we're proud of the reputation San Joaquin Valley College has garnered with its high standards of instruction and superior service to students," states Mark. In response to this mission, the college has continued to build a broad-spectrum vocational training curriculum in the health, business and technical fields that leads to an associate's degree.

In June 1995 its educational excellence was rewarded when all campuses received regional accreditation from the Accrediting Commission for Community and Junior Colleges of the Western Association of Schools and Colleges. In addition, the college maintains accreditation for many individual programs.

Owners Mark Perry, President, and Mike Perry, CEO

In 1997 at the suggestion of the Tulare/Kings Dental Society, the original Visalia campus expanded to include a new 16,000-square-foot health science facility, and became the first private junior college in the nation to offer a dental hygiene program. Here students receive professional training while utilizing public participation in strengthening their skills. The following services are offered to the public at large and individuals referred through agencies and businesses: clinical exams and medical histories, X-rays, teeth cleaning and polishing, fluoride treatments, sealants and preventative dentistry education.

San Joaquin Valley College's programs are offered under three learning divisions: health, business and technology. Health programs in the fields of dental assisting and dental hygiene, health technology, medical assisting, vocational nursing, respiratory care, surgical technology and veterinary technology prepare students for many opportunities in an expanding job market. These classes give students experience in hands-on learning, using modern equipment and supplies under actual working conditions. Professionals in a variety of health care fields also act as advisers to each program, ensuring academic quality.

The business division consists of varied classes covering business administration, administrative office professions, corrections, health care administration, health care insurance, travel and hospitality, and emergency services and safety management. Students develop the ability to use the latest office technology and computer software in organizing tasks and managing information for a number of working environments. Continuing to focus on hands-on training, students are able to take advantage of the school's fully equipped computer labs for practical applications.

The technical division offers training in computer support technology, electronic engineering technology, refrigeration and air conditioning technology, and information systems engineering. These specialized fields use technical theory, as well as applied concepts, to prepare students for careers that meet the changing needs of employers. The refrigeration and air conditioning technology program is one of the highest rated in the nation.

Year-round enrollment, accelerated programs and flexible class hours accommodate students' lifestyles er period of time than traditional higher education. In addition to rigorous coursework, San Joaquin Valley College offers student development, advising and guidance programs that are designed to assist students in discovering their aptitudes, vocational preferences and life goals. The employment services department prepares graduates to present themselves and their qualifications to prospective employers after comprehensive job search training that includes resume preparation, interview coaching, networking skills, salary negotiation and self-marketing.

Through ongoing development of instruction and services, Robert and Shirley Perry's vision for the college is steadily being fulfilled. San Joaquin Valley College has grown into an institution that is vital to the lifeblood of the Central Valley's business community. Eloquently articulating the Perry philosophy, Shirley Perry stated, "Whether it be San Joaquin Valley College or some other college, you will never receive anything so important as an education, our country's most important resource." The school's success continues to be the shining reality of their hard-fought dream.

Urology Associates of Central California

Urology Associates of Central California premiered in 1998 as the only facility of its kind in the Central Valley, representing the collaboration of nine of the valley's finest urology physicians. This state-of-the-art facility provides thousands of Central Valley residents a specialized setting for patient examinations, diagnostic testing and minor treatment, and offers a licensed ambulatory surgery center.

The synergy and convenience of having nine urological specialists available at one location also allow patients to have access to the finest, most technologically advanced equipment available. For example, until recently surgery was the only method available to remove kidney stones. Today, a new noninvasive technique is available and has been hailed as a revolutionary medical advancement in patient safety and comfort. Lithotripsy therapy generates low-energy shockwave impulses that focus on breaking the kidney stone into tiny particles that can be passed through the urinary tract. The lithotripter at Urology Associates is the only one stationed in the Central Valley.

Urology Associates of Central California is located off Maple and Herndon avenues in northeast Fresno.

Urology Associates keeps 70 employees and physicians busy serving the needs of more than 1,000 patients a week. The beautiful facility includes comfortable patient examination rooms, a laboratory, a special-procedures area, plus radiology and ultrasound departments. Located in the east wing of the building, the ambulatory surgery center includes three surgery suites and a soothing recovery area. Urology Associates also operates satellite offices in several communities surrounding Fresno.

Historically, the practice of urology has focused primarily on men. However, with advancements in treatment options, more women are seeing urologists for a variety of conditions. Patients seek the expertise of Urology Associates for such conditions as kidney stones, urinary incontinence, impotence, cancer, infections and birth defects, and to provide surgical procedures such as vasectomies and circumcisions, to name a few.

The Wave of the Future: Physician Perspectives

Gilbert Dale, M.D., president of Urology Associates, recognizes the need for a specialized urological center. "Medicine is becoming more technology oriented, and the business of medicine is becoming too complex for a physician to successfully remain in private practice," Dr. Dale reveals. "Physicians who combine their resources and expertise can effectively offer the quality of care and progressive medical techniques patients desire."

William Schiff, M.D., is a third-generation urologist. His father, Jack Schiff, M.D., also works at one of the center's satellite offices. Father and son enjoy having medical discussions almost daily. The younger Schiff views himself as a general urologist specializing in "quality of life issues" such as erectile dysfunction and urinary incontinence. According to Bill, "People are beginning to be less embarrassed about urological concerns. They're happy to know that these issues are not a result of personal failures and something can be done."

Irwin Barg, M.D., Urology Associates' vice president, explains the reason why he joined other urologists to develop the facility. "I wanted to continue to deliver the highest quality medical service and to have a comfortable environment for my patients. Today, businesses that are grouped together can operate more efficiently and provide higher levels of service. That concept extends to health care and patients are the beneficiaries."

Artin Jibilian, M.D., also sees a specialized one-stop-shop for patients as the future of practical medicine. "Becoming a part of this team has allowed me the ability to focus on the needs of my patients. As a group, we have hired the expertise to deal with the business aspects of medicine such as Medi-Cal, Medicare, private insurance and HMO contracting."

Narayana Ambati, M.D., has a busy practice that includes teaching new physicians/residents about urology through University Medical Center and providing pediatric urology at Valley Children's Hospital. The evolution of medicine has come a long way during his career. Dr. Ambati says, "Physicians now have more treatment tools. Of course we incorporate our education and training, but we now have access to drugs such as Viagra, or equipment such as the lithotripter. I value my collaboration with the physicians of Urology Associates. My students and patients can readily see that the future of medicine is being practiced here."

H. Greg Rainwater, M.D., believes his patients are getting great service at the center. "Patients come to me to help them. It is much more convenient for the patient to receive all the tests needed, to receive the physician's evaluation and recommendation, and if necessary, surgery — all under one roof and often in the same visit. Procedures done at Urology Associates can cost less than 60 percent of what the same procedure would cost if performed in a hospital, even when the procedure is performed on an outpatient basis," says Dr. Rainwater. From the practitioner's perspective, he sees the benefits of physician collaboration as "ready access to the wisdom and experience of other urologists."

After his 20-plus-year tenure in Fresno, **Robert Julian, M.D.**, can see that patient needs have changed over the years. "People want to know all about their medical conditions and what alternatives are available. My patients often go onto the Internet to seek information about a cancer, a drug or treatment alternatives. Urology Associates represents the physical embodiment of expertise to many of these patients," shares Dr. Julian.

Chris Julian, M.D., Robert Julian's son, agrees. "We now have both the educational resources and the medical tools to effectively serve our patients. Patients and families can take advantage of our video rooms to learn more about specific medical conditions and treatment choices. We believe that an informed patient is a satisfied patient."

Kuldip Behniwal, M.D., believes in the collective vision of his physician colleagues. Dr. Behniwal also provides medical services in Madera and says, "Urology Associates is here to serve the diverse needs of people throughout the Central Valley. We provide care to all patients, regardless of economic status. I am happy that we offer the same high quality care to the entire community."

Urology Associates of Central California invites Central Valley residents to visit the new facility, just off Herndon and Maple avenues in Fresno, and looks forward to being a valued leader in health care services for years to come.

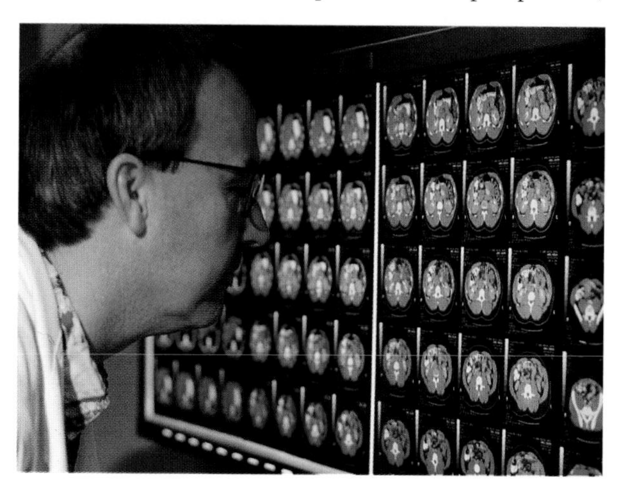

Patients can take advantage of specialists who offer state-of-the-art technology and diagnostic services at the center.

Ag One

While farming may still hold the romance of outdoor life, the virtue of honest labor and the sense of being drawn to a vocation by destiny, modern agriculturalists must also be scientists, engineers and economists. Today's agribusiness deals with a host of diverse factors, from international trade and competition in world markets to physics and biotechnology.

Agriculture in the San Joaquin Valley ranges from 20-acre family farms to the holdings of industry giants. Even many small farms employ advanced technological methods, such as using the global positioning system (GPS) to pinpoint areas that need more seed, fertilizer or water.

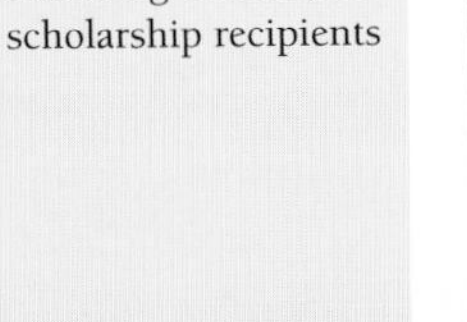

Some of Ag One's 2,000 scholarship recipients

The world's expanding population has increased humanity's need to produce more food from the same or less available land. The ability to meet these needs has come from technological advancement and the new skills, methods and products that have created this technology have been the result of education.

It is education that has transformed the ancient art of tilling the soil into the modern miracle of abundance. In 1979 an important idea sprouted in one of the world's most abundant farming regions, the San Joaquin Valley. The idea was to grow education.

It began when some friends — two professors and a farmer — talked over ham and eggs about creating a foundation that would award scholarships to students at California State University, Fresno's College of Agricultural Sciences and Technology. Their intention was to assist deserving students and help make the college the best agricultural school in the state.

Ag One was incorporated as a nonprofit foundation in 1979 and is the perfect conduit for the expression of gratitude and generosity of the university's alumni and friends. The funds it raises provide scholarships that not only help individual students, but by attracting the best students, help enrich valley agriculture.

The program has created a cycle of benefits: students work in the valley after graduation and contribute to the foundation to help students that follow them. This was exemplified in October 1997 when then Ag One President Erik Roget announced at a dinner for donors and supporters that the foundation had passed the $1 million mark. Roget, who graduated from California State University, Fresno, in 1980, was himself an Ag One scholarship recipient.

The $2 million mark was broken only a couple of years later, largely due to the estate of Dr. Lloyd Dowler, a former dean of the College of Agricultural Sciences and Technology. This substantial endowment of $730,000 honors Dowler's lifelong devotion to the agricultural school and its students.

The Ag One endowment fund comprises more than 60 named funds. Funds can be earmarked per donors' requests to establish scholarships in support of whichever of the college's fields of study they desire.

By its 21st year Ag One had awarded more than 2,000 scholarships. The College of Agricultural Sciences and Technology, with an enrollment of 1,200 students, grants the most scholarships of all the colleges at the university, awarding more than $200,000 per year.

Ag One gathers seed money to raise one of the world's most important crops — well-educated agriculturalists. As Alcidia Gomes, Ag One's executive director says, "What better place to grow them than in the agricultural center of the world — the San Joaquin Valley."

Department of Veterans Affairs Central California Health Care System

"The Price of Freedom is Visible Here." These words are seen at the entrance to the Department of Veteran Affairs Central California Health Care System (VACCHCS), demonstrating that those who have served their country honorably, and whose sacrifices were the price paid for its freedom, are entitled to excellent service. To this end, VACCHCS offers veterans high quality health care with respect and dignity.

The impetus for the Fresno VA Hospital began on March 6, 1941, when U.S. Rep. Bud Gearhart of Fresno introduced a bill in Congress that would provide a 150-bed facility in the Central Valley. On September 17, 1947, Victor Maghakian, the San Joaquin Valley's most decorated hero of World War II, turned the first shovel of dirt for the new seven-story, earthquake-resistant VA Hospital in Fresno. The facility was completed in March 1950.

Expanded and upgraded since its inception, the VA added a four-story outpatient clinic building, a University of California, San Francisco (UCSF) Medical Education Building and a 60-bed Geriatric Extended Care Unit. Upgraded with fiber-optics, this medical center is linked internally to the most complex diagnostic equipment and technologies, and externally to the most comprehensive health data information computer system in the nation. Two newly opened community-based outpatient clinics located in Atwater and Tulare help provide primary care health services to veterans in the surrounding communities.

The VA's affiliation with UCSF incorporates teaching residencies in specialties such as surgery, psychiatry and radiology. As a teaching hospital, VACCHCS is affiliated with a number of medical and dental schools, including Stanford, University of California, Los Angeles (UCLA), UCSF, University of California, Davis, University of California, Berkeley, and University of the Pacific. Many physicians, on completion of their training, remain in the area, setting up practices to serve the residents of the San Joaquin Valley.

The VA today is a model of excellence for health care, providing 175,000 outpatient visits and 3,000 inpatient visits to Valley veterans annually. In addition, the VA is unrivaled in its ability to deal with veterans' unique needs. Conditions such as Post Traumatic Stress Disorder (PTSD), Gulf War Syndrome, spinal cord injury, substance abuse and mental illness are treated utilizing the latest findings in VA research.

VA medical centers are among the best in the nation. Scores given to the VA by the Joint Commission for the Accreditation of Hospital Organizations (JCAHO) have been generally higher than those given to other public and private hospitals. In 1998 the Fresno facility's scores, on a scale of zero to 100 percent, were extremely impressive with 100 percent marks for ambulatory care and alcohol/ drug abuse treatment programs, 99 percent for long-term care and 98 percent for home care provision.

By 1999 the UCSF Medical Education Building and outpatient buildings had been added to the grounds of the VA. The large lawns had been replaced with additional parking lots.

The VA Central California Health Care System's spirit of caring also extends to the community in many ways. Numerous outreach services include free screenings for upper respiratory disease and depression, smoking cessation classes and participation with valley high schools and colleges in career development and student job experience.

Dedicated to the values of respect, commitment and compassion, VACCHCS delivers a grateful nation's promise of high quality health care to those who have paid the price for this nation's freedom.

First Armenian Presbyterian Church

The First Armenian Presbyterian Church of Fresno celebrated its first 100 years as a congregation in 1997. It is a vibrant, growing church that averages between 400 to 500 in attendance at its Sunday services. It is a youthful church filled with 150 Sunday School attendees and a youth group of 137. It is a caring church that ministers to new refugees and immigrants arriving in this country. The early morning services are spoken in Armenian for the benefit of the recent arrivals from Armenia. It is a giving church that funds many programs for the city and people of Fresno. It is a prosperous church of business professionals, educators and philanthropists who form a good, solid body doing the work of God in its community and homeland.

The original church building, made famous by member William Saroyan, graced the Fresno landscape for many years. At right is the present-day sanctuary.

The way has not been an easy one. Several Armenian families came to settle in Fresno beginning in the autumn of 1883, when the city was a small town of 1,300 people. A few who came before felt the area was a delightful land of opportunity. The early settlers greatly struggled to eke out a living and found much discrimination. There were no meetings of any kind in the early years, but the population grew and in 1897, 40 gathered in an upper room of Nicholls' Hall in downtown to hear the Rev. Lysander Tower Burbank of the Presbytery of Denver preach a sermon in the Armenian language. These 40 people were enrolled as charter members of a new Presbyterian church. Most of these came from other Presbyterian churches in the area. With the help and guidance of the Stockton Presbytery, the young church grew.

Within a few years after its charter was adopted, the small congregation built its first church. The three-story, octagonal building was completed in April 1902, and was depicted in developer M. Theo Kearney's illustrated brochure as part of the attractions in Fresno. It was this sanctuary that Pulitzer Prize-winning author William Saroyan attended as a boy and wrote about years later. When the congregation later relocated, this building served as a reception hall and meeting place. On October 30, 1985, this last remaining wooden church building in the city was gutted by fire.

The new century was marked by welcoming many new members into the fellowship. The 1895, 1909 and 1914 massacres of Armenians in Turkey accelerated the growth. In the decades that followed, Armenians from Europe, Egypt, Syria, Lebanon, the Soviet Union, the Americas and Armenia immigrated to Central California and joined the fellowship of the First Armenian Presbyterian Church.

The church continues its ministry today with one senior pastor, an associate pastor and a director of Christian education, in addition to those who serve in the areas of music and those who teach young people. The halls of the annex are decked with photographs of members who have gone before. The youth are able to identify with their roots and grow within a warm family atmosphere.

In 1978 the Rev. Bernard Guekguezian came to pastor the church and continues in service today. The ministry of the First Armenian Presbyterian Church is the story of God's mighty hand at work generation after generation.

FRESNO CITY & COUNTY CONVENTION & VISITORS BUREAU

Fresno County lies nestled in the San Joaquin Valley, a fruitful vale of blossoms guarded by majestic towers of snow and stone. Since prospectors first rushed to the Sierra foothills in search of gold, the area's natural grandeur and hometown charm have made people feel welcome. The beautiful setting draws more than 3 million visitors annually, many on their way to one of the nearby national parks — Yosemite, Sequoia and Kings Canyon.

The agribusiness capital of the world, with over 250 commercial crops and more than $3 billion in production, Fresno County is a land of beautiful contrasts: snow-capped Sierras on the horizon, flowering fruit trees, vineyards and vegetable fields — a vision of rural splendor, a stunning array of museums and galleries, theaters and the Fresno Philharmonic Orchestra, a cultural treasure trove.

The Fresno City & County Convention & Visitors Bureau works to benefit the local economy by bringing visitors and conventions to the region. The history of conventions in the area dates almost from its beginnings. As far back as 1895, just 10 years after the city of Fresno was incorporated, the Fresno County Chamber of Commerce allocated $100 for badges and promotional materials. In 1926, the chamber set aside $40 per month to solicit convention business and appointed a committee to pursue that goal. The next year, J.C. Hinton, the committee chair, reported 15 major conventions. The convention bureau became a separate entity from the chamber in 1962.

Nature made Fresno a paradise; the Fresno City & County Convention & Visitors Bureau has done its best to make it a convention paradise as well. The award-winning convention center complex encompasses more than five city bocks and is regarded as one of the most versatile in the western United States. The new exposition center, completed in 1999, provides state-of-the-art convention amenities. With an 11,000-seat arena, a 32,000-square-foot unobstructed exhibit hall/ballroom, almost 70,000 square feet of exposition space, a 13,000-square-foot conference center and 40 meeting rooms, it is a grand facility. Accompanied by new hotels and restaurants, it helps stake Fresno's claim as a premier state convention venue.

Situated midstate and easily accessible from north and south, Fresno provides a pleasant geographical compromise. Conventions need convenience. They require ample provisions for lodging, dining and activities. The bureau is responsible for planning, organizing and stimulating the development necessary for a successful convention business, which contributes to the local community both financially and by creating amenities useful to all.

Conventions produced an estimated economic impact of more than $67 million for fiscal year 1997-98. The bureau has also helped many movie production companies discover the area's impressive scenery and 19th-century rural American spirit. Fresno is becoming an increasingly popular location for the film, commercial and television industries.

Neither the glamour of filmdom, nor the frenzy of the gold rush, has or will change Fresno's down-home sense of itself. The stately Fresno Water Tower represents the area's solid values. It is now a visitor center run by the Fresno City & County Convention & Visitors Bureau. Architect George Washington Maher designed it in 1894, just one year before the chamber allocated that first $100 to attract conventioneers. The Fresno City & County Convention and Visitors Bureau continues to invite all to come and enjoy the beautiful central San Joaquin Valley.

The Fresno Water Tower, built in 1894 and home of the Fresno Convention & Visitors Bureau's Visitor Information Center.
Fresno Convention & Visitors Bureau

Microcomputer Education Center

To list an educational institution's curriculum and requirements is standard, but often its underlying story says more than its statistics. So it is for Microcomputer Education Center.

In 1974 Ricardo Trevino Sr. received word that he had been laid off from his job of 12 years. Losing a livelihood is never easy, but in this case Ricardo was the father of nine children. A decision had to be made, so Ricardo huddled with his wife and the two discussed their limited options. The end result was that the family was loaded into a 1969 Chevy four-door Impala, along with all the possessions they could squeeze into the trunk, and traveled 1,500 miles to Fresno looking for work. They had been told by Ricardo's uncle that money grew on trees, and when they arrived they found out the rumor was true. However, what they were picking off trees wasn't dollar bills but fruit, and the money received from the picking was slim, even with most of the family members working.

Keeping class size small means students get individual attention.

When the Trevino family first came to Fresno, they stayed with Ricardo's uncle, who had encouraged the family to make the move. As the oldest of the children, Rick Trevino slept in the car with his father while the rest of the family crowded into the house, sleeping on floors and doubling up on couches. Having little money wasn't the only challenge. Although natives of the United States, young Trevino, along with the rest of his family, spoke little English.

Determined to make the move a success, the Trevino children were signed up for school according to their respective ages, and the family eventually settled into a house of its own. After three years though, the family decided it wanted to see home again and packed up for the return trip to Laredo, Texas. By that time, Rick was a senior at Roosevelt High School and decided he wanted to stay. He said goodbye to his family, and at the age of 17 was all on his own. The decision turned out to be the right one because it set the young man on a path toward securing an education, success as a business owner and a contentment with life he'd never dreamed possible.

Rick Trevino maintains an open-door policy to students and staff.

After graduating from high school Trevino went to work at a gas station on Ventura Avenue in downtown

Fresno while attending California State University, Fresno. He majored in industrial technology with an emphasis in computers and finished his education in less than four years by attending summer classes and taking the maximum class load every semester. His ambition didn't go unnoticed, and in 1983 his mentor and professor, Dr. Skip Adrian, recommended him for a job at Hughes Aircraft Company in Southern California. In 1984 he became an assistant project manager and spent the next four years with Hughes.

Trevino met his wife, Manuela, while still in college and they married in 1988. The couple resettled in Fresno and Trevino decided to start his own business while his wife worked as a teacher. The first business entailed setting up, installing and maintaining computers, but the venture turned out to be less than lucrative so Trevino began to look at other opportunities. He had been running the business during the day and teaching computer classes at night, and that gave him the idea to blend both worlds. Microcomputer Education Center began in one room with just two students in 1989. A photograph of one of those students still sits in a frame atop Trevino's desk. The man was a displaced worker and came to Trevino for training. The two men still stay in contact and the former student is doing well.

In barely a decade, the school has grown to accommodate 160 graduates a year and boasts 19 employees, including 10 teachers. Students now have access to certification in such fields as office automation technology, microcomputer operations, medical office administration, computer accounting and electronic technology. In total, the school offers 10 different types of certificates.

Trevino need no longer worry about his wife paying the bills and takes every opportunity to credit her with seeing them through the lean times. "If it hadn't been for her, we wouldn't have made it. I owe her a lot."

In keeping with the Trevino family tradition, Anna Trevino also pitched in and worked for her brother free of charge when the school first opened. She is still there as the school's controller.

The school offers some services that students don't always find at other institutions. Trevino said that many of the students reach adulthood without guidance from their families so the school provides training in general employee development and practices. There are workshops in building self-esteem, setting goals and constructively managing personal problems.

Trevino's wife, Manuela, supported the family when Trevino opened his first one-room business school. "I owe her a lot," says Trevino.

MICROCOMPUTER EDUCATION CENTER BEGAN IN ONE ROOM WITH JUST TWO STUDENTS IN 1989. IN BARELY A DECADE, THE SCHOOL HAS GROWN TO ACCOMMODATE 160 GRADUATES A YEAR AND BOASTS 19 EMPLOYEES, INCLUDING 10 TEACHERS.

Trevino's father, Ricardo, brought his family to California hoping for a better life. Rick fulfilled his father's hopes.

The student body consists of people from all age groups and walks of life. The oldest student ever to graduate from the school was 72 and the youngest 17; but most students are in their early 30s. Well aware that most students are either just beginning a career or training for a new one, Trevino and his staff constantly research government and private funding allocations for students. After securing funding, the school then matches the source with the student. Many students qualify for funding because of income levels or work displacement. For those who do not qualify for a grant, the school helps with securing student loans.

"The training in personal growth coupled with occupational training not only changes the future for the student," said Trevino, "it changes the future for their families."

To help students jump start their new careers, the school provides placement assistance. An on-site placement office provides students with employment leads, in addition to training in presentation and interview skills, resume writing, and using the Internet as a tool for the job search. The school has established a rapport with a number of companies that frequently call to announce job opportunities and invite graduates to interview for positions. Trevino assures students that job placement assistance is available to graduates for as long as the school remains open. Another amenity offered to students is the opportunity to return to the school and refresh their skills at no cost.

MICROCOMPUTER EDUCATION CENTER IS ACCREDITED BY THE ACCREDITING COMMISSION OF CAREER SCHOOLS AND COLLEGES OF TECHNOLOGY (ACCSCT).

Funding sources look for a school that has the necessary credentials and representatives come to the actual facility to inspect the classrooms, teaching techniques and resources. The teachers and curriculum must meet certain standards. The school is closely examined for past performance, with special attention paid to how quickly students are able to obtain permanent jobs. According to Trevino, the strongest measurement used by state and federal agencies to award funding is the number of students who find work after finishing the courses.

To further help students, Trevino includes a computer in the cost of tuition. The cost can be deducted if the student already has access to a computer, but for those who don't, the inclusion puts them even farther down the road to success.

Microcomputer Education Center is accredited by the Accrediting Commission of Career Schools and Colleges of Technology (ACCSCT), which is listed by the United States Department of Education as a nationally recognized accrediting agency.

In 1995 Trevino purchased a four-building complex totaling 15,000 square feet of classrooms and offices. Fearful of growing too fast and jeopardizing the quality of teaching for which the school has become known, class sizes are restricted to no more than 16 students. The complex can eventually accommodate up to 270 students as the school continues to grow. For the year 2000, Trevino expects to enroll 200 students.

Within the perimeters of the school there is a library with books and magazines related to classroom subjects. A student lunchroom is bright and clean and papered with job announcements and information. There is also a lush park with grass, trees, flowers and benches where students can go to nibble a snack or just relax between classes. Situated throughout the grounds are brick planters holding rainbows of roses. Trevino planted the roses himself and does the watering, believing that beauty inspires learning. All of the classrooms have floor-to-ceiling or bay windows, giving the rooms an open and airy feel.

There is no doubt that the classes will continue to grow. While the state of California is expected to double its population by 2040, Fresno is projected to triple its population in the same amount of time. That increase is coupled with another projection: the San Joaquin Valley will become the next Silicon Valley.

For a city the size of Fresno, the cost of living is relatively lower than anywhere else in California, and technical industries as well as many other types of businesses are looking closely at the area for expansion. As salaries climb to meet the cost of living in such places as San Jose and San Francisco, companies are looking to cut costs by locating in areas where employees can fulfill the American dream without needing $100,000 a year to do it. Fresno and the surrounding area offers that sort of solution. As more companies arrive needing more trained workers, schools like Microcomputer Education Center are predicted to have bulging enrollment lists.

Never forgetting where he came from and how it all began, two of the classrooms still hold the original tables Trevino started with in his first school. They are actually doors that were painted and nailed to support planks. Trevino keeps them around not only for their sentimental value but because of what they have come to represent. The desks are where the work is done, opening a door to the future.

As a leader in advocating education, Trevino himself has not stopped learning. He graduated from the Small Business Administration Executive Education Program and devoted a year to Leadership Fresno, a program sponsored by the Fresno Chamber of Commerce. Leadership Fresno is composed of a group of business owners and community leaders who commit to spending one year working on community improvement projects. Along with other community leaders, Trevino established a leadership program for high school seniors patterned after Leadership Fresno. The program was successful and is still in place today.

Twelve years after graduating from California State University, Fresno, Trevino was honored as Alumnus of the Year by the industrial technology department. His old mentor, Dr. Adrian, had been the one who nominated him.

The amazing growth of the school can only be attributed to word-of-mouth advertising. With 83 percent of the graduates obtaining jobs, the school's reputation draws certificate candidates from all over the San Joaquin Valley. Trevino points to his staff when discussing the success of the school. "The people who work here care about the students. They are very capable and I know that they would do just fine without me because they are very good at their jobs. I believe too, that God gave me this school so all of us here could help others have a better life. It's really a gift from God; I'm just the caretaker."

This classroom holds the tables (left) Trevino made from doors when he first began his business school.

BIBLIOGRAPHY

Allen, Stan. Coalinga Chamber of Commerce. Interview. September 15, 1999.

American Association of University Women. *Heritage Fresno Homes and People.* Pioneer Publishing Co., Fresno, 1975.

Ainsworth, Ed. *Pot Luck.* George Palmer Putnam, Inc., Hollywood, 1940.

Atkin, William T. "Agriculture, Lumber Gave Clovis Its Start." *Fresno Past & Present.* Vol. 30. No. 2. Fresno City and County Historical Society Quarterly Journal.

Baker, George L. "Morton — The Power In Fresno Politics." *The Fresno Bee*, March 21, 1971.

Belluomini, Thomas. Interview. September 24, 1999.

Bier, Jerry. "Aldredge named city manager." *The Fresno Bee*, December 24, 1986.

Bier, Jerry. "Christofferson Hands Council His Resignation." *The Fresno Bee,* July 23, 1986.

Boren, Jim. "3 incumbents forced into runoffs." *The Fresno Bee,* March 6, 1991.

Boren, Jim. "Doig bowing out." *The Fresno Bee,* December 27, 1988.

Boren, Jim. "Doig claims he'll survive political crisis." *The Fresno Bee,* July 9, 1987.

Boren, Jim. "Humphrey will run for mayor." *The Fresno Bee,* August 23, 1988.

Boren, Jim. "Humphrey wins; no runoff." *The Fresno Bee,* March 8, 1989.

Boren, Jim. "Patterson grabs mayoral lead." *The Fresno Bee,* March 6, 1993.

Boren, Jim. "What next for Little Hoover report?" *The Fresno Bee,* March 26, 1992.

Bort, James H., Jr. "The Doig Story." *The Fresno Bee,* August 24, 1986.

Bright, William. *1500 California Place Names.* University of California Press, Berkeley, 1998.

Bunnell, Lafayette Houghton, M.D. *Discovery of the Yosemite and the Indian War of 1851 Which Led to That Event.* Yosemite Association, Yosemite National Park, 1990.

Calkins, Royal and Jim Boren. "Doig and cocaine dealer: more than just neighbors." *The Fresno Bee,* August 13, 1986.

Calkins, Royal. "Doig's first 2 years get dark review." *The Fresno Bee,* December 21, 1986.

Calkins, Royal. "Phone record probe asked by Macmichael." *The Fresno Bee,* September 17, 1986.

Carter, La Verne A. "Sanger Marks Its Centennial in 1988." *Fresno Past & Present.* Fresno Historical Society. Vol. 30, No. 1. Fresno City and County Historical Society Quarterly Journal.

Caruthers High Future Business Leaders of America. *The History of Caruthers.* 2nd edition. Caruthers High Future Business Leaders of America, Caruthers, 1976.

Caughey, John Walton. *California.* Prentice-Hall, Inc. Englewood Cliffs, N.J., 1960.

"Change in the City Council." Editorial. *The Fresno Bee,* May 7, 1987.

Cleland, Robert Glass. *Pathfinders.* Powell Publishing Company, Los Angeles, 1929.

Clemings, Betsy. "Humphrey: Her pluses minuses." *The Fresno Bee,* April 22, 1990.

Clemings, Betsy. "Little Hoover Commission a step closer." *The Fresno Bee,* December 24, 1990.

Clemings, Betsy. "Will council see new era or same old politics?" *The Fresno Bee,* March 8, 1989.

Clingan, Helen and Forest. *Oak to Pine to Timberline.* Word Dancer Press, Fresno, 1985.

Clough, Charles W. and William B. Secrest, Jr. *Fresno County: The Pioneer Years.* Panorama West Books, Fresno, 1984.

Clough, Charles W., et. al. *Fresno County in the 20th Century.* Panorama West Books, Fresno, 1986.

Clough, Charles W. *Madera.* Madera County Diamond Jubilee Committee and the Madera Historical Society, Madera, 1968.

"Council backs bond issue to acquire river land." *The Fresno Bee,* March 11, 1987.

Crampton, C. Gregory, editor. *The Mariposa Indian War 1850-1851, Diaries of Robert Eccleston: The California Gold Rush, Yosemite, and the High Sierra.* University of Utah Press, Salt Lake City, 1957.

Doughty, Jim. community development director, city of Huron. Interview. April 19, 1999.

Dudley, Anne. "Decade delivers growth, grime to valley." *The Fresno Bee,* December 31, 1989.

Dudley, Anne. "Little Hoover members satisfied year's work successful." *The Fresno Bee,* March 22, 1992.

Dudley, Anne. "What next for Little Hoover report?" *The Fresno Bee,* March 26, 1992.

Eaton, Edwin. *Vintage Fresno.* The Huntington Press, Fresno, 1965.

Elliot, Wallace W. *History of Fresno County, California.* Reprinted edition, Valley Publishers, Fresno, 1973.

Farquhar, Francis P. *History of the Sierra Nevada.* University of California Press, Berkeley and Los Angeles, 1965.

"Fast Facts on the City of San Joaquin." Informational material provided by the city of San Joaquin.

Fannon, Dorice. Firebaugh city clerk and president of the Firebaugh Chamber of Commerce. Interview. September 15, 1999.

Fremont, Brevet Capt. J.C. *Report of The Exploring Expedition to The Rocky Mountains in the Year 1842, and to Oregon and North California in the Years 1842-44.* Gales and Seaton, Washington, 1845.

Fresno County Centennial Committee. *Fresno County Centennial Almanac.* Fresno County Centennial Committee, Fresno, 1956.

Geringer, Linda. executive director, Kerman Chamber of Commerce. Interview. April 1, 1999.

Gomes, Sharlene. *Danish Creamery Association 1895-1995.* Fresno, 1995.

Henson, Bob and Frances. *Bits & Pieces of Riverdale's History.* Riverdale, 1996.

Hoagland, Doug. "Shoring up the future." *The Fresno Bee.* June 27, 1999.

"Humphrey for mayor." Editorial. *The Fresno Bee.* February 28, 1989.

Humphrey, Karen. Interview. November 16, 1999.

Katz, Andy. "Escape to 'Pleasantville.' " *The Fresno Bee.* June 13, 1999.

Kean, David W. *Wide Places in the California Roads.* Vol. 4. The Concord Press, Sunnyvale, 1996.

Kearney, M. Theo. *Fresno County California and the Evolution of the Fruitvale Estate.* Facsimile Reproduction. Fresno City and County Historical Society, Fresno, 1979.

Keeler, Guy. "It's all in the Family." *The Fresno Bee.* May 9, 1999.

Kershaw, Rosellen. Interview. November 23, 1999.

Klisch, Rebecca E. city clerk, city of Fresno. Interview. November 17, 1999.

"Last Rites Are Held in L.A. for W.G. Kerckhoff." *The Fresno Bee.* February 25, 1929.

Latta, Frank F. *Dalton Gang Days.* Bear State Books, Santa Cruz, California, 1976.

Latta, Frank F. *Handbook of Yokuts Indians.* Reprinted edition, Coyote Press, Salinas, 1999.

"Little Hoover Commission members." *The Fresno Bee,* March 22, 1992.

Long, Bob. "Who in the World is William S. Chapman?" *Fresno Past & Present.* Fresno Historical Society. Vol. 39, No. 2. Fresno City and County Historical Society Quarterly Journal.

Long, Bob. "William S. Chapman: The Unknown Builder of Fresno County." *Fresno Past & Present.* Fresno Historical Society. Vol. 39, No. 3. Fresno City and County Historical Society Quarterly Journal.

Marott, Robert. administrator, Calwa Recreation and Park District. Interview. September 21, 1999.

Mayhew, Don. "Expanding Views." *The Fresno Bee,* August 22, 1999.

McCubbin, John C. *The McCubbin Papers.* Edited with Introduction and Notes by Kenneth Zech. Reedley Historical Society. Reedley, 1988.

McFarland, J. Randall. *Centennial Selma.* J. Randall McFarland, in association with The Selma Enterprise. Selma, California, 1980.

McFarland, J. Randall. "City in the Country." *Fresno Past & Present.* Fresno Historical Society. Vol. 34, No. 4. Fresno City and County Historical Society Quarterly Journal.

McFarland, Randy. "The Early Days in Reedley." *Fresno Past & Present.* Fresno Society. Vol. 29, No. 4. Fresno City and County Historical Society Quarterly Journal.

McFarland, Jon R. (Randy). *Village on the Prairie.* The Ensign Publishing Company, Fowler, 1972.

Miller, Howard. "From Green Bush Spring Flows the Story of a City Called Fresno." *Fresno Past & Present.* Fresno Historical Society. Vol. 27, No. 2. Fresno City and County Historical Society Quarterly Journal.

Mitchell, Annie. *Jim Savage and the Tularenos Indians.* Westernlore Press, Los Angeles, 1957.

Morison, William. *The Alta Empire.* Alta. Irrigation District, Dinuba, 1988.

Myers, William A. *Iron Men and Copper Wires.* Trans-Anglo Books. Glendale, 1983.

Olsson, Cindi. "Kingsburg: From 'Tough Place' to 'City of Churches.'" *Fresno Past & Present.* Fresno Historical Society. Vol. 30, No. 3. Fresno City and County Historical Society Quarterly Journal.

Orozco, Roy. "Where Time Stands Still." *The Fresno Bee.* August 8, 1999.

Panter, John. "Central California Colony: 'Marvel of the Desert.'" *Fresno Past & Present.* Fresno Historical Society. Vol. 36, No. 2. Fresno City and County Historical Society Quarterly Journal.

Philbrick, Gary. *Engineer.* State Division of Oil and Gas, Coalinga. Interview. September 15, 1999.

"Philosophy and History of the Calwa Recreation and Park District." Written material provided by the Calwa Recreation and Park District.

Pinkerton, Scott. *Mariposa County Courthouse.* Mariposa Heritage Press, Mariposa, 1989.

Pipes, William V., R.G. Principal Geologist/Central Valley Manager. Geomatrix Consultants. Interview. July 1999.

Preston, Brenda Burnett. *Andrew Davidson Firebaugh & Susan Burgess Firebaugh California Pioneers.* Rio Del Mar Press, Rio Del Mar, 1995.

Prieto, Jerry. Fresno County Ag commissioner. Interview. August 19, 1999.

Rehart, Catherine Morison. *The Valley's Legends & Legacies.* Word Dancer Press, Fresno, 1996.

Rehart, Catherine Morison. *The Valley's Legends & Legacies II.* Word Dancer Press, Fresno, 1997.

Rehart, Catherine Morison. *The Valley's Legends & Legacies III.* Word Dancer Press, Fresno, 1999.

Rehart, Burton Schyler, Jr. *The Lincoln-Roosevelt League: A Study of the Progressive Insurgency Within the Republican Party in California, 1906-1910.* Master of Arts thesis. Department of History, Fresno State College, February, 1966.

Rehart, Schyler. "Dr. Chester Rowell — Crusading Newspaperman, State Political Leader and Mayor of Fresno." *Fresno Past & Present.* Vol. 28. No. 1. Fresno City and County Historical Society Quarterly Journal.

Rehart, Schyler. "Fresno's City Halls." Part II. *Fresno Past & Present.* Vol. 33. No. 1. Fresno City and County Historical Society Quarterly Journal.

Rehart, Schyler. "J.C. Forkner Turned Fresno's 'Hog Wallows' Into 'Garden of Eden.'" *Fresno Past & Present.* Vol. 19. No. 3. Fresno City and County Historical Society Quarterly Journal.

Rehart, Schyler and William K. Patterson. *M. Theo Kearney Prince of Fresno.* Fresno City and County Historical Society, Fresno, 1988.

Rehart, Schyler. "The Man Who Was M. Theo Kearney New Facts Revealed."*Fresno Past & Present.* Vol. 36. No. 3. Fresno City and County Historical Society Quarterly Journal.

Richter, Bertina. *Fort Miller, California, 1851-1865.* Peter Lang Publishing, New York, 1988.

Rosato, Joe. "Ted Wills held sway from Ike to Reagan." *The Fresno Bee,* May 10, 1987.

Rose, Gene. *Reflections of Shaver Lake.* Word Dancer Press, Fresno, 1987.

Rowell, Chester H. "A Brief Account of the Life of Chester H. Rowell." Unpublished manuscript. Courtesy of Schyler Rehart.

Salley, Harold. *History of California Post Offices 1849-1990.* 2nd edition edited by Edward L. Patera. The Depot, La Mesa, California, 1991.

Secrest, William B. "Church Wars." *Fresno Past & Present.* Vol. 37, No. 4. Fresno City and County Historical Society Quarterly Journal.

Seeger, Diane. "Historical Background and Importance of Kearney Boulevard." *Fresno Past & Present.* Vol. 22, No. 1. Fresno City and County Historical Society Quarterly Journal.

Shekoyan, James E. Interview. November 15, 1999.

Simmons, Ed. *Westlands Water District The First 25 Years.* Westlands Water District, Fresno, 1983.

Smith, Wallace. *Garden of the Sun.* California History Books, Fresno, 1939.

Solis, Al. director, Development Department, city of Fresno. Interview. November 17, 1999.

Solis, Al. "HPC After the San Adreas." Memorandum. August 24, 1981.

Sun-Maid Growers of California. "The World's Favorite Raisin." Promotional brochure.

Trask, Bonnie. Interview. September, 1999.

Treadwell, Edward F. *The Cattle King.* Western Tanager Press, Santa Cruz, 1981.

Vandergon, Robert D. "1998 Fresno County Agricultural Crop and Livestock Report." Fresno County Department of Agriculture.

Vandor, Paul E. *History of Fresno County.* Vol. I. Historic Record Company, Los Angeles, 1919.

"W.G. Kerckhoff Buried in L.A." *Fresno Morning Republican.* February 26, 1929.

Waiczis, Michael R. *A Portrait of Fresno 1885-1985.* Val-Print, Fresno, 1985.

Walker, Ben R. *Fresno Community Book.* Arthur H. Cawston, Fresno, 1946.

Walker, Ben R. *The Fresno County Blue Book.* Arthur H. Cawston, Fresno, 1941.

Wash, Robert M. "Timber!" *The Fresno County Employee.* Vol. VIII-IX. September, 1955.

Washington Union High School Centennial 1892-1992. Easton Historical Society, Fresno, 1992.

"Welcome to Parlier." Material provided by the city of Parlier.

Westlands Water District. Pamphlet.

Wood, Raymond F., PhD. "The Origin of the Name of Fresno." *Fresno Past & Present.* Vol. 2, No. 4. Fresno City and County Historical Society Quarterly Journal. October, 1960.

Wooster, C.M. Letter to George Cosgrave stating how Fresno was named. October 18, 1928. California State University, Fresno, Madden Library, Special Collection.

Zylka, Claire Baird, Ken Greenberg and Jessie Myers Thun. *Images of an Age Clovis.* Pacific Printing Press, Fresno, 1984.

The Fresno Bee, January 16, 1950.

The Fresno Bee, May 2, 1952.

The Fresno Bee, May 5, 1952.

The Fresno Bee, July 23, 1986.

Fresno Morning Republican, July 7, 1898.

Selected readings on the subject of agriculture and labor:

Daniels, Cletus E. *Bitter Harvest: A History of California Farm Workers 1870-1941.*

McWilliam, Cary. *Factories in the Field, Story of Migratory Farm Workers.*

Taylor, Ron. *Chavez and the Farm Workers.*

INDEX

PARTNERS INDEX